STUDIES IN HISTORICAL GEOGRAPHY

English Parliamentary Enclosure

STUDIES IN HISTORICAL GEOGRAPHY

Editors: Alan R. H. Baker and J. B. Harley

Also published in this series

Southern Africa

A. J. CHRISTOPHER

Finland

MICHAEL JONES

Rural Settlement in Britain

BRIAN K. ROBERTS

Mirrors of the New World

J. M. POWELL

English Towns 1500–1700

JOHN PATTEN

Climatic Change, Agriculture and Settlement

M. L. PARRY

Planning the Past

ROBERT M. NEWCOMB

STUDIES IN HISTORICAL GEOGRAPHY

English Parliamentary Enclosure

Its Historical Geography And Economic History

MICHAEL TURNER
Department of Economic and Social History
University of Hull

DAWSON · ARCHON BOOKS

First published in 1980

Wm Dawson & Sons Ltd, Cannon House
Folkestone, Kent, England

Archon Books, The Shoe String Press, Inc
995 Sherman Avenue, Hamden, Connecticut 06514 USA

British Library Cataloguing in Publication Data

Turner, Michael
English parliamentary enclosures.
– (Studies in historical geography).
1. Inclosures – Economic aspects – History
I. Title II. Series
333.7'6 HD594.6 79–92508

ISBN 0 7129 0982 6
ISSN 0308 6607

Archon ISBN 0–208–01786–0

Printed litho in Great Britain
by W & J Mackay Limited, Chatham

Contents

To
Ali, Kate, and James

Figures

Tables

Appendixes

Preface and Acknowledgements

If justification is required to write a book for the series 'Studies in Historical Geography' then my credential as a geography graduate is perhaps justification enough. If justification is required to write a book which claims also to be an economic history then perhaps my credentials as first a postgraduate and now a teacher of economic history answer that justification. But perhaps the greater justification is not in the credentials of the author but rather in the weight of the subject. That there is in the two disciplines a gap which a book of this kind will breach I hope will become clear as the book proceeds. Historical geography and economic history are happy bedfellows and long may they continue to be so, but this book has been prepared with neither especially in mind, and yet both in mind. My hope is that the reader treats it in this way, an individual piece of work which does not fall readily into primary classification.

The main reference work on which this book draws and out of which it naturally grew is my own edition of W. E. Tate, *A Domesday of English Enclosure Acts and Awards*. This work came out in November 1978 through the imprint of the Library of the University of Reading, but my editorial tasks began in the summer of 1972. I would like to thank Professor J. C. Holt who as head of the History Department at Reading invited me to become the editor of Tate's manuscripts. I would also like to thank James Thompson, the University librarian, and his staff but in particular his archivist Jim Edwards. Finally, as far as my stay in Reading was concerned I would like to thank the Social Science Research Council for the award of a research fellowship for the academic year 1972–3.

While the revised manuscript of the *Domesday* was being processed for publication I exercised the author's prerogative of being the first to work on the raw data. All the computational work was completed between 1973 and 1976, during which time I held a research and teaching post in economic history at the University of Durham. I would like to thank the computer unit at Durham for much-needed assistance. Some of the writing was completed at Durham but most of it was composed, as time permitted, while I held successively two temporary research posts in London at Ealing College of Higher

Education and the Institute of Historical Research, in 1977 and 1978 respectively. On both occasions I received valuable library facilities and for these I record my thanks.

The writing and rewriting of this book was completed at the University of Hull. I would like to thank the drawing office of the Department of Geography and the Photographic Department of the Library for transforming my 'sketches' into efficient maps and figures. Mrs Irene Baldwin typed some twenty pages of the final script but the main bulk of the typing I completed myself.

My prefatory date is August 1979. This was a happy month, the birth of a book and of a son, but the origins of the book in going back at least seven years and almost as many institutions caused more pains and gave fewer joys than the creation of a son. My wife will disagree with me because she had to bear that son and also a daughter three years earlier. I cannot claim that the book became one of Alison's sources of joy but I can thank her and Kate and James for giving me my joys and for sharing my pains.

Department of Economic and
Social History, the University
of Hull
August 1979

1

Introduction

Prologue

'God made the country, and man made the town.' It may be unwise to tear lines rudely from their text, but as a statement of casual thought this was a very disappointing reflection from one of Buckinghamshire's most illustrious poets, William Cowper.[1] He wrote that line in 1783 in the village of Olney in north Buckinghamshire where fifteen years earlier he had witnessed the transformation of the landscape as the parish was enclosed by enclosure commissioners. He must have seen the former open fields transposed into numerous enclosures, subdivided by hedgerows, and he must have travelled frequently along the newly formed roads, bridlepaths and footpaths. It was the same in many other parishes in the south midlands, as it was also in many other English counties. If it was not already, then it was rapidly becoming a man-made landscape: 'The landscape of Olney, like the English countryside in general, is as artificial as any urban scene.'[2]

There are numerous ways in which the actions of man have been fossilised in the present-day landscape–the cultural landscape. These have commanded considerable attention from historical geographers, archaeologists, and economic and agricultural historians alike. Studies abound of deserted villages, of the works of landscape gardeners, and perhaps of the most widespread vestige of human interference, the distribution of ridge and furrow features. In the county of Buckinghamshire it has been estimated that there are 35 square kilometres of ridge and furrow, covering 28 per cent of the land area, and involving the displacement of about 3½ million tons of earth on average by ½ metre.[3] But if it is a question of scale then possibly it was the actions of the enclosure commissioners in the eighteenth and nineteenth centuries that produced the greatest areal change in the shortest comparable time span. Research by the late W. E. Tate demonstrated that this transforming hand of man was concentrated between about 1720 and the mid-Victorian period, but in particular during the six decades of the reign of King George III.[4] It is rightly known as a Georgian enclosure movement producing a Georgian landscape.

The regional expression of this enclosure movement varies considerably. For example there were different ways of raising a boundary; the quickset hedge of much of the midlands contrasts vividly with the heavy stone walls of the Pennine counties and the combination of enclosure and drainage schemes so typical of the fenland parts of Lincolnshire, Norfolk, Cambridgeshire, and Somerset. In the midlands it was essentially a land reform which transformed a traditional method of agriculture by some notion of co-operation in communally administered holdings, usually in large fields and devoid of physical territorial boundaries, to a system of agricultural holding in severalty, that is the separation by a physical boundary of one person's land from that of his neighbours. At the same time certain communal obligations and privileges and rights were declared void for all time. It could also mean the subdivision of areas of commons, heaths, moors, fens, and wastes into separate landholdings and again the abandonment of obligations, privileges, and rights; but this was less a feature of the midlands enclosures though more commonly found on the marginal areas of England.

The landscape that was produced had, and still has, a distinctive and discernible character, but it is one that is being severely eroded. The Milton Keynes Development Corporation in creating the new city of Milton Keynes will eventually obliterate the whole or parts of fifteen enclosure schemes in Buckinghamshire, and the development of Slough has laid six enclosures under concrete since the mid-nineteenth century. The giant midlands reservoirs such as Grafham and Rutland Waters have in turn drowned dozens of eighteenth- and nineteenth-century enclosures.

There are a number of outstanding features that the twentieth century has inherited from the enclosure commissioners. They and their surveyors have been credited with considerable skill and proficiency, though very often this is unmerited. It is not very difficult to compare the fields they produced with the apparent haphazard arrangement of fields found in ancient enclosures. A perusal of many enclosure maps and a subsequent view of the present-day landscape will sometimes show a hideous arrangement of field sizes and shapes. It is clear that on many occasions the commissioners appeared to show little appreciation for topography with respect to the subsequent disposition of the fields. Long narrow fields are as common as a well-ordered chequerboard of square or nearly square fields. Certainly they have straight sides, which is unlike most fields of old enclosure, but their shape with respect to topography is not always well suited to the vagaries of the plough, though of course since the period of parliamentary enclosure considerable consolidation of holdings has taken place and the grubbing-up of hedgerows has been, and still is, a common feature. On the other hand it should not be such a surprise to find that the enclosure landscape is less ordered on a closer inspection. Some parishes contained large numbers of allottees ranging in ownership size from hundreds of acres to a few acres or even parts of an acre. The Buckinghamshire parish of Haddenham springs to mind. This was enclosed in 1830–4 and the commissioners had to accommodate 105 allottees. At Bierton, enclosed in 1779–80, there were 72, at Wendover, enclosed in 1794–6, there were 74, at Stewkley, enclosed in 1811–16, there were 95 and at Princes Risborough, enclosed in 1820–4, there were 172. It must have been difficult to satisfy all claims.[5] Some allottees had to be content with tiny misshapen corners of larger fields, others were allotted two or three separate pieces of land perhaps at opposite ends of the parish, and others still were allotted a massive piece of land up to two or three hundred acres in extent which might remain that way for many years before funds became available to finance further hedgerows and therefore adjust the land to more manageable proportions.

Very often the commissioners took advantage of the 'natural' boundaries of the open fields, the balks and the headlands that defined the many furlongs and strips. It is evident that in many instances the new field boundaries have fossilised the former furlong boundaries.[6] The Bierton enclosure map of 1779–80 actually superimposes the furlong pattern on the new system of fields and roads.[7] To an even greater extent the commissioners used these balks and headlands to define the future courses of the new roads and other communications arteries, such as the footpaths and bridlepaths.[8] The ancient furlongs were often disposed at right angles to each other and therefore the new enclosure roads of the midlands typically had straight stretches interspersed with right-angled bends, sometimes double right-angled bends where the roads crossed parish boundaries, or reversed 'S' shaped roads and paths as they followed the courses of the old pre-enclosure strips.[9] It was not until 1801 that the

Standing Orders of the House of Commons on the presentation of enclosure bills insisted on the inclusion of a clause stating that the roads in the future were to be formed in the most commodious way.[10] An inspection of the widths of enclosure roads can also be very informative. Before about 1790 the major carriageways created at enclosure were invariably formed at a total width of 60 feet. This would be about 20 feet of carriageway flanked with up to 20 feet of grass verge on either side. The less important roads were usually about 40 feet wide in similar proportions. Today those same roads survive with the same expansive grass verges. After about 1790 all new roads were laid out with a maximum width of 40 feet, though occasionally up to 50 feet.

It is not very clear why the road widths change in the 1790s. It is unlikely that there was a change in the parliamentary standing orders but it may have arisen because the expansive verges became convenient resting places for the homeless who set up hovels of a semi-permanent nature on the roadside. If allowed to settle, every such pauper was a potential drain on the parish rates. The reduction in the size of the grass verges may therefore have been an attempt to discourage 'gypsies, vagabonds and wastrels', as eighteenth-century parlance would have it. Whatever the reasons the result is that in some respects it is possible to date the enclosure landscape of the midlands by an inspection of the road widths. A 60-foot road is probably of pre-1790 or even pre-1780 origin since the decade of the 1780s was relatively dormant in enclosure history. Where a road narrows from an overall width of 60 to 40 feet a boundary change might be suspected, due to two contiguous parishes being enclosed at quite widely separated dates, though I would not claim this as a hard and fast rule.

The actions of the enclosure commissioners, their surveyors and road and hedge contractors, have therefore left an indelible mark on the English countryside, in mountain and in vale, in clay and in sand, in fen and in heath. If for no other reason than that we constantly tread upon and traverse eighteenth- and nineteenth-century relict features, the study of parliamentary enclosure has aroused much interest among both amateur and professional historians.

The collection and presentation of the enclosure statistics

The publication of this book has been primarily motivated by the need to revise the basic statistics in use concerning parliamentary enclosure.

At a time when new methods of research are being applied to well-worn fields of historical inquiry, in particular by using quantitative statistics, any new interpretations regarding parliamentary enclosure will remain wanting as long as the basic information in use remains unrevised, accepting of course that it requires revision. The main sources for the location of bare facts and crude statistics, in the sense of estimates, are the official Government *Blue Books* of 1904 and 1914.[11] The main published accounts of the parliamentary enclosure movement are found in the two notable volumes by E. C. K. Gonner (1912) and G. Slater (1907). Subsequently there has appeared the work of W. H. R. Curtler (1920) and more recently W. E. Tate (1967).[12] All these volumes, except the last named, were in turn based on the various official and semi-official estimates contained in the *Blue Books* and in other parliamentary returns and sources.[13] The main objection regarding the utility of all these sources, apart from their by now exhausted use, is that they relied very heavily on estimates and were not substantiated enough by the primary enclosure documents. This is a problem recognised by M. Williams in his work on the national incidence of wasteland enclosure and its local occurrence in Somerset.[14] Most recently there has appeared J. A. Yelling's *Common Field and Enclosure in England 1450–1850* (London 1977). As the title suggests, it has a wider chronology than the present study and deals specifically with common fields but not with common and waste to any great extent.[15] It is a synthesis of published work and of Yelling's own researches, and clearly a book of this size contains much new material, but nevertheless the basic statistics on the chronology and extent of parliamentary enclosure rely heavily on Slater, Gonner and others. The book was 'written in the belief that a new general treatment of the subject is now required' and what the reader receives is not only a new general treatment but also a good general treatment.

The volumes referred to thus far will remain as important landmarks in the historiography of enclosure but it is surely time that many of their findings were revised or even replaced altogether (except Yelling's book). So much have they been regarded as the major sources that H. C. Darby's *Historical Geography of England* published in 1936 used Gonner's maps of 1912 to describe the incidence of enclosure. This of course is not at all remarkable, but when Darby came to revise his work, published as *A New Historical Geography of England* in 1973, he was in no better position to revise the maps and they appeared once more virtually unchanged.[16] Yelling's maps also follow the fashion of Slater and Gonner. When publications which refer to the national incidence of parliamentary enclosure appear it is invariably Slater or Gonner or the *Blue Books* which provide the statistical background. To illustrate the most recent incidences the reader might usefully consult L. J. White, M. Williams, G. S. L. Tucker, and G. Philpot, and one of the most popular and widely used reference volumes, *British Economic Growth, 1688–1959* by Phyllis Deane and W. A. Cole.[17] It is only when an approach is made at the more specific county level that better statistics are available. For example there are the excellent works on Warwickshire, Leicestershire, Somerset, South Lincolnshire, and West Yorkshire by J. M. Martin, H. G. Hunt, M. Williams, D. B. Grigg, and W. S. Rodgers respectively, to mention only a cross-section of what is available.[18] The county, artificial though it is in many respects, represents an ideal research unit for a monograph or university thesis.

Seemingly we shall have to wait many years and many publications before the 42 eighteenth-century English counties have been covered in a thorough and systematic way, that is unless some one person undertakes the mighty task himself. I do not claim this distinction for myself, but perhaps a share in its inauguration.

The pioneer figure in the revision of the statistics relating to parliamentary enclosure was W. E. Tate. Before his death in 1968 he had published statistical handlists for 27 of the 42 English counties.[19] In these he showed the dates of the individual enclosure acts, listed them in chronological order and subdivided them into those enacted by private or public local acts and those enacted under the umbrella of the General Acts of 1836, 1840, and 1845. For each entry he included details of the townships, villages, hamlets, manors or merely 'places' involved in the enclosures. He also included many of the gross acreages enclosed based either on the estimates in printed sources or on the acreages quoted in the enclosure awards.[20] There then followed details about the dating of the enclosure awards and the location in record repositories of the enclosure awards and maps which were known to have survived. In addition he sought to distinguish between the enclosure of lands that included *some* open field arable and the enclosure of lands that were *exclusively* commons and wastes. He envisaged his life's work in one volume to be called *A Domesday of English Enclosure Acts and Awards*, that is, bringing together all the statistics and details for all parliamentary enclosures for all the English counties.[21] In fact from 1951 until his death in 1968 Tate did not publish a single new county handlist; he was preoccupied with correcting and completing his earlier lists and constructing afresh the unpublished ones. At the same time he held an important academic post with Leeds University and towards the end of his life was hampered by failing health. His unfinished manuscripts were deposited in Reading University library archives some time after his death to await an editor. In the academic session 1972–3 I was appointed as a research fellow at the University of Reading through the generous offices of the Social Science Research Council. The brief was to act as editor of the unfinished and unpublished manuscripts. The task was to check, and if necessary correct and add to, the existing published county reports, and to revise or construct afresh the information for the unpublished counties. A year is a short period in which to complete a work which had occupied another person for an academic lifetime. This is said by way of an apology because almost certainly some errors will exist. While a single error will upset the enclosure history of a single entry I do not think that the aggregate effect of all errors will seriously distort the temporal and spatial history of parliamentary enclosure which is presented in this volume.

The reader is referred to the complete volume of Tate's *Domesday* for details about individual enclosures and for an introductory summary of the methods of research employed.[22] The statistics in the present volume are an aggregation and analysis of the spatial and temporal incidence of parliamentary enclosure, and an analysis of the possible economic and social determinants of parliamentary enclosure. The enclosure data used are based almost entirely on Tate's *Domesday*. It was Tate's method throughout his academic life to treat enclosure in a piecemeal fashion. This was inevitable in an age when the organisation of record repositories was in its earliest stages of sophistication, in an age which was divided by a world war, and with a man whose formal academic training was, by modern standards at least, somewhat basic. He accepted the methods employed by central government in the presentation of enclosure evidence in their Blue Books and his piecemeal study took the form of the relatively inflexible county base. The precedent was already set by government, both nationally and locally, since the enclosure awards were enrolled upon completion with the respective *county* clerks of the peace. As editor of Tate's manuscripts it was convenient to adopt his county division; indeed the terms of acceptance as editor contained the unwritten clause that Tate's organisation of the material would remain relatively unchanged. Accordingly, the intimate relationship this present volume has with Tate's *Domesday* will in the first instance dictate that a county approach will be maintained and will inevitably suffer the criticism proffered by F. M. L. Thompson in review.[23] However, in all the chapters which follow this imposed rigidity will be slowly eroded as both the county and regional incidence of parliamentary enclosure will be dissected and examined, and cross-county comparisons made. The data must be presented in some form, and while the county unit may not be the most satisfactory one it suits initially the existing method of collection. It should be stressed that this is only the initial method of presentation and it will not blur the significance of the findings and conclusions.

Appendix 1 is a categorised summary of parliamentary enclosure, first by private and public local acts (combined) and second by the General Acts of 1836, 1840, 1845 and those following. Sections A and B of the Appendix embody the former and sections C, D, E, and F the latter categories. In addition sections A, C, and E embody enclosures which included *some* open field arable lands and sections B, D, and F summarise the enclosures *exclusively* of commons and wastes, including their many definitions such as moors, fens, mosses, heaths, and others.[24] The counterpart of Appendix 1 which translates the acts into acreages is contained in Appendix 2. The distinction between open field arable and common and waste was not very easy to make for all enclosures. They cannot all be readily identified as one or the other. In the midlands counties, which were predominantly open field arable enclosures (regardless of subsequent land use changes), a number of enclosures were composite land reforms involving other land uses. These different land uses are not always precisely distinguishable, not even by an inspection of the original documents. For example, a typical enclosure petition might recite that the

> Open arable fields, meadows, pastures, commons and waste grounds within the parish (manor, lordship, liberty etc.) of. . . in the county of. . . are intermixed and dispersed in small parcels and in their present state are incapable of any considerable improvement.[25]

The act might borrow the very same wording and this might in turn be found as the preamble to the award, recited in full without any further explanation or measurement of the different land types. Where it has been possible to identify the acreages of different land-use types from an inspection of the documents, the appropriate adjustments in all the Appendixes have been made. To illustrate this we notice that many Norfolk parliamentary enclosure awards distinguish between different land uses, showing quite clearly how many acres of open field arable were being enclosed and how many acres of common and waste. The appropriate arable acreage has been included in section A and the common and waste acreages in section B; at the same time care has been taken not to double count the number of acts. The problem between common and waste and open field arable is more easily solved for enclosures under the General Acts in sections C, D, E, and F, because more accurate descriptions of the land uses are given in the documents. Occasionally it is difficult to distinguish between C and D. The appropriate General Act for D is the 1840 Act which deals specifically with the enclosure of common and waste. This is the counterpart of the 1836 General Act which dealt specifically with open field arable. However, on inspection of some enclosure documents under these two Acts it seems clear that the terms of the Acts were sometimes misapplied. For example, in Cornwall there were eleven enclosures by authority of the 1836 Act though it is evident that they were not enclosures of open field arable; similarly with one Devon enclosure. In Essex the single enclosure under the 1840 General Act included only ¾ of an acre of common and waste out of a total enclosure of 89 acres. Similar misapplications of both the Acts occur with enclosures in Gloucestershire, Lancashire, Lincolnshire, Nottinghamshire, Staffordshire, Westmorland, and the West Riding of Yorkshire.[26] In the present study the appropriate transfer of details has taken place.

In some counties some enclosures have been included under section A, although in fact it is strongly suspected that they contained only a small proportion of open field arable. This problem does not arise when enclosures wholly concerned with common and waste are concerned since the wording of the documents is usually unambiguous.

There is therefore an admitted error in some of the figures presented in Appendix 2, sections A and B. For example, compare my entry for Somerset with the more intensive work on that county by Williams. He says that

> Between 1770 and the end of the nineteenth century, 144,369 acres of land, previously considered to be waste or commonable pasture, were enclosed by Parliamentary act throughout Somerset.[27]

From my Appendix the aggregate acreage of B, D, and F, which under my definition is common and waste, is 133,028 acres. The difference between this and Williams's estimate may be a real error on my part for overestimating the amount of open field arable and therefore underestimating the amount of common and waste, or it may be that Williams includes Exmoor Forest, which was 20,014 acres enclosed in 1815–17, as wholly in Somerset whereas I divide it equally with the county of Devon.[28] I am prepared to accept that I am in error, even to the extent of over 11,000 acres misallocated. However Somerset, along with one or two other counties where open field arable and common and waste were enclosed side by side and where common and waste was the more important, are few in number. Besides, the 11,000 acres error, if indeed it is real, may be uniquely high, but even so only represents 1·1 per cent of the county area. More seriously perhaps, such an error represents 6·6 per cent of all Somerset enclosures.

Other instances where this distinction between open field arable and common and waste may be somewhat blurred recently came to light at a meeting of the jointly held conference of the British Agricultural History Society and the Historical Geography section of the Institute of British Geographers. The discussant was Dr John Chapman of Portsmouth Polytechnic.[29] Chapman is currently analysing a 10 per cent sample of all English and Welsh enclosures, extracting from this sample every detail about every type of land which was being enclosed, as far as the enclosure awards allow such close definition to apply. Thus far he has compared a proportion of his 10 per cent sample with the earlier lists that Tate compiled. Taking issue with Tate's rather constricting structure of land type, in other words the inevitable fact that by lumping together all those places where *some* open field arable was enclosed will obscure the extent of common and waste enclosure, Chapman has found that for Berkshire and Cambridgeshire the extent of open field arable enclosure is not as important as Tate would have us believe. Whereas the total acreage enclosed will probably be quite accurate (see below, pp. 29–30 where I pose this question again) the true distinction between open field arable enclosure and common and waste enclosure may be blurred. In the case of Berkshire the Tate lists suggest that by acreage 94 per cent of parliamentary enclosure was open field arable enclosure; Chapman suggests that something like 53 per cent is nearer the truth. For Cambridgeshire the Tate lists suggest 85 per cent open field arable enclosure and Chapman suggests 72 per cent. In the case of the former county obviously the discrepancy is very large, but less so for the latter. The counties where this type of error occurs and will be most keenly felt are at the margin of the extensive open field arable country, such as Berkshire and its association with heaths and downs and Cambridge in the middle of the fens. Some doubts might also arise therefore over the distinction between open field arable and common and waste enclosure for the counties of Middlesex and Wiltshire. In both of these counties, as also with Berkshire and Cambridgeshire, over 20 per cent of the land area was subject to parliamentary enclosure. The West Riding of Yorkshire may also prove difficult of definition. Dr Chapman may have identified the two most wayward counties, and though he may, and almost certainly will, revise to a greater or less degree for nearly every county, perhaps such revisions will not necessarily be very great.[30] A recently published (1979) essay on Durham enclosures estimated that 106,785 acres were enclosed by Act of Parliament, which was encouragingly close to if not indistinguishable from my own estimate of 106,800 acres.[31]

In spite of this illustrated disclosure of errors I suggest that for most counties it will be small enough not to interfere seriously with the general impressions of density, distribution, and chronology of the two types of enclosure to be presented in the later appendixes, maps and analysis below.[32]

A second problem, though a smaller one for the compiler than for the user of the enclosure statistics, is that the classifications in use and the analysis of them convey no impression of what happened to the land after enclosure. Did it remain either as arable or as common and waste, or was the former converted to pasture and the latter ploughed up for tillage? This question may be partially answered for certain counties or parts of counties for specific moments in time, and it may be possible in the final chapters to draw conclusions as to the consequences of enclosure on land use or possibly the prospective changes in land use which may have acted as an incentive to enclose. Substantially however this question remains the province of another study.

Appendix 1 will indicate that there were 5,286 acts of enclosure, private, public, and under the General Acts. In fact this is a slight overestimate because some acts involved lands in more than one county. For example, Exmoor Forest enclosure was split between Somerset and Devon; Malvern Chase enclosure and disafforestation in 1664 involved land in Gloucestershire, Herefordshire, and Worcestershire; and the enclosure of Bishop's Stortford and Farnham in 1820–6 concerned 387 acres in Hertfordshire (Bishop's Stortford) and 235 acres in Essex (Farnham). There are 21 duplicates of acts in this sense and so the number of separate enactments was 5,265, as summarised in Table 1.

The final totals may differ from the estimates of other researchers; town improvement acts, unless they included some enclosure, have been omitted, so also have a number of other 'apparent' enclosures because on closer inspection they were found to be other than strict enclosures.[33] Full details can be found in the *Domesday.* Enclosures, or rather improvements enacted under the 1876 Commons Regulation and Improvement Act have also been omitted. There was a strong case for including them since they also relate to the appropriate year

Table 1. SUMMARY OF ENCLOSURES BY PARLIAMENTARY ACT

Type of act	Number of acts	Number of acts after correction for double counting
A	2,778	2,767
B	1,388	1,381
C	158	158
D	98	98
E	169	168
F	695	693
Total	5,286	5,265

where A is acts containing some open field arable
B is acts for common and waste only
C is enclosures of open field arable under the 1836 General Act
D is enclosures of common and waste under the 1840 General Act
E is enclosures of open field arable under the 1845 General Act et seq.
F is enclosures of common and waste under the 1845 General Act et seq.

of the 1845 Annual General Enclosure Act but nevertheless they have been excluded as not being ordinary enclosures. The interested reader is referred to the fuller details in the *Domesday* and in Baron Eversley (Sir G. J. S. Lefèvre), *English Commons and Forests* (London 1894).[34]

Appendix 1 indicates that the acreage information for some 218 enclosures is not known. This is mainly because the relevant documents, the enclosure awards and/or maps, have not survived or at least have not yet come to light.[35] Also, in some cases the information may not be available because the relevant acts and/or entries in the *Journal of the House of Commons* do not adequately attempt to estimate the size of the prospective enclosure. In Appendix 2 and subsequently the missing information has been inserted by means of the average of the known enclosure acreages. Thus the 101,192 acres of open field arable in Derbyshire (section A) has been derived by aggregating the 68 known acreages, dividing by 68 to give a mean size of enclosure and multiplying by 71 to give a final estimate which includes the three unknown acreages.[36] Where there is missing information a mean size of the known acreages is calculated and used as a notional mean for all like enclosures from which an estimate is derived. In all cases the calculations remain exclusive to the individual counties and also exclusive to the internal A–F subdivision within the counties. In this way it is hoped to eliminate as much as possible any misrepresentation because of regional differences or differences between types of enclosure. If both the actual acreage as mentioned in the award and the estimated acreage as mentioned in the act or the *Journal of the House of Commons* are known then it is the award acreage which is used if the two happen to differ. As Appendix 1 shows, most of the missing acreages occur in sections A and B. Even so, the subsumation of 218 guesstimates within a total population of 5,265 acts is a considerable advance on the 1,040 guesstimates out of a total population of 4,240 acts as calculated by G. Slater.[37]

Appendix 3 is a revision of Appendix 1 in terms of the county density of enclosure, that is the density measured as the percentage of county area enclosed by act of Parliament. There is another problem of definition here, namely precisely what is the county area from which to calculate percentages? Modern (1979) counties have resulted from radical reforms in local government administrative boundaries since 1974; reforms in terms of size, shape, and even nomenclature. Modern Tyne and Wear, Avon, Cleveland and others are herein ignored in preference for the counties as they were defined, by name at least, prior to 1974. Thus they number 42 for England, to include three separate ones for the three Ridings of Yorkshire, the Isle of Wight coupled with Hampshire, and Monmouthshire reckoned as part of England as indeed it was for enclosure purposes, at least in the eighteenth and nineteenth centuries. The enclosures which today fall within the Greater London area have been divided appropriately between the Home Counties to which they were historically affiliated, thus resurrecting the erstwhile county of Middlesex. There were strong claims for dividing both Sussex and Suffolk each into their two halves of east and west, and Lincolnshire into its three divisions of Lindsey, Kesteven and Holland. While the temptation has been resisted in the appendixes, in the discussion in the chapters below the opportunity has been taken to look at Lincolnshire and Suffolk separately in some detail to indicate the different regional characteristics of enclosure. I have included the enclosures of each parish in the counties in which they existed prior to 1974. This presented no great problems or errors except that some parishes in certain west midlands counties were formerly in an adjacent county, for example at the time of enclosure. On balance, however many parishes each county has lost in the nineteenth and twentieth centuries it has regained them in like numbers from other counties. At its worst, Warwickshire has gained more than it has lost with the effect of slightly overestimating the extent of parliamentary enclosure in that county.

Where the land in an enclosure was split between two or more counties, as in the case of Exmoor Forest outlined earlier, the acreage concerned has been divided equitably between the counties unless the enclosure documents assign the acreages between counties separately, as with

with Bishop's Stortford and Farnham assigned to Hertfordshire and Essex respectively, also mentioned above.

Recent, that is to say 1974, county boundaries do not necessarily conform to their historical counterparts, for there were a number of administrative county changes in the nineteenth century as well as in the twentieth.[38] The county acreage figures given in the 1831 Census volumes are inaccurate, a fact which the volumes readily admit, yet a definition of the county for the year 1831 probably most accurately defines the counties of this study.[39] The Census came at the end of the main waves of parliamentary enclosure activity and includes nearly all of those enclosures defined under sections A and B of the appendixes. Other estimates of county area simply do not agree with one another. For example, Bartholomew's 1903 *Survey Atlas of England and Wales* gives three estimated areas for the counties:

(a) based on the ancient (undefined) county;
(b) based on the administrative county;
(c) based on the registration county.[40]

The aggregate acreage for England is the same in all three cases but within the counties there are differences. The 1873 *Returns of Waste Lands* quotes yet another set of acreages which in turn differ from the acreages used in the Census of 1951.[41] As far as any maps produced in this volume are concerned, most county boundary changes are not very important since on the scale that the maps have been drawn such changes in boundary could easily be obscured by the thickness of a cartographic line. However, in that the maps refer to broad ranges of grouped frequency data (in the sense that the density of enclosure is categorised in divisions ranging from 0 to 100 per cent), the choice of base county acreage becomes important in those cases where the density of enclosure approximately coincides with a change in group size. Thus calculating from the 1831 Census acreages it appears that 40·2 per cent of Lincolnshire was enclosed by act of Parliament, whereas by calculating from the 1873 Census returns the density of enclosure was 38·8 per cent. If 40·0 per cent marks the boundary between two groups of density for cartographic purposes then the choice of base county acreage can be important. Similar problems occur with Warwickshire and the North Riding of Yorkshire. Appendix 4 can be used to compare the effect on the density of enclosure of the counties by using different base county acreages. For the remainder of this book the calculations with respect to density are based on the 1873 county acreages if for no other reason than that they seem to be the most reliable of the earlier official estimates and to all intents and purposes the 1870s mark the very end of the era of parliamentary enclosure. But to illustrate that the differences between the different base counties are small and do not misrepresent the relative importance of the different counties in terms of density, Appendix 4a is a rank correlation coefficient matrix comparing the ranking of each county density of enclosure in each of the five base county estimates with its relative position in the other four. Thus in one estimate Oxfordshire is the leading county and in another it is second to Cambridgeshire. A perfect correlation in rank order would give a coefficient of 1·0. The worst correlation coefficient obtained was 0·969, which was a comparison between the 1831 Census base county and the 1956 estimate. The worst correlation involving my 1873 base county standard was 0·971, which was a comparison with the 1956 county.[42]

It should be realised at this stage that certain admissions of error have been made over the presentation of enclosure evidence in this book. There have been difficulties in distinguishing open field arable from common and waste; in defining the county in use; but in particular there is the difficulty that 218 enclosure acreages have been estimated, and a number of others rely on possibly dubious estimates from the acts of Parliament and from the *Journal of the House of Commons*. Even so, the evidence is more reliable, more accurate than the evidence heretofore in use from Slater and Gonner. However, suppose that all of the estimates are plus or minus 5 per cent in error, or even plus or minus 10 per cent in error. To what extent would such errors still give acceptable tolerance limits from which to form crucial conclusions regarding the spatial and temporal history of parliamentary enclosure? The county densities with plus or minus 5 and 10 per cent error limits are given in Appendix 5. At the 10 per cent level the leading county, Oxfordshire, fluctuates between 48·9 per cent and 59·8 per cent of the county enclosed by act. Even if Oxfordshire was overestimated by the full 10 per cent and all other counties similarly underestimated by the full 10 per cent, the county would still be listed in the top eight counties enclosed by act. At the more realistic 5 per cent error level Oxfordshire falls within the range 51·6–57·1 per cent, and whichever way all the other counties are treated it would always be at least among the top five counties. Lincolnshire was the leading county in terms of acreage and at its worst, 10 per cent overestimated, was 34·8 per cent enclosed, and at its best, 10 per cent underestimated, was 42·5 per cent enclosed (or at the 5 per cent level, between 36·7 and 40·6 per cent enclosed).

The worst feelings of doubt perhaps can be expressed over the figures calculated for Gloucestershire where there are 46 estimated acreages out of a total of 195 enclosures for the county, and for Herefordshire where there are 19 estimated acreages out of a total of 72 enclosures. Together these two counties account for 30 per cent of all the estimated acreages. For whatever contemporary administrative reason the enclosure commissioners and their clerks who drew up the Gloucestershire awards give no indication of aggregate acreage enclosed after about 1805, or at least rarely so.

A plan of the book

Perhaps the most important question that needs to be asked, because the most comprehensive, is Why was there so much Parliamentary enclosure between about 1730 and about 1870? Before an answer can be attempted it is first necessary to ask and attempt to answer a number of subsidiary questions. The 'why' must remain subordinate at this stage because the remainder of the question presupposes, at least qualitatively, that:

(1) a lot of enclosure took place (so much) and that it was of a special sort (Parliamentary);

(2) it took place in a particular locale (England);

(3) it took place in a particular chronology (c. 1730–1870).

The question conveys no impression of *how much* of the *special sort* was enclosed; *where* it was enclosed unless it assumes uniform distribution over England; or *when* it was enclosed unless it assumes uniform enclosure over time. The 'why' will therefore be the last element of the question to be answered once it is known how much, where, and when parliamentary enclosure occurred.

The following chapters tackle in turn each of the elements of the main question. Chapter 2 establishes the size of the parliamentary enclosure movement in terms of acres and densities of enclosure and relates this to the geographical distribution of (1) total enclosure; (2) open field arable enclosure; (3) common and waste enclosure. The counties can also be ranked in order of importance into those where parliamentary enclosure was very important and those where it was insignificant. Chapter 3 establishes when parliamentary enclosure occurred and again it is treated on a county basis. It also discusses the different types of enclosure, whether open field arable or common and waste. The overriding result will be the establishment of two separate enclosure movements each of approximately 20 years' duration, thus condensing 140 years of parliamentary enclosure history into 40 years of intensive (temporal) and extensive (spatial) activity. Chapters 4–7 will then try to answer the 'why' element of the question. First of all there will be some model building and econometric testing of the model to establish the possible determinants of enclosure. Prices, money supply, population, war, food self-sufficiency will all be offered separately or in association with one another as possible determinants. The book will conclude by discussing two alternative determinants of enclosure. The first will discuss land shortage in the century before 1750 as a reason for the first wave of intensive enclosure activity up to 1780. It will suggest that this land shortage was keenly felt in the heavy-soiled areas, the counties of the midland clays, where in view of the depression of grain prices in the second quarter of the eighteenth century there was insufficient land available to extend pastoral activities as long as the land remained in open fields. The second study will investigate the relationship, if any, between landownership and the chronology of parliamentary enclosure.

2

The Spatial Setting

The overall spatial setting

The statistics presented in Appendixes 1–5 contain the bare facts about parliamentary enclosure; they are important in their own right as a body of hitherto unknown information, but their function should now be as a springboard for other investigations. They convey only a marginal explanation of geographical distribution in that they display the information under county headings, but they give no sense of chronology except to be bracketed between starting and terminal dates. For a fuller insight into the ramifications of spatial and temporal differences it is useful, even necessary, to submit the statistics to a different kind of manipulation and present them in other forms, that is to say in maps of spatial differentiation and density of enclosure, and graphs of temporal differentiation, and to investigate the individual histories of enclosure for at least a small proportion of the counties. In this way it may be possible to appreciate better the important variations in time and space that took place.

From the first act of Parliament for the enclosure of the Dorset village of Radipole in 1604 to the last act in 1914, there were 5,265 private and public acts, and enactments under the several General Acts, for the enclosure of land in England.[1] In particular this land reform can be compressed into the period from 1750 to 1819 inclusive when 3,828 acts were passed, all of which were private or public local acts.[2] Over all time the 5,265 acts accounted for the enclosure of 6·8 million acres (to the nearest 100,000 acres) which was 20·9 per cent of the surface area of England, though of course a very much higher proportion of the surface area available for agricultural use.[3] In terms of acres enclosed the leading counties in descending order of importance were:

County	Number of acts	Acreage enclosed
Lincolnshire	362	667,099
Yorkshire, West	362	432,278
Norfolk	322	420,363
Northampton	210	335,587
Yorkshire, East	186	335,333
Total	1,442	2,190,660

In each of these counties there were over 300,000 acres enclosed by acts of Parliament. In only five counties, therefore, i.e. a little over 12 per cent of the English counties, there were 2·2 million acres enclosed which taken together accounted for 32·2 per cent of all parliamentary enclosure and 27·4 per cent of all enclosure acts passed. If Yorkshire was treated as one county then in acreage terms it was the leading county with 1,022,361 acres or 15·4 per cent of all parliamentary enclosure. At the opposite end of the scale, the counties with fewer than 50,000 acres enclosed by Act of Parliament were:

County	Number of acts	Acreage enclosed
Middlesex	38	49,956
Essex	76	41,818
Devon	71	41,643
Rutland	30	41,376
Sussex	85	40,969
Hereford	72	32,972
Cheshire	55	29,179[4]
Monmouth	13	16,370
Cornwall	31	10,539
Kent	34	8,071
Total	505	312,893

From a little under 25 per cent of all English counties this group yields only 4·6 per cent of all parliamentary enclosure or 9·6 per cent of all enclosure acts. As will be demonstrated, there is an alternative, possibly more justifiable and certainly clearer way to present these enclosure statistics, that is as proportions or densities of the respective county areas.

Parliamentary enclosure was possibly the largest single aggregate landscape change induced by man in an equivalent period of time. In a number of ways it surely warrants this weight of significance, producing as it did scattered farmsteads where once nucleated villages proliferated, hedgerows or stonewalls and thus a mosaic of geometrically shaped fields, and ordered landownership patterns where once existed the relatively disorderly open fields with their complicated ownership patterns and equally complex tenurial or occupational and farming patterns. The fast rate which this process of change attained did not begin until 1750 and it was not maintained beyond 1830. In fact by this last date 18·4 per cent of England had submitted to the gavel of Parliament and its army of enclosure commissioners and surveyors, out of a final total of 20·9 per cent which was ultimately enclosed by acts.

Enclosure was by no means a continuous process in time or across space, and there were important temporal and spatial variations. Appendix 3 reinterprets the gross acreages of Appendix 2 into proportions or densities of enclosure expressed as a density of county area. This allows an easier comparison of importance between the counties based on the ranking of densities. The final column of Appendix 3 is presented as a map of relative density of enclosure in Fig. 1.

The 20·9 per cent of England that was enclosed by parliamentary Act varied from the seemingly and relatively insignificant 0·8, 1·2, and 2·5 per cent for Kent, Cornwall, and Devon, to the seemingly and relatively very significant 54·3, 53·4, and 53·0 per cent for Oxfordshire, Cambridgeshire, and Northamptonshire. Bearing in mind that isolated buildings, villages, towns, standing water, waterways, and highways existed and must therefore have consumed a certain percentage of county area, the last three mentioned counties were conceivably enclosed by Act to the extent of 70 per cent or more of the land available for possible agricultural use. The stated proportions do not mean that most of Kent, Cornwall, and Devon still await enclosure, since they were enclosed at other periods of time, mainly before the eighteenth century, and in many cases may in fact in large measure have never been 'open'.[5] Nor is enclosure in the widest sense of the word yet complete; there are still lands that are in many respects open and subject to common rights of varying distinctions. Perhaps the most famous surviving example of the open fields with many of the ancient field rules and regulations still in operation is to be found in the Nottinghamshire village of Laxton, though many would argue that there the preservation of the open fields is maintained artificially as a kind of living museum piece.[6]

The Law of Property Act of 1925 and the Commons Registration Act of 1965 are the most recent major enactments regarding commons. The former related to metropolitan commons, manorial wastes, commons situated within boroughs or urban districts and other commons to which it would subsequently apply. It allowed the public a general right of access for air and exercise over those lands covered by it, subject to the protection of the common itself and to the

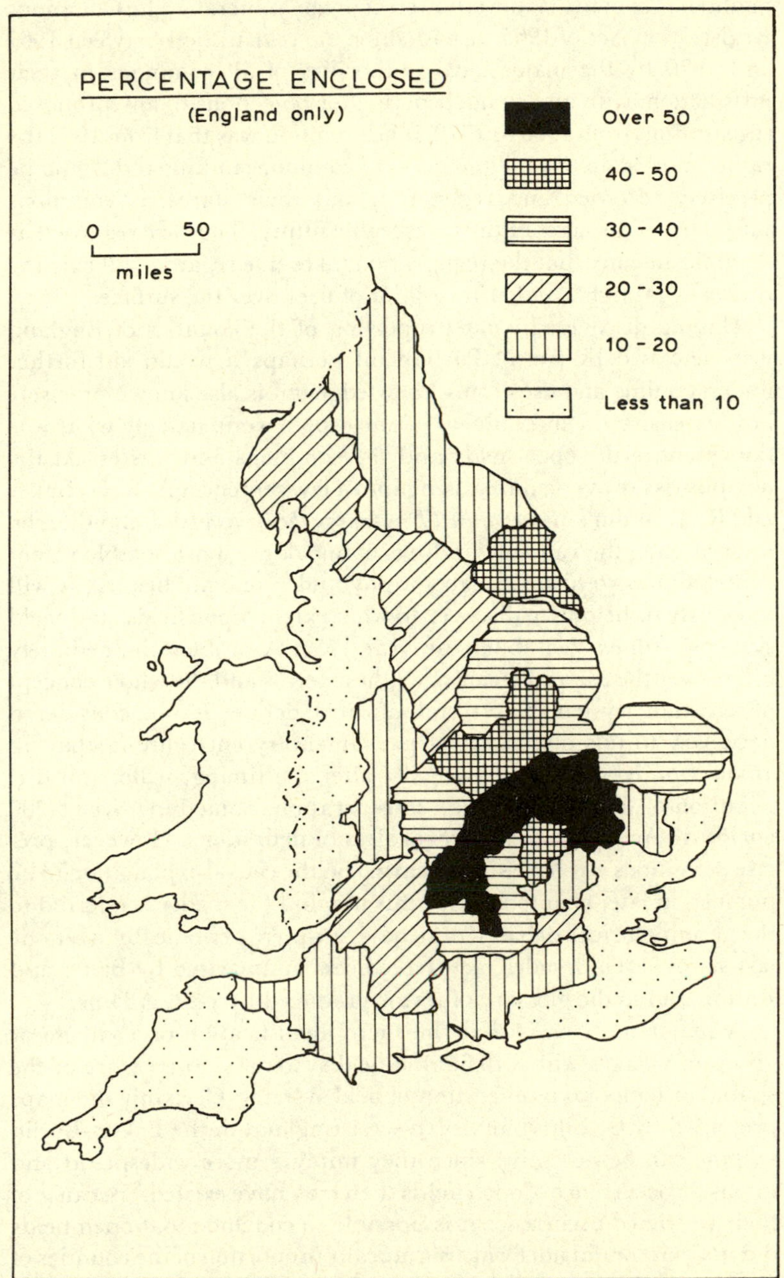

Fig. 1. Density of parliamentary enclosure in England.

maintenance of the manorial interest in any minerals. The Commons Registration Act of 1965 provided for the registration between 1967 and 1970 by the major local authorities of all commons in their jurisdiction, with an extended period for objections to any proposed registrations from 1968 to 1972. The intention was that from 1972 the rather more than one million acres of commons in England would be precisely recorded and registered, and their status as commons safeguarded throughout the foreseeable future. They are regarded as a public amenity, but the registration takes due regard of all existing proven legal rights, either in soil, or of user over the surface.[7]

Having discovered what proportion of the counties of England were enclosed by Act of Parliament perhaps it would aid further understanding and use of this knowledge if it is also known precisely how extensive the forerunners of enclosures were, namely what was the extent of the open fields and the commons and wastes. At the obvious risk of over-summarising into a few sentences A. R. H. Baker and R. A. Butlin's *Studies of Field Systems in the British Isles*, and thereby undermining the valuable findings of one of the most notable recent contributions to historical geography and economic history, it will obviously be helpful to discover to what extent 'open fields' and 'field systems' still existed about the year 1750. A problem immediately arises over the use and meaning of these terms and the whole concept of agrarian 'systems'. A terminological debate is not considered necessary to this discussion of parliamentary enclosure in that no amount of definition will radically alter the timing, scale, and distribution of the change under consideration. Something over 5,200 enclosure Acts were passed regardless of definitions. However, precise definitions *may* have some bearing on the causal explanation to be pursued in later chapters. With this in mind the reader is referred to the terminological debates that have erupted periodically over the last six or seven decades, and have been summarised by Baker and Butlin, and to the glossary of terms produced by I. H. Adams.[8]

A major problem is that the mere identification of a village or group of villages with a definable field system is no measure of the spatial or temporal proliferation of field systems. Certainly the maps presented by G. Elliott for north-west England in the Baker–Butlin volume can be deceptive since they imply a more widespread and intensive occurrence of open fields than may have existed.[9] Because of their restricted occurrence it is possible to conclude that open fields did not exist or did not form a significant proportion of the counties of Cumberland, Westmorland, Lancashire, and Cheshire, though in the first two the highly localised coastal disposition of the open fields was obviously important. The open fields of Durham and Northumberland in turn were located mainly in the eastern third of those counties. By a similar process, some may say of arbitrary segregation, it is possible to construct a list of counties from Baker–Butlin in all of which the open fields were of lasting importance, being extensive in spatial terms until at least 1750. Apologies must be extended to the contributors to the Baker–Butlin volume if it appears that their endeavours have been too much reduced. This treatment in no way detracts from the value derived from the book.

In order as they appear in the Baker–Butlin book it is possible to identify the following as important open field counties about the year 1750:[10] Yorkshire, West Riding; Yorkshire, East Riding; Warwickshire; Worcestershire; Nottinghamshire; Leicestershire; Rutland; Lincolnshire; Northamptonshire; Cambridgeshire, and Norfolk. Though David Roden in his chapter on the 'Chiltern Hills and Environs' discusses the counties of Oxfordshire, Buckinghamshire, and Bedfordshire, one is left with the impression that these were not important open field counties on the eve of the great parliamentary enclosures. This impression must be corrected and these counties must join our list because the open fields were, in all three, very extensive well into the eighteenth century north and north-west of the Chiltern cuesta, that is in about 75 per cent of Oxfordshire, 65 per cent of Buckinghamshire and practically all of Bedfordshire. But the Baker–Butlin volume is by no means complete and to the list must be added the counties of Gloucestershire, Huntingdonshire, Derbyshire, and Wiltshire, and possibly Hampshire as well, in all of which to varying degrees the open fields still abounded in the mid-eighteenth century. They may have abounded even more except for some periods of specific enclosure activity as for example occurred in the Cotswolds of Gloucestershire where court rolls of the sixteenth century 'teem with notices of enclosure', at the height of the Cotswold woollen trade.[11] The remainder of the county stayed in open fields until the eighteenth century. Baker, in H. C. Darby's *A New Historical Geography of England*, points to the fact that some districts which from evidence in the 1334 lay subsidy returns were midlands open fields were, by 1600, enclosed. He is referring mainly to the western counties of Herefordshire and Shropshire and parts of Staffordshire, Worcestershire, Warwickshire, Gloucestershire, and Somerset.[12] Elsewhere we learn that

> The bulk of Somerset was enclosed by hedges at an early date, the only unenclosed ground being in the great commons and wastes which were the hard core of difficult lands then left.[13]

F. V. Emery, also in the Darby volume, establishes that the coastal lowlands, for example of Durham and Cumberland, and from Lancashire to the Cheshire plain, was an enclosed countryside in 1600. Some land had always been so and had probably been taken in directly from the waste. He extends the area to confirm Baker's evidence about the Welsh Borders and to include the south-western counties and much of south-east England. For the last he says that by 1600 Essex, Kent, Suffolk, Hertfordshire, Surrey, and Sussex were almost entirely enclosed.[14] There was much early enclosure in Hertfordshire because it was a highly esteemed corn county with a close proximity to the largest market, London. It can be considered 'several' for the purposes of a study of parliamentary enclosure except for the open chalk plateau in the north-east of the county on the Cambridgeshire border.[15] As Arthur Young remarked, Hertfordshire was a county 'generally enclosed *of old time*'.[16] In neighbouring Middlesex the two centuries which elapsed between Norden's acclaim of it as a great corn county and the Board of Agriculture's *General Views* of the 1790s and 1800s were ones of great construction for buildings, roads, estates, and parks as well as for enclosures. In other words Middlesex can be eliminated as an open field county perhaps for reasons other than the usual pre-1750 enclosure.[17] Kent, Essex, and Devon became known as the three counties where 'inclosures be most',[18] and in the last named,

> at all times (and especially after the enclosure movements of the Middle Ages) open fields were to be found at only a small proportion of the total number of settlements within the county.[19]

Thus for the present study Devon, along with a number of other counties, can be conveniently treated as though it was *never* in open fields.

There is a broad similarity between the list compiled above and the main counties of parliamentary enclosure illustrated in the Appendixes and in the map of density of parliamentary enclosure. Not altogether an earth-shattering conclusion, but perhaps indicative of the fact that *non-parliamentary enclosure* after 1750 took place in the same areas as parliamentary enclosure. The characteristics of the differing field systems that evolved in different places commanded that by about 1750 the map of density of parliamentary enclosure should also represent the relative survival or density of those archaic systems, intermixed with common and waste. These last land classifications call for serious qualifications to the general conclusion, namely to what extent field systems ever existed in upland, fenland, or heathland England, though this may become clearer in due course as the story unfolds.

Some regional examples

The south midlands

The list of open field counties culled from Baker and Butlin needs serious amendment because within those counties the open fields and common grounds were not necessarily evenly distributed. So much can be gathered from a close reading of Elliott's contribution on Cumberland and Westmorland and from Butlin's contribution on Durham and Northumberland.[20] Further illustration of this point can be made with reference to many other counties. Thus in Buckinghamshire and Oxfordshire the distribution of open fields in time and space can seriously disfigure the general impression of parliamentary enclosure derived from county statistics. In Buckinghamshire for example there are three broad physiographic regions within and between which there were considerable differences in the occurrence and/or survival of the open fields. The county can be divided broadly into: the clays to the north and north-west of the county to incorporate the gault of the Vale of Aylesbury, the Kimmeridge and Oxford clays of central Buckinghamshire and the glacial boulder clays which overlie the Oolitic succession in the north; the chalk escarpment of the Chiltern Hills with its south-east facing dip slope, in some places overlaid with a superficial covering of clay-with-flints; and lastly, in the southernmost part of the county a region of lighter soils dominated by the river terrace gravels of the rivers Thames and Colne. Open fields so described could be found in all three of these regions but broadly speaking the county can be resolved into two, the clays of the midland plain and the Chiltern uplands, Leland's 'champaine' and 'Chilterne'. The latter was mainly early enclosed, that is before 1750, and was only touched by parliamentary Act with the enclosure of scattered commons and wastes.[21] The clays, in direct contrast, were dominated by parliamentary enclosures, and these clays continued into the adjacent counties of Northamptonshire, Oxfordshire, and Bedfordshire in all of which more than 45 per cent of the land area was enclosed by Act after 1750. Yet for Buckinghamshire the comparable density of enclosure was only 35·3 per cent.

Figure 2 illustrates the essential difference between the Chilterns and the adjacent clay vale and is in part an explanation of why the

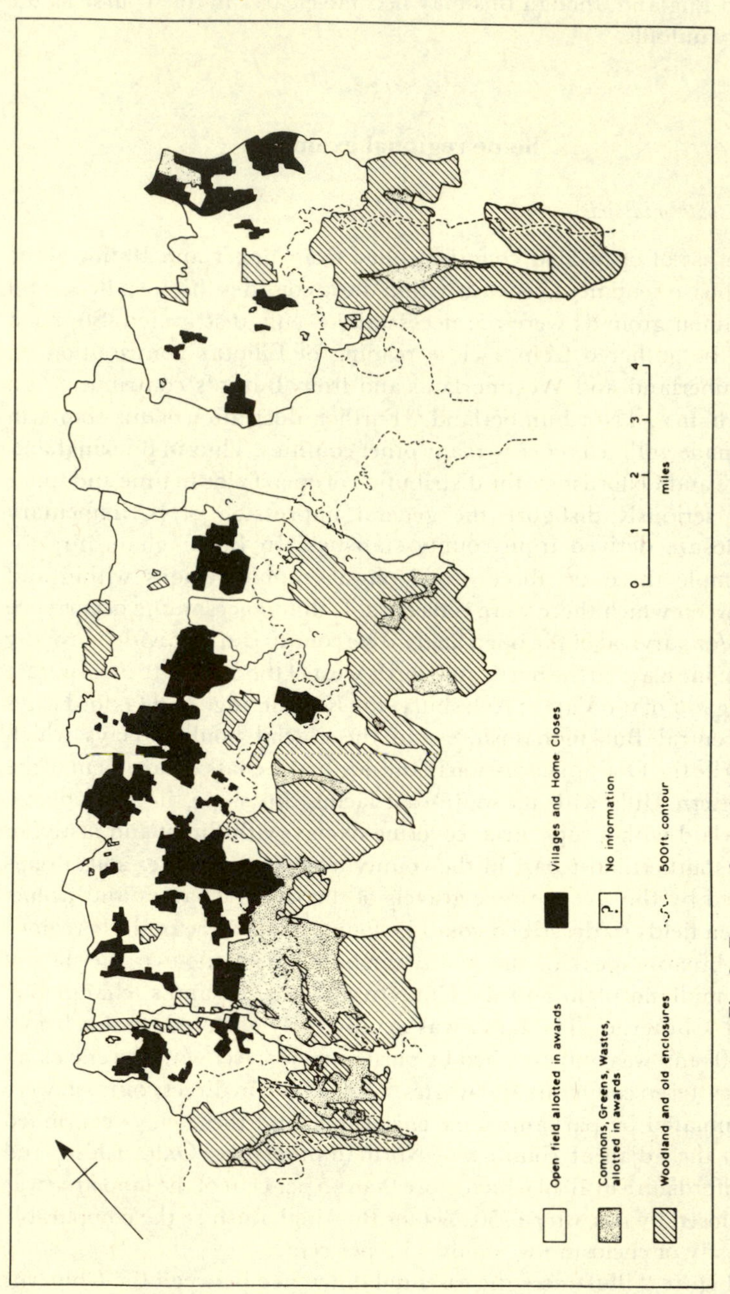

Fig. 2. Extent of open field in the Chiltern/Vale parishes of Buckinghamshire.

density of enclosure in Buckinghamshire as a whole does not compare very favourably with the other midland plain counties.[22] J. T. Coppock has also drawn a sharp distinction between the Chilterns and the Vale: the early enclosure of the former produced isolated farmsteads or 'court' farms and demesne farms, whereas the later enclosures of the Vale produced village farms.[23] See also David Roden's map in Baker and Butlin which shows the location of common arable fields mainly in the north and north-west shadow of the Chiltern escarpment.[24]

If Buckinghamshire is divided into its eight constituent ancient hundreds and separate densities of enclosure calculated for each it reveals that four of the five northern or 'clay' hundreds had densities well in excess of the county average of 35·3 per cent, giving figures comparable with Northamptonshire, Bedfordshire, and Oxfordshire, thus:

Hundred	Density of enclosure
Cottesloe	57·7 %
Newport Pagnell	43·7
Buckingham	40·8
Aylesbury	48·4
Ashenden	27·3

The exception in north Buckinghamshire is the hundred of Ashenden which is long associated with the ancient royal forest of Bernwood and parts of the extensive old enclosed estates of the Earls of Verney and the Earls and Dukes of Buckingham. The average density of enclosure for north Buckinghamshire was therefore approximately 44 per cent, which is much more representative of the midlands open fields and would place the county eighth in ranked order of all counties, assuming that not such a large correction was necessary for other counties. The two Chiltern hundreds of Burnham and Desborough were only enclosed by Act to the extent of 7·0 and 9·1 per cent respectively of land area, and the enclosure of Stoke hundred situated in the southernmost part of the county on the light soils of the river terrace gravels was also less than the county average. The neighbouring county of Oxfordshire also contains parishes within the Chilterns but far fewer than those in Buckinghamshire such that in the seventeenth century the county was 'with the exception of a small area of Chiltern country in the extreme south an almost entirely open field county'.[25] This comes out to a certain extent in the following table, though using number of townships as a measure of density of enclosure clearly overstates the case since the 'number' of townships will include areas of land which were not in open fields.

Table 2. CHRONOLOGY OF ENCLOSURE IN OXFORDSHIRE (BY TOWNSHIP)

Region	Before 1640	1640–1730	After 1730	Number of townships
Redlands	13%	Nil	87%	39
Cotswolds and Stonebrash	15	21	64	100
Chilterns	35	17	48	23
Clay Vales	21	10	69	121
Oxfordshire	19	13	68	283

Source: F. Emery, *The Oxfordshire Landscape* (1974), 111.

The densities of enclosure for the Buckinghamshire hundreds of Aylesbury and Cottesloe itemised above would be even higher if the presence of the Chilterns could be eliminated altogether. Both of these hundreds include parishes which share both Chiltern and Vale topographies, that is they are long and narrow in shape, typical of scarpland Britain, extending from deep in the Vale of Aylesbury, up the scarp slope of the Chilterns and then deep into the south-easterly facing dip slope.[26] The enclosures of the parishes of Princes Risborough (1820–3), Monks Risborough (1830–9), Bledlow (1809–12), Cheddington (1853–7), Ivinghoe (1821–5), Pitstone (1853–6), and Wendover (1794–7) were all large in acreage and almost entirely consisted of open field arable which was concentrated in the shadow of the Chilterns in the clay Vale of Aylesbury. This is clearly illustrated in Fig 2, the transect along the crest of the Chiltern escarpment showing the influence of the Chilterns, an area dominated by woodlands and old enclosures, though also with areas of commons, greens, and wastes which were allotted at enclosure. The plan attached to the Wendover enclosure award clearly shows a distinct boundary as the old enclosures of the hills gave way to the open fields of the Vale.[27]

The west midlands

Such regional variations within the same county are not peculiar to Buckinghamshire and Oxfordshire, however, and J. M. Martin has described the soil and topographical complexities of Warwickshire. The Felden in the south was different from the pastoral Arden forest in the north and within the Felden there was the difference between the fertile Avon valley and the heavy intractable clays of the south-east, towards the Northamptonshire border (and from hence on to the clays of north Buckinghamshire and Oxfordshire).[28] This distinction in Warwickshire, which can also be traced into neighbouring Staffordshire and Worcestershire, is well illustrated by B. K. Roberts in his contribution to the Baker–Butlin volume.[29] For Worcestershire J. A. Yelling draws the similar distinction between the woodland and the champion country. The latter, in the south of the county, contained extensive open fields such that the density of parliamentary enclosure was as high as 43 per cent, easily in the mainstream of midlands enclosures, compared to the woodland in the north and west of the county where the density was only 4 per cent. These are figures taken from Yelling's own study of the county.[30] My own figures, while agreeing with the general impression given by Yelling, show a lower density of enclosure. For example, the highest density discovered was for Blackenheath (Lower) Hundred with a density of 40·7 per cent and Pershore (Upper) Hundred also with 40·7 per cent. If Staffordshire can be counted as a northern extension of the woodlands of Worcestershire and Warwickshire then its enclosure history accords well with that of its neighbours. Enclosure proceeded apace in Staffordshire in the centuries before the eighteenth, such that only 3·3 per cent of the county was enclosed by Act of Parliament.[31]

West Yorkshire

The West Riding of Yorkshire is a county with enormous regional variations. This is inevitable considering its size. It contains the extensive uplands of the Pennine chain and the Dales where no widespread open field system ever existed, or at least where if it did exist it was relatively restricted to the valley bottoms. Instead permanent pasture, either regulated in stints or existing as waste, predominated in these upland areas but was sharply juxtaposed with the Vale of York which was characterised by a recognisable open field system. This is well illustrated when the different types of parliamentary enclosure – the open field arable as distinguished from the commons and wastes–are investigated. While the enclosure of the county as a whole appears to be uniform in terms of density, with a low of 13·0 per cent for the Liberty of Leeds and a high of 89·9 per cent for the Soke of Doncaster but with all other divisions ranging more narrowly from 14·3 to 36·7 per cent, when the type of enclosure is investigated more closely it is noticeable that in the east towards the Vale of York the enclosure was mainly of open-field arable, while in the west and north in the Pennines and Dales, it was mainly the enclosure of commons and wastes. For example, Asbrigg Upper Wapentake on the Lancashire border, in the south-west, was enclosed to the extent of 32·7 per cent of area, which when subdivided was 11·4 per cent open field arable and 21·4 per cent common and waste; and in Staincliff West Wapentake where 23·3 per cent was enclosed only 1·0 per cent was open field arable and 22·3 per cent common and waste. In contrast, in the east of the Riding into and towards the Vale of York the corresponding densities of enclosure for Barkstone Ash Upper Wapentake were 29·7 per cent total enclosure composed of 29·3 per cent open field arable and 0·4 per cent common and waste, and for Osgoldcross Lower Wapentake the densities were 30·9, 22·8 and 8·1 per cent respectively. The only West Riding division which does not conform to this general pattern is Staincliff East Wapentake in the north-west, where the densities were 32·1, 18·6 and 13·5 per cent. The general pattern for the county would predict a lower second and correspondingly a higher third figure, but this Wapentake embraces Airedale and Wharfedale where much of the enclosure was open field arable in the floors of the valleys.[32] Williams's analysis of Somerset enclosures also shows that 97·6 per cent of all common and waste enclosure occurred in only four areas, all of them marginal for one or other reason, either hills as in the Mendips or lands liable to floods like the Levels.[33] This method of highlighting the topographical characteristics of commons enclosures is corroborated to some extent by S. R. Eyre in his study of part of north Derbyshire where he found that the upward limit of cultivation on the uplands could be traced to the enclosure of commons and wastes between 1775 and 1855. In other words the maximum altitudinal extent of cultivated land predated the mid-nineteenth century and was marginal land brought into cultivation by parliamentary enclosure.[34]

Lincolnshire

In Lincolnshire seemingly, the density of enclosure was 38·7 per cent of the land area, but this is a county with considerable diversity within its borders. Consider the three divisions of Lincolnshire, that is Holland, Kesteven and Lindsey, summarised as follows. Of the 362 enclosure acts for the county only 37 were concerned with the division of Holland, the south-eastern division containing the extensive fenlands and bordering the Wash, but these few Acts affected 37·8 per cent of the division. More specifically 27·4 per cent of Holland was

Table 3. TYPES OF ENCLOSURE IN LINCOLNSHIRE (ESTIMATED ACREAGE, AND AS A PERCENTAGE OF THE DIVISION)

Division (acres)	A[a]	B	C	D	E	F	Total[c]
Holland (263,120)	27,259	71,363				776	99,398 (37 Acts)
	10·4%	27·1%[b]				0·3%	37·8%[b]
Lindsey (972,796)	283,610	58,692		14,516	5,592	2,454	365,864 (222 Acts)
	29·2%	6·1%		1·5%	0·6%	0·3%	37·6%
Kesteven (469,377)	183,977	19,820		274		527	204,598 (107 Acts)
	39·2%	4·2%		1·5%		0·1%	43·6%
County	28·7%	8·6%		0·9%	0·3%	0·2%	38·7%

a. Categories A–F are the same as used in Appendixes 1, 2, and 3 and Table 1.

b. Of which 14·3 per cent comprises the four enclosures of four very large fens, Haut Huntre 1767, Market Deeping 1801, Wildmore 1801, and East and West Fen 1801. See note 35.

c. The total aggregate acreage does not equal the aggregate given in Appendix 2 because the 11 pieces of missing information have been re-estimated within their separate divisions. The total number of Acts is 365 whereas in Appendix 1 only 362 are entered; this is because four of the Acts embraced two or more of the three divisions and are therefore double-counted in this Table.

common and waste enclosure of which 14·3 per cent was enclosed by the four large fen enclosures of Haut Huntre 1767 (18,052 acres), Market Deeping 1801 (8,790 acres), Wildmore Fen 1801 (8,086 acres but shared with Kesteven and Lindsey) and East and West Fen 1801 (16,059 acres but shared with Lindsey).[35] Holland therefore, though superficially in the mainstream of parliamentary enclosure, was in fact far removed from counties like Buckinghamshire and Norfolk, in both of which also over 30 per cent of the county area was enclosed by act. It was far removed because of the overwhelming influence of enclosure of other than open field arable and in particular because of the four large fen enclosures. Indeed the role of drainage in land reclamation was as important or even more important than the role of enclosure, but in fact that drainage could not take place without also recourse to enclosure.[36] In direct contrast, in Kesteven 43·6 per cent of the division was enclosed by act of Parliament of which 39·2 per cent was open field arable. Lindsey also was predominantly open field arable but its importance in terms of density is reduced somewhat because it is such a large division. There were more acres involved at enclosure in Lindsey and overall the division contained about 55 per cent of all Lincolnshire enclosures.

Thus we see the open field arable enclosures which embraced the midland counties extending up the east coast to include the greater part of Lincolnshire, the East Riding of Yorkshire, the Vale of York, and the eastern half of the West Riding. The North York Moors and the Cleveland Hills acted as the effective northern boundary of extensive open field arable. We also see how artificial it is to consider an area as large as Lincolnshire or the three Ridings of Yorkshire as single units for even within the sub-regions it is possible to find different expressions of enclosure both in type and chronology.[37]

Some eastern counties

Perhaps Cambridgeshire is the county where the problems presented by size of study unit and changing topography within study unit can give a most misleading impression of the distribution of parliamentary enclosure. In brief – since fuller illumination appears later[38] – perhaps as much as 70 per cent of south Cambridgeshire was enclosed by act of Parliament compared with only 10–20 per cent of the northern or fenland half. The density for the whole county therefore is reduced to 53 per cent which, though it makes it one of the top three counties, nevertheless hides the importance of the fact that the southern half of the county was predominantly in open fields in 1750, or even in 1790, and that in the following 60 years it underwent what can only be described as the most concentrated agricultural organisational change that there had ever been, certainly in that county and probably in any county.

In neighbouring Suffolk also there was a considerable regional variation in the distribution and density of enclosure. Only 10 per cent of the county was enclosed by act of Parliament but this obscures the important fact that there was considerable concentration of the different types of enclosure with open field arable mainly in west Suffolk and common and waste in east Suffolk. This is illustrated in Table 4.

There was nearly four times the acreage of parliamentary enclosure in west Suffolk as there was in east Suffolk, in other words 19 per cent of the land area of west Suffolk, which is approaching the national average of 20·9 per cent. If this distribution of enclosure was mapped it would show a much greater concentration of enclosure activity in west Suffolk, in particular on the lighter sands and fens in the north-west of the county, that is to say in the areas known as the Breckland and the Fens.[39] M. R. Postgate informs us that the Breckland is a ‘combination of porous basal chalk and a low annual

Table 4. DISTRIBUTION AND DENSITY OF PARLIAMENTARY ENCLOSURE IN WEST (W) AND EAST (E) SUFFOLK

Type of[a] enclosure	Number of acts		Number of acres			Acres expressed as percentage of respective half county		Acres expressed as percentage of whole county
	W	E	W	E		W	E	
A	41½[b]	6½[b]	65,229	4,028		16·7	0·7	7·3
B	11	24	5,367	14,931		1·4	2·7	2·2
C					Nil			
D					Nil			
E	3	1	2,757	67		0·7	0·01	0·3
F	8	17	836	1,394		0·2	0·3	0·2
Total of open field arable; i.e. A+ C+ E	44½[b]	7½[b]	67,989	4,092		17.4	0·7	7.6
Total of common and waste; i.e. B+ D+ F	19	41	6,203	16,325		1·6	3·0	2·4
Grand total	63½[b]	48½[b]	74,189	20,420		19·0	3·7	10·0

a. Categories A–F are the same as used in Appendixes 1, 2 and 3, and in Table 1.
b. Half acts because on one occasion the Act included land in both East and West Suffolk.

rainfall', causing 'an aridity that makes the region marginal for cultivation', and it is the extensive heaths which characterise the Breckland giving 'an environment that was marginal for arable cultivation', and it is 'even today, an area that is regarded as sub-marginal for cultivation.'[40] There was in consequence little pre-parliamentary enclosure in this region, in contrast to the claylands of both central Norfolk and Suffolk.[41] In fact, 'The heavy clays of central Suffolk probably never lay in open fields',[42] or at least, 'only a small amount of open field had still survived in the central and eastern districts of East Anglia by the end of the seventeenth century.'[43] Thus 'The majority of parishes with remnants of open field lay in the western sector of the county, on the poorer sands which had only recently become improvable. In brief, the better quality farmland was enclosed well before the days of Parliamentary Acts.'[44]

The corollary of this was that there was very little land remaining to be enclosed in mid-Suffolk or mid-Norfolk by the time of the parliamentary enclosure movement but a great deal of parliamentary enclosure of the Breck still to come. This was certainly the case for

Suffolk but less so for Norfolk. Certainly mid, south and east Suffolk was devoid of open field enclosure during the parliamentary enclosure period. However, the history of parliamentary enclosure in Norfolk was one of more regular spatial distribution with less concentration on the Suffolk border and also less in Norfolk Breckland. What concentration there was, was more central and oriented to the east in contrast to the westerly concentration in Suffolk. In addition of course, north Norfolk in the Good Sands was *the* area of agricultural improvement associated with the rise of the Norfolk Husbandry. It was an area much enclosed and improved by the so-called 'popularisers' in the early to mid-eighteenth century before the main wave of parliamentary enclosure began; as a result there was very little enclosure to follow, apart from a scattering of small commons.[45]

The Suffolk Breckland was heavily enclosed by parliamentary Act and in fact the hundreds of Lackford and Risbridge had higher densities of enclosure than the national average. Tables 5 and 6 illustrate this very well, showing the predominance of open field arable enclosure in west Suffolk, especially in Lackford and Risbridge. In fact almost half of all Suffolk arable enclosure took place in the hundred of Lackford, situated in the north-west corner of the county, and indeed this hundred along with many midland county hundreds was in the vanguard of parliamentary enclosure activity.

Table 5. DISTRIBUTION OF PARLIAMENTARY ENCLOSURE IN WEST SUFFOLK BY HUNDRED

Hundred or Division	Acreage enclosed	As percentage of land area	Of which was mainly open field arable	Of which was common and waste
	acres	%	%	%
Babergh	885	1·3	0·7	0·6
Blackbourn	9,503	14·1	11·5	2·6
Cosford	170	0·6	—	0·6
Lackford	35,054	43·9	42·2	1·7
Risbridge	12,636	21·4	18·5	2·9
Thedwestry	7,311	18·4	16·8	1·6
Bury St. Edmunds[a]	1,057	34·8[a]	34·8	—
Sudbury	—	—	—	—
Thingoe[a]	7,523	23·8[a]	23·3	0·5
Total	74,189	19·0	17·4	1·6

a. Bury St Edmunds, although enclosed to the extent of 34·8 per cent of its area, is too small a division from which to draw any great conclusions. Thingoe is also quite small.

Table 6. DISTRIBUTION OF PARLIAMENTARY ENCLOSURE IN EAST SUFFOLK BY HUNDRED

Hundred or Division	Acreage enclosed	As percentage of land area	Of which was mainly open field arable	Of which was common and waste
	acres	%	%	%
Blything	2,331	2·8	—	2·8
Bosmere and Claydon	157	0·3	—	0·3
Carlford	233	1·0	—	1·0
Colneis	1,042	6·0	—	6·0
Hartismere	1,808	3·3	1·1	2·2
Hoxne	294	0·6	—	0·6
Loes	—	—	—	—
Mutford and Lothingland	8,780	26·6	9·4	17·2
Plomesgate	498	1·2	0·2	1·0
Saniford	325	0·7	—	0·7
Stow	80	0·4	—	0·4
Thredling	—	—	—	—
Wangford	4,806	13·6	0·7	12·9
Wilford	14	Neg.	—	Neg.
Ipswich	52	0·7	—	0·7
Total	20,420	3·7	0·7	3·0

The result of locating more precisely the enclosure statistics in this way is to draw as sharp a distinction as possible between areas predominantly of open field arable agriculture in the year 1750 and those areas where open fields had disappeared at an earlier date or had never existed at all.

Another major characteristic of Suffolk parliamentary enclosure was its temporal concentration.

> By the end of the eighteenth century the general distribution of land holdings in Breckland was little altered from the pattern that prevailed during the Middle Ages.[46]

Breckland was to be enclosed in a great rush, especially between 1796 and 1816. Postgate ascribes this to 'the economic conditions that prevailed during the Napoleonic Wars when the improvement of arable land was at a premium.'[47] This viewpoint demands further inquiry and it will be touched upon in later chapters. In brief, the explanation is that the sandy, agriculturally marginal soil was made, perhaps for the first time, very profitable at the prevailing high wartime prices, even at the prevailing high cost of enclosure. The main enclosures of common and waste also occurred during the war and were mainly concentrated on the coastal sandy soils of eastern Suffolk, possibly for the same reason. In support of this theory the evidence in Thirsk and Imray is obviously very important. They point to the change which occurred away from dairying and into corn production and which they attribute to a response to high grain prices during the war, when even the heavy clays were ploughed up because corn became more profitable than dairying and where the evoked response in sandy regions was for a plough-up of marginal lands.[48]

Some northern counties

The demonstration in the foregoing pages of highlighting the enormous differences that occurred within counties but which a solely county approach hides, is of course not a new thing. In the Baker–Butlin volume on field systems, Butlin and Elliott for the north-eastern and north-western counties respectively have in a different way also established the more specific incidence of enclosure. They have mapped evidence indicating the former existence of common arable fields from which it is perfectly clear that in Northumberland and Durham the common arable fields were mainly found (at some unspecified point in antiquity) in the eastern third of these counties, that is, on the coastal plain at altitudes below 400 feet, and with some western penetration along the major valleys such as the Tyne and Tees. The Pennines were virtually devoid of common arable fields. The picture is further illuminated by R. I. Hodgson who clearly shows that most of the 70,000–80,000 acres enclosed in Durham between 1550–1750 was open field arable and located in the coastal or lowland eastern third of the county, and that nearly all of the 107,000 acres enclosed by act of Parliament between 1750 and 1870 was common and waste and located in the western two-thirds, the high Pennines or Pennine spurs.[49]

In Cumberland and Westmorland also, the greatest incidence of enclosure was coastal with again some inland valley penetration. The 'Lakes' environs, like the Pennines, were virtually devoid of common arable fields. In fact 'even today the bulk of the Lake District and Pennines are uncultivated', let alone enclosed.[50]

Even this exercise of establishing the broad areas of high or low density of enclosure within the counties still does not give the true picture of parliamentary enclosure. Ideally what is required is an even smaller unit to work with, preferably at the parish level. However, to plot the necessary data for all the English counties would be both a lengthy task and result in a map or series of maps which for casual reference purposes would be so full of detail and of such a scale as to be relatively meaningless. The method can be demonstrated however by plotting the density of enclosure, and/or the distribution and/or the chronology of enclosure for individual counties. This is shown in, for example, Slater's chronological map of England and in greater detail his maps of the east Midlands, east Anglia, and the three counties of Hampshire, Surrey, and Sussex; also in Rodgers' map for West Yorkshire and Hunt's for Leicestershire, among others.[51] Figure 3 is a similar type of map for Buckinghamshire showing the density of enclosure on a parish basis for the whole county. It seems clear from this that some parishes were almost entirely enclosed by parliamentary act while others were relatively or totally untouched. The latter may have been enclosed in former times or contemporaneously by private agreement. Either way such a map poses several questions. For example, why did the open fields persist in some villages into the eighteenth century and not in other, perhaps even neighbouring parishes? Why is there parliamentary enclosure in some and agreements in others? And, as later chapters will investigate, why is there different timing?

It is hard to conceive an orderly system in which a mosaic of land uses, of different landownership distributions of open and closed parishes, and of different stages in the disintegration of the peasantry existed, and may have influenced the timing of enclosure, but nevertheless we try to give it considerable order by umbrella-style classifications. The prevailing national and local economic circumstances must also be considered and indeed may have been the most important influence. These are questions that will be touched upon in the chapters which follow. The maps of county density show, for the present purposes, that in many villages mere vestiges of the open fields remained to be enclosed. Very few had been left totally untouched by earlier piecemeal or more extensive enclosure, for example enclosures by medieval intakes, the so-called depopulating enclosures of the fourteenth to sixteenth centuries and enclosure agreements of the seventeenth century and thereafter. Even in those localities where parliamentary enclosure was the most important form of enclosure there were neighbouring parishes where it was a trivial finale to what had been a more protracted enclosure movement spread over several centuries before 1750. Such maps therefore represent a simplified mosaic cross-section of one aspect of rural life about the year 1750 in which land organisation and farming was not only about to embark on a period of great flux, but also in which all

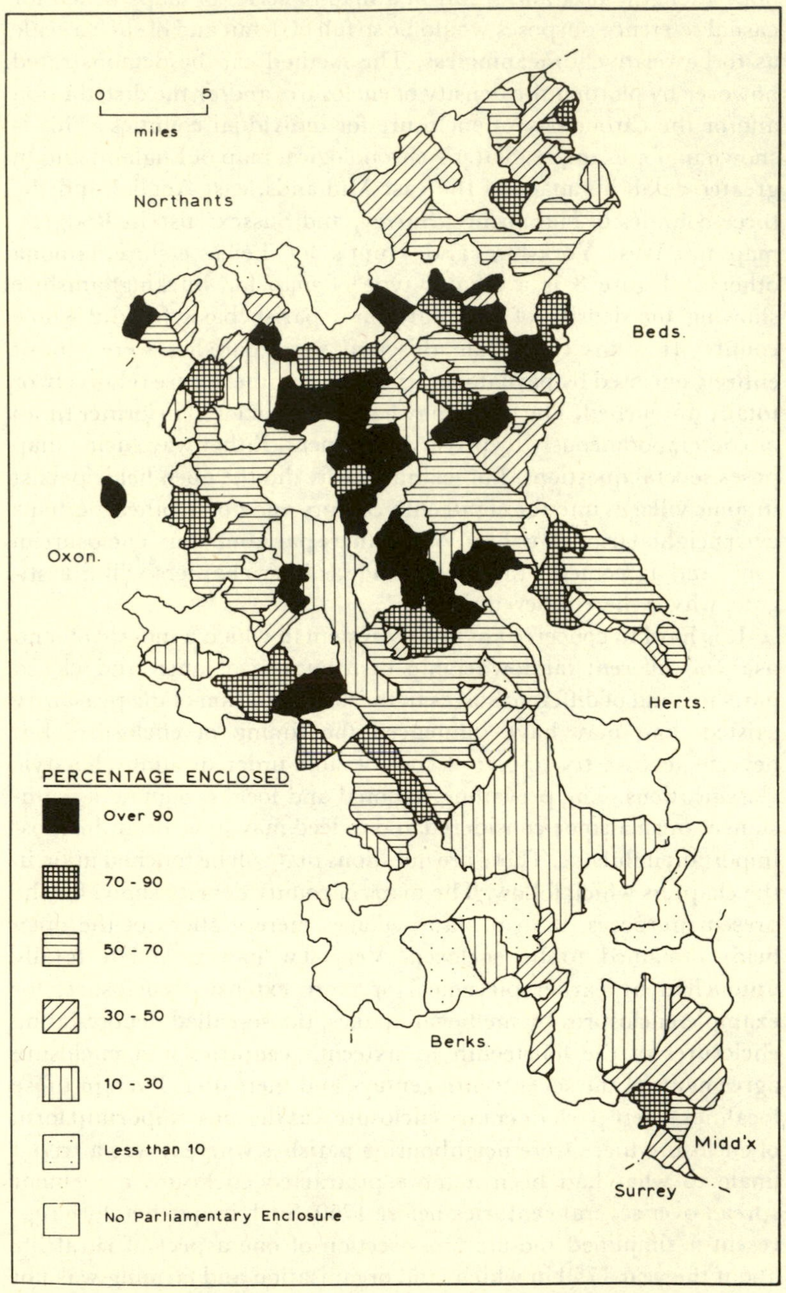

Fig. 3. Density of parliamentary enclosure in Buckinghamshire.

elements of the changes wrought over the centuries before and to some extent after 1750 existed side by side in their manifold forms. This mosaic of change also very often defies any order which topography or soil differences might be expected to impose, calling into question the environment as a determinant of enclosure and reinforcing any thoughts that entrepreneurial instincts may have been more important. Parliamentary enclosure may have been the final act in the dissolution of the open fields, but in many places and villages it was a trivial finale to what had been a continuous process. In other villages however it was the major method of organisational change.

Density of parliamentary enclosure

Parliamentary enclosure was greatest in terms of concentration of activity, if by this we measure it as density, in the counties of Oxfordshire, Cambridgeshire, and Northamptonshire, ranked in that order and in all of which over 50 per cent of the land area was affected. By including those counties where over 40 per cent of land area was enclosed the number of counties increases to eight: the three mentioned plus Huntingdonshire, Bedfordshire, Leicestershire, Yorkshire East Riding, and Rutland in descending order, with Lincolnshire a close ninth. By allowing for a certain percentage of each county occupied by standing buildings in the form of cities, towns and villages, running and standing water, roads and other highways in the eighteenth century, it is easy to imagine that approaching or exceeding 50 per cent of the land available for agricultural uses in all these counties was enclosed in the century after 1750. This puts into serious doubt some early estimates of pre-parliamentary enclosure. For example, there simply would not have been enough land available for 44 per cent of Northamptonshire to have been enclosed by 1675, as Gonner suggested, or for 47 per cent of Leicestershire to have been enclosed by 1710.[52] By also allowing for a certain amount of enclosure by agreement after 1750 it is clear that open field agriculture survived on a very wide scale a mere two centuries ago. The group of counties where the density of enclosure exceeded 40 per cent of land area formed a very distinct wedge in the east and south Midlands centred on Rutland and Huntingdonshire, though with Yorkshire East Riding somewhat isolated.

This area of predominantly open field agriculture in 1750 could so easily be extended by including counties like Lincolnshire (density 38·8 per cent), Nottinghamshire (36·4 per cent), Buckinghamshire north of the Chilterns, eastern Warwickshire, perhaps south Derbyshire, and the eastern West Riding. This gives a broad swath of counties concentrated in eastern central and south central England. By increasing the catchment to include all counties where over 30 per cent was enclosed and further broadening the range for counties with over 25 per cent of land area enclosed by Act of Parliament produces a pattern not unlike concentric growth rings, with Northamptonshire or Leicestershire at the centre. Taking this growth ring analogy to its ultimate conclusion, it can be said that parliamentary enclosure was insignificant in the south-western counties (Devon and Cornwall), the south-east (Essex, Surrey, Kent, and most of Suffolk and Sussex) and in the Welsh border counties (Cheshire, Shropshire, Herefordshire, and Monmouthshire, and including Lancashire). No doubt devotees of the study of field systems and their origins can see an ethnic relationship emerging in the way expounded by H. L. Gray at the start of this century.

A review of literature might indicate that this brief summary attaches too much spatial importance to parliamentary enclosure. Historians of Tudor and Stuart England and of the late seventeenth and early eighteenth centuries might fairly point to the evidence of anti-enclosure committees, pamphleteers, depopulation inquiries and leveller activity, as well as to known enclosure agreements, in order to undermine the importance attached in this book to parliamentary enclosure. It is very probable that the weight of words in public outcry and public inquiry was inversely proportional to the number of acres affected. The inspired widom of Darby in reviewing the period from 1600 to 1800 sums up the conflict.

> At this point in time, on the verge of the great changes brought about by Parliamentary enclosure we may pause to ask what had been the effect upon the landscape of the enclosing activity of the years since, say 1450. In view of the outcry about depopulation in the Midland counties, and in view of the flood of pamphlets, the sustained legislative activity and the many deserted villages, it may seem strange to find that, after all, the Midlands were the main area of Parliamentary enclosure. The counties which had produced such a volume of complaint in Tudor times were the very ones in which open fields flourished triumphantly right on into the eighteenth and even into the nineteenth century. How is the paradox to be explained?[53]

The answer is that much of England outside the midlands, for a variety of reasons of mainly cultural or environmental origin, was already enclosed before the fifteenth and sixteenth centuries or had never been open. This is illustrated in the earlier summary of Baker–Butlin, the map produced by Gonner and redrawn with minor amendments in Darby, and Emery's summary in the same work.[54] The pamphleteers did not mean that *all* the open fields had disappeared; on the contrary much or even most of the midlands was still in open fields in the middle of the eighteenth century, but the political message they were broadcasting may have distorted the magnitude of the events.

Distribution and density of open field arable enclosure

Heretofore it has been established what proportion of England, and similarly what proportion of each county, was enclosed by act of Parliament. This is of course vital information and an obvious starting point in any discussion of parliamentary enclosure, but the analysis can now be taken a stage further by ascertaining the relative importance spatially of open field arable enclosure as distinct from the enclosure of commons and wastes (including moors, stinted pastures, heaths, fens, etc). The two may be radically different in distribution, density, and chronology, and indeed there has already been an unavoidable discussion of them in the foregoing analysis.

The example of Cambridgeshire

Cambridgeshire can be described as *the* county of parliamentary enclosure and *the* county of open field arable farming even though it lies second to Oxfordshire in a ranked list of density of enclosure and fifth in a ranked list of density of open field arable enclosure.[55] This is bound up with the fact that Cambridgeshire is an awkward county to analyse since it could so easily be confused with the other land-use changes which were taking place in the fenland counties which fringe the Wash. We refer here mainly to the considerable drainage schemes that occurred in the Holland division of Lincolnshire, and also in west Norfolk and to some extent in north Cambridgeshire. The reservations outlined in the Introduction aptly apply to Cambridgeshire, namely the difficulty of distinguishing arable from common and waste enclosure. In this context the reader is referred back to the Introduction and the work currently being pursued by John Chapman. Some of the Cambridgeshire enclosures may have been linked with drainage and reclamation schemes and might easily have been incorrectly included as arable enclosures. Nonetheless, the county will still emerge as one of the leaders of open field arable counties. The calculation of density of enclosure for the county is misleading and understates the case for the county because there is a topographical anomaly associated with Cambridgeshire which is more important than the ones already outlined for Warwickshire, Suffolk, Worcestershire, Buckinghamshire, and other counties.

Of the 154 Cambridgeshire parishes at the time of the 1831 Census, 107 were affected in some large or small way by one or more parliamentary acts for the enclosure of open field arable. In the two hundreds of Staine and Thriploe every parish was affected and in many others the majority of parishes were involved, in particular in the hundreds in the south of the county. In contrast, in the northern hundreds there was either no enclosure by act whatsoever, as in Wisbech, or there was very late enclosure (after 1830) of common and waste. The fens in other words were relatively devoid of open field arable lands. In contrast, the southern half of the county was very heavily enclosed. The data summarising the history of parliamentary enclosure in Cambridgeshire are set out in Table 7.

The southern half of the county was very heavily enclosed; in fact it appears from the table that the two hundreds of Thriploe and Whitlesford were enclosed by more than 100 per cent of their respective land areas. This was clearly impossible and we can point to two reasons for this. First it seems clear that the acreages quoted in the enclosure awards *sometimes* included the amount of old enclosure in the respective parish as well as the newly allotted land. This was pointed out to me by the Cambridgeshire county archivist when the *Domesday* was being compiled.[56] On the other hand, we are told by C. Vancouver in 1794 that on the eve of the Napoleonic wars, of 147,000 acres of arable in the county 132,000 was in open fields, and of 98 parishes described 83 were still in an open state.[57] In other words the county clearly was heavily in open fields. The second reason is that the base acreage used for the hundreds and the subsequent calculation of density is the one quoted in the 1831 Census Enumeration Abstract.[58] This quotes an aggregated acreage for the county of 536,853 acres. In a footnote to the Census it is explained that the real area of the county was 857 square statute miles, and consequently 584,480 acres. The aggregate therefore is 8·2 per cent underestimated. This error may be specific to a group of hundreds or parishes but on the other hand it may be evenly diluted throughout the county. Suppose that it is evenly diluted and is therefore a consistent 8 per cent error in the sense of an underestimate. The figures in the table therefore can be corrected by this amount. Thus the 68·2 per cent density of enclosure for Armingford Hundred when deflated by 8 per cent becomes 62·6 per cent, the 51·6 per cent for Chilford becomes

Table 7. SUMMARY OF PARLIAMENTARY ENCLOSURE IN CAMBRIDGESHIRE[c]

Hundred or Division	Number[a] of parishes in hundred	Type of enclosure as a percentage[b] of hundred area						Total open field arable	Total common and waste
		A	B	C	D	E	F		
Armingford	14(8)	68·2		5·9				74·1	
Chesterton	6(4)	76·3						76·3	
Cheveley	5(4)	99·0						99·0	
Chilford	11(9)	51·6				10·4		62·0	
Flendish	5(4)	83·0						83·0	
Longstrow	14(13)	81·5				8·9		90·4	
Northstrow	11(10)	85·8		4·7		1·0		91·5	
Popworth	11(10)	76·7	8·2	2·7				79·5	8·2
Radfield	9(7)	78·7						78·7	
Staine	6(6)	105·5						105·5	
Staploe	9(7)	38·9				3·4		42·3	
Thriploe	10(10)	91·2				5·4		96·6	
Wetherley	11(9)	80·9						80·9	
Whittlesford	5(5)	101·2						101·2	
Ely	2(2)			5·1				5·1	
Wisbech	9(6)		1·5				0·4		1·8
Witchford North	3(3)	2·7	44·9				Neg	2·7	44·9
Witchford South	11(10)	21·9	0·9	1·6		2·5	2·8	26·0	3·7
Cambridge	1(1)	63·4	1·9					63·4	1·9
Ely City	1(1)			4·5				4·5	
Total	154(129)								

a. Figures in brackets refer to the number of parishes covered in some way by an act of Parliament for enclosure.
b. Categories A–F are the same as those used in Appendixes 1, 2 and 3 and in Table 1.
c. See Chapter 1 and the passages concerning Chapman, pp. 24–5.

47·4 per cent, the 105·5 per cent for Staine becomes 96·8 per cent and so on. After a consistent deflation of this sort throughout the county it is still evident that there was a lot of open field arable enclosure in the county. In eleven hundreds there seemed to be 70 per cent of land area enclosed in this way, of which four had over 80 per cent. After allowing for land occupied by water, buildings, and routeways it can justifiably be said that perhaps as much as three-quarters to four-fifths of south Cambridgeshire was in open fields about the year 1770 but that by about 1860 it had been enclosed by acts of Parliament.

Cambridgeshire as a county lies second to Oxfordshire in terms of ranked density of enclosure, but the relatively small area of the Chilterns in south Oxfordshire does not distort the distribution and density of enclosure perhaps as much as the fens understate the case for Cambridgeshire. Bearing in mind the strong reservations which apply to this county, perhaps we can say with some due caution that we have located the area of England most densely enclosed by act of Parliament, or conversely the most densely open field area of England in the mid-eighteenth century. What is more, compared with other open field enclosure it was relatively late enclosure in Cambridgeshire, but that will form part of the story in the chapter which follows.

In summary, of the 154 Cambridgeshire parishes in the 1831 Census Enumeration Abstract some 129 were affected by acts of enclosure. And to re-emphasise the importance of south Cambridgeshire in the history of parliamentary enclosure, of all the hundreds in the southern half of the county it seems that only one, Staploe, with a density of 42·3 per cent, experienced less than 60 per cent enclosure of open field arable. Even after correcting for errors in the 1831 data only two hundreds, Staploe and Chilford, experienced less than 60 per cent density of open field arable enclosure. The remaining hundreds of south Cambridgeshire, it appears, were in the vanguard of open field arable husbandry. Even if some of the Cambridgeshire enclosures have been misinterpreted and should rightly be counted as mainly drainage schemes, and even if some enclosure acreages include also areas of old enclosure, it would take a lot of errors of this kind seriously to undermine these conclusions.

Density of open field arable enclosure

Figure 4 is a map of density of enclosure for the English counties depicting the parliamentary enclosure of open field arable. It is not

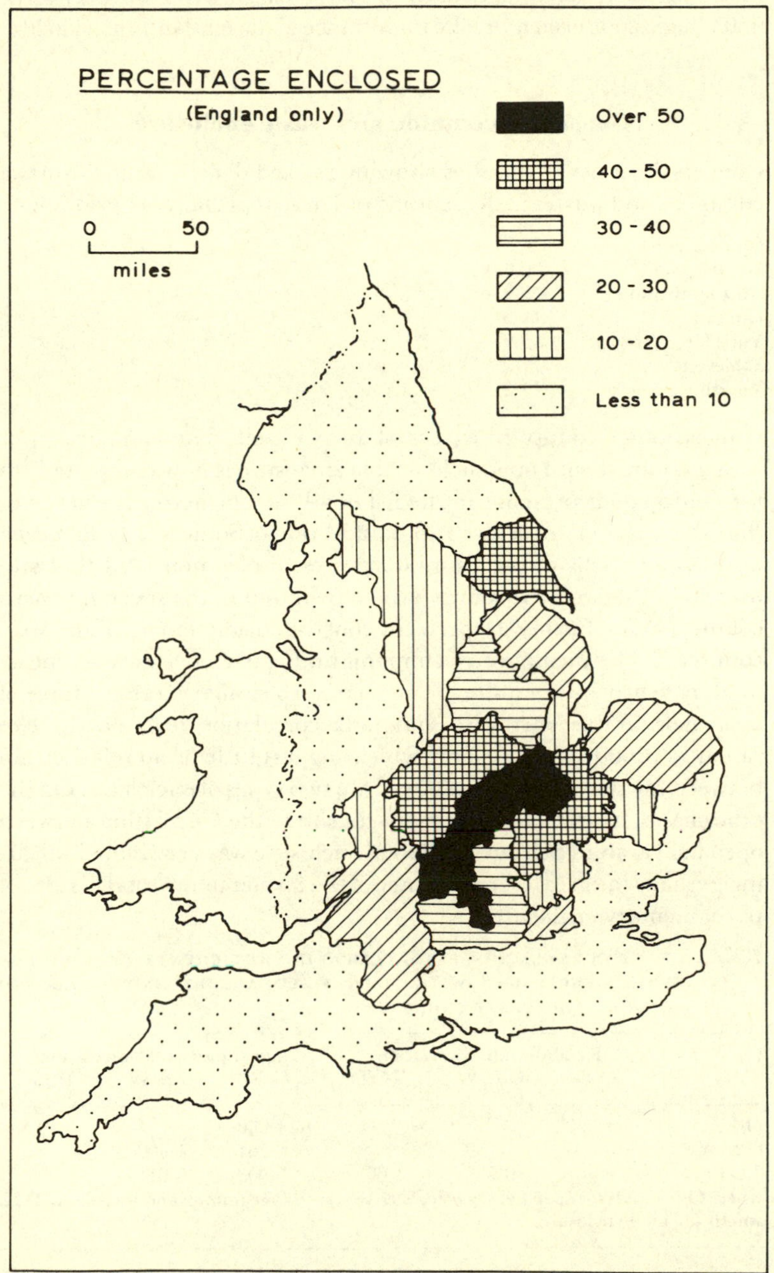

Fig. 4. Density of parliamentary enclosure of open field arable in England.

unlike the earlier map of density of total enclosure in Figure 1 except that it highlights even more the importance of the midlands open fields.

Density of common and waste enclosure

Conversely, a list of counties showing ranked density of enclosure of commons and wastes in descending order of importance is as follows:

Cumberland	26·5%
Westmorland	20·8
Northumberland	15·9
Durham	14·9
Yorkshire, West	13·0
Somerset	12·7
Yorkshire, North	12·6

with no other county in excess of 10 per cent. The comparison or rather contrast with open field arable enclosure is now complete with the conspicuous presence in the list of all the northern counties with the exception of Lancashire and the addition of Somerset. In fact even by the mid 1950s of the 1½ million acres of common land that still existed in England two-thirds was to be found in the seven northern counties and a further 13 per cent constituted the moors of the west country.[59] The incidence of common and waste enclosure as measured by density is not quite the converse of a similarly ranked table of open field arable enclosure, but rank correlation tests on the two rankings produces coefficients which suggest little or no relationship between the spatial distributions of the two types of enclosure. On the other hand, as the following matrices show, the correlation between open field arable enclosure and total enclosure was very high, indicating perhaps the greater importance of the former in the total history of parliamentary enclosure.

Table 8. RANK CORRELATION TESTS COMPARING THE COUNTY RANKING FOR TOTAL ENCLOSURE WITH OPEN FIELD ARABLE ENCLOSURE AND COMMON AND WASTE ENCLOSURE

	Kendall rank correlation			Spearman rank correlation		
	O/F	C & W	TOT	O/F	C & W	TOT
O/F	1·000			1·000		
C & W	−0·193	1·000		−0·261	1·000	
TOT	0·781	0·035	1·000	0·908	0·011	1·000

where O/F stands for open field arable, C & W stands for common and waste and TOT stands for total enclosure.

Figure 5 is a map of density of parliamentary enclosure of common and waste for the English counties. The void that was the arable

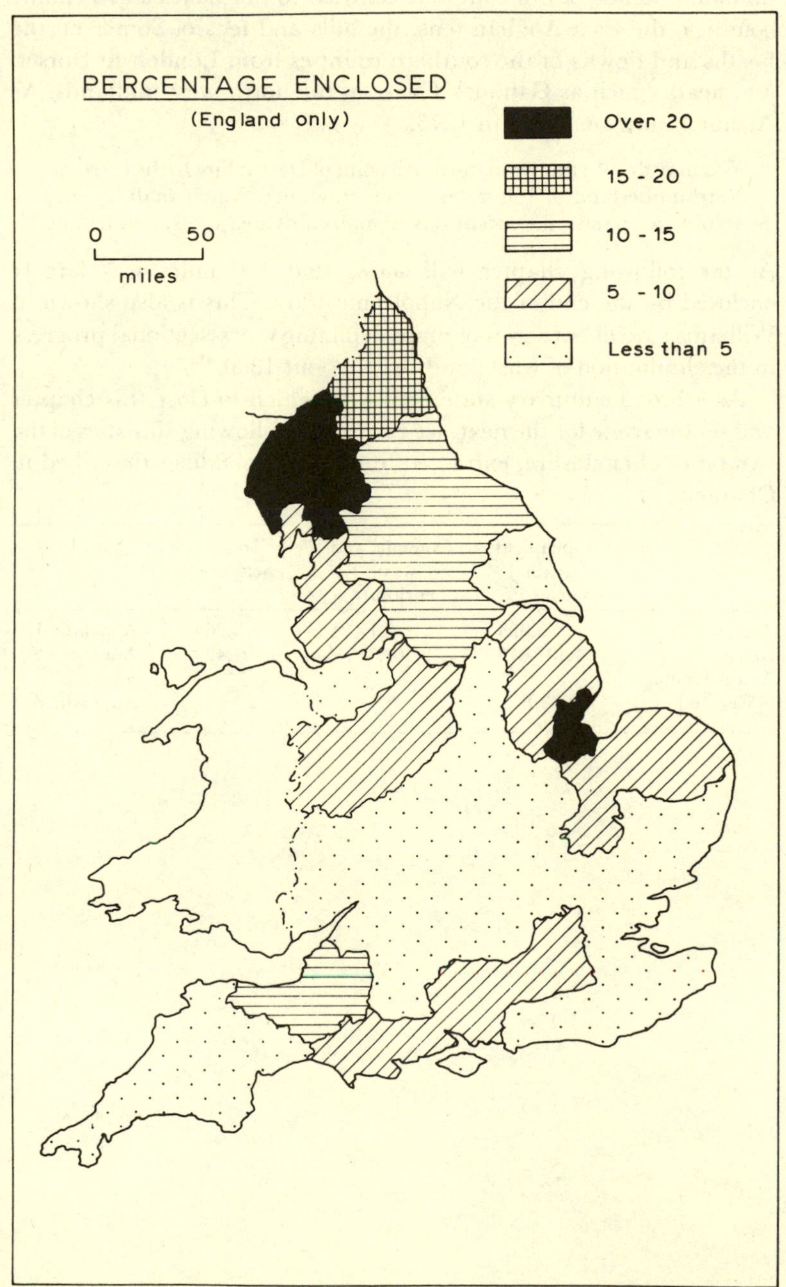

Fig. 5. Density of parliamentary enclosure of common and waste in England.

midlands stands out in complete contrast to the Lakes and Pennine counties, the East Anglian fens, the hills and fens of Somerset, the heaths and downs of the southern counties from London to Dorset, and heaths such as Cannock Chase in the north-west midlands. As Arthur Young observed in 1773,

> You may draw a line from the north point of Derbyshire to the extremity of Northumberland of 150 miles as the crow flies, which shall be entirely across wastelands; the exceptions of small cultivated spots, very trifling.[60]

As the following chapter will show, that 150 miles was largely enclosed by the end of the Napoleonic wars. This is also shown in Williams's excellent series of maps depicting cross-sectional progress in the elimination of wastelands from about 1800.[61]

As a broad summary statement with which to close this chapter and set the scene for the next, we can list the following statistics of the two types of enclosure, extracted from the Appendixes described in Chapter 1.

	Open field arable enclosure	Common and waste enclosure	Total enclosure	See also
Acts	3,093	2,172	5,265	Appendix 1
Acres	4,487,079	2,307,350	6,794,429	Appendix 2
As a percentage of England	13·8	7·1	20·9	Appendix 3

3

The Temporal Sequence

The overall temporal sequence

In the same way that the density and distribution of parliamentary enclosure varied spatially so also did the temporal sequence vary. Figures 6 and 7, the respective chronologies of parliamentary enclosure for Buckinghamshire and Oxfordshire, illustrate this very well. Even though on closer inspection broad patterns can be seen, it is still true to say that many neighbouring parishes were enclosed many decades apart. This has been demonstrated for other counties, by H. G. Hunt for Leicestershire, W. S. Rodgers for West Yorkshire, and M. Williams for Somerset, and on the national scale by Slater and Gonner.[1] The maps produced by the last two named have been reprinted with some revisions by Darby.[2] If the different chronologies *within* counties were so different even where very often topography, soil, and other variables were similar, then the differences *between* counties could be greater.

Appendixes 6–10 are different ways of demonstrating the importance of different periods of time for the enclosure of open field arable and common and waste for the English counties. It should be noted at this stage however that the date of an act did not mark the beginning and end of the enclosure process; there was often a pre-act period of negotiation when parish opinion on the desirability of enclosure was canvassed and support or opposition weighed up. The date of an act might be two, three, or more years after the initial idea was mooted.[3] This point of course is important in view of the analysis to come in later chapters, but unfortunately in most of the more than 5,200 cases of parliamentary enclosure it is not possible to say when the first steps towards the successful passing of an act were made. Ideally this was

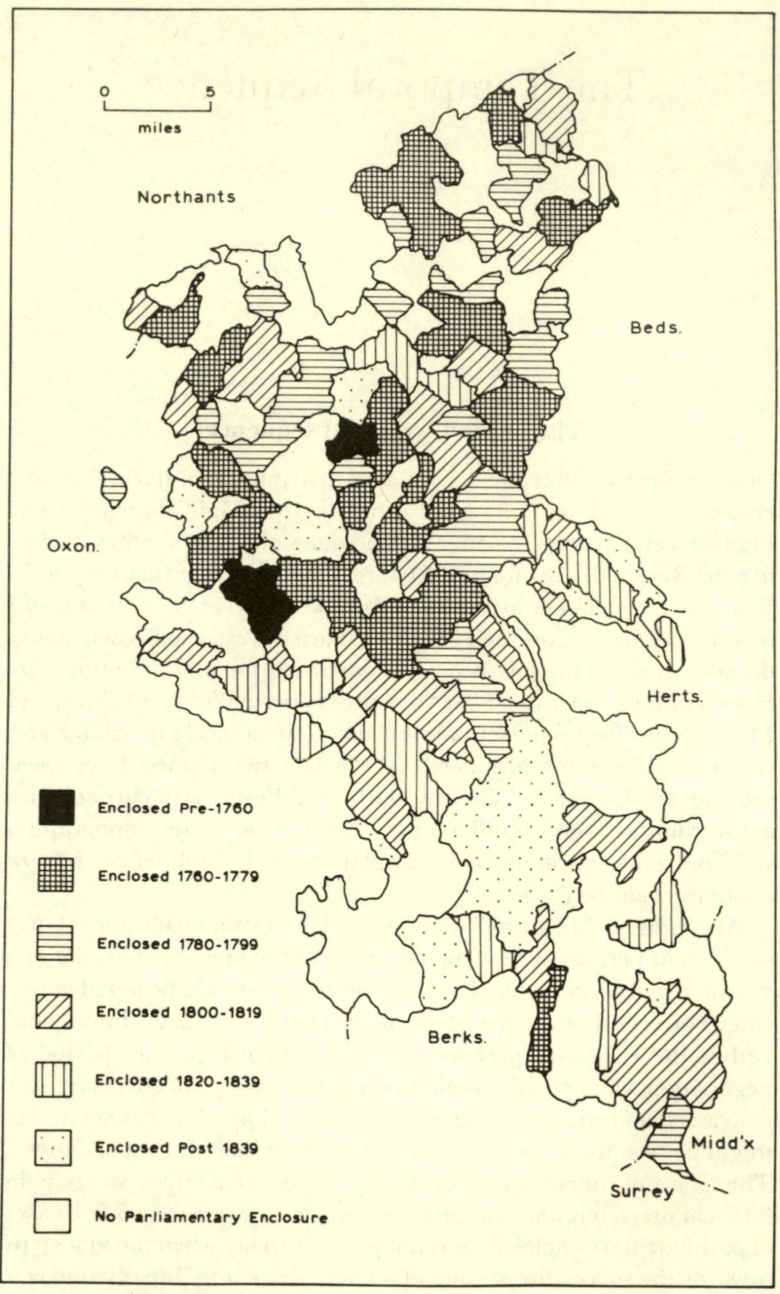

Fig. 6. Chronology of parliamentary enclosure in Buckinghamshire.

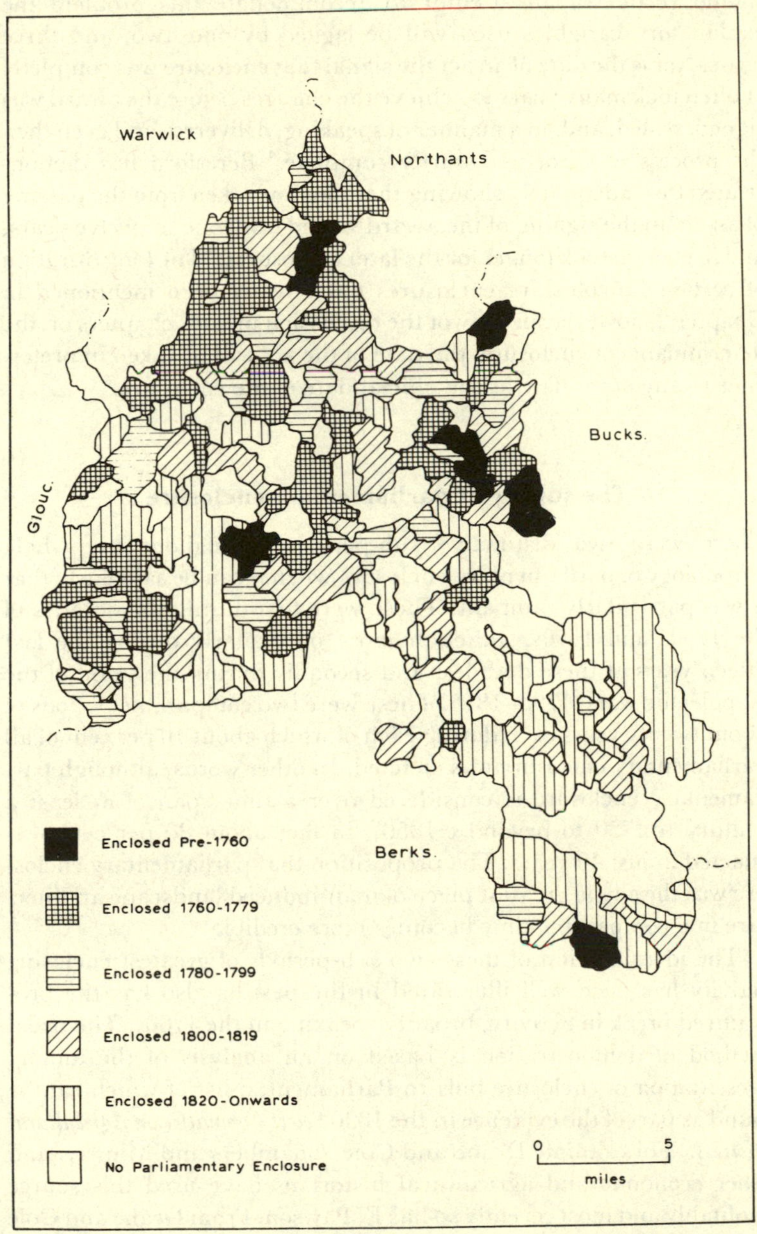

Fig. 7. Chronology of parliamentary enclosure in Oxfordshire.

the date to which the determinants of enclosure under discussion later should relate. In an attempt to accommodate this problem the explanatory variables used will be lagged by one, two, and three years. Nor is the date of an act the signal that enclosure was complete. It often took many years to achieve the changes before the award was signed, sealed, and, in a manner of speaking, delivered, and even then the process was not necessarily complete.[4] Beresford has demonstrated this, adequately showing that the time taken from the passing of an act to the signing of the award varied from one to twelve years, and in general took longer for the later enclosures.[5] The long duration of certain Lincolnshire enclosures has already been mentioned in Chapter 2; however, in view of the discussion in later chapters on the determinants of enclosure, the date of the act will be taken in preference to any other date as the official date of the enclosure.[6]

The supply of parliamentary enclosure

There were two distinctive sub-periods throughout the whole chronology of parliamentary enclosure when it can be said fairly that it was particularly rampant. These were first during the decades of the 1760s and 1770s, although more particularly during the last fifteen years of these decades, and secondly during the years of the Napoleonic wars, 1793–1815. These were two comparable periods of about twenty years each during each of which about 40 per cent of all parliamentary enclosure was enacted. In other words, although parliamentary enclosure is considered over a time span of at least a century (c.1750 to beyond c.1850), in fact about 80 per cent was enacted in just 40 years. The proposition that parliamentary enclosure was the single greatest piece of man-induced landscape architecture in a comparable time becomes more credible.

The identification of these two sub-periods of greatest enclosing activity has been well illustrated in the past as also has the pronounced break in activity, broadly speaking in the 1780s. The usual method of demonstration is based on an analysis of the annual presentation of enclosure bills to Parliament, a list of which can be found as part of the evidence in the 1836 *Select Committee on Agricultural Distress*.[7] For example Deane and Cole, Chambers and Mingay, and other economic and agricultural historians have used this source profitably and most recently so has E. Pawson. From Deane and Cole we are able to conclude that the zenith of enclosure activity was during the decade of 1805–14 when 983 bills were presented to

Parliament, followed by 660 in 1770–9, compared with only 246 during the 1780s.[8] After 1815 the number of enclosure bills rapidly declines. From Pawson, and Chambers and Mingay, we are shown these figures in graphical form.[9] Thus far therefore our impression of the progress of parliamentary enclosure is based on the annual presentation of bills to Parliament. This is not the same as enclosure *per se*. It might indicate the demand for enclosure but it does not measure the supply, and also there may be an element of double counting. For example there were a number of failed bills which on resubmission at a later date may have been more successful, and a number of bills were presented in one physical year but were not translated into acts until the following physical year (the distinction here is made between physical and regnal year where the latter in following the course of a Parliament may encompass parts of two physical years). My own figures, taken from Tate's *Domesday*, are given in Table 9 and measure the number of acts passed; that is they approximate to or may even be identical to the supply of parliamentary enclosure. A half-decadal summary of the supply of parliamentary enclosure is given in Table 10.

The most important year for open field arable enclosure was 1801 when 86 acts were placed on the statute books, and the most important half decade was 1800–4 with 321 acts. This may be only coincidentally associated with the period of almost annual harvest failure which preceded 1800 in the second half of the 1790s. This culminated in the 1801 inquiry by the Home Office, the 1801 crop returns, an inquiry motivated not only by harvest failure but by the continuing Napoleonic war and feelings of insecurity about future food self-sufficiency. In other words it took the form of an arable crops

Table 9. THE SUPPLY OF PARLIAMENTARY ENCLOSURE – MEASURED AS THE NUMBER OF ACTS PASSED IN THE TEN MOST IMPORTANT YEARS

Year	Number of acts	Of which open field arable	Of which common and waste
1811	122	67	55
1801	117	86	31
1809	115	74	41
1813	112	68	44
1812	110	58	52
1814	106	58	48
1803	103	66	37
1810	97	64	33
1802	95	71	24
1777	92	58	34

Table 10. THE SUPPLY OF PARLIAMENTARY ENCLOSURE–AS MEASURED IN ACTS IN HALF-DECADES, 1730–1844

Half decade	Number of acts	Of which open field arable	Of which common and waste
1730–4	24	19	5
1735–9	15	8	7
1740–4	26	19	7
1745–9	13	9	4
1750–4	26	12	14
1755–9	91	75	16
1760–4	130	107	23
1765–9	263	209	54
1770–4	319	250	69
1775–9	321	231	90
1780–4	105	68	37
1785–9	132	84	48
1790–4	235	168	67
1795–9	344	245	96
1800–4	450	321	129
1805–9	430	270	160
1810–14	547	315	232
1815–19	232	115	117
1820–4	115	54	61
1825–9	101	53	48
1830–4	66	39	27
1835–9	59	40	19
1840–4	62	38	24

resources census.[10] Nevertheless an analysis of these returns shows that compared with its predecessors 1801 was a bumper harvest year but that this may have been partly due to a feeling of uncertainty over future arable supplies resulting in a general move to increase arable output.[11] The opportunity that enclosure gave to increase arable output and the proximity of the busiest half decade for arable enclosure to the 1801 inquiry therefore needs to be highlighted if only to suggest the coincidence. On the other hand we should also note the 1801 General Enclosure Act. This was an act designed to make enclosure cheaper by making it administratively easier to guide through Parliament, and therefore its proximity to the busiest half decade for enclosure may be significant. But it is often regarded as a clause amendment act only, which only marginally made enclosure less costly.

The most important year for the enclosure of common and waste was 1811 when 55 acts were placed on the statute books, and the most important half decade was 1810–14 when 232 acts were passed. During this half decade there were also 315 acts for the enclosure of open field arable, thus making it the most important five-year period for parliamentary enclosure as a whole. In this period also falls the most important year for parliamentary enclosure, 1811, when 122 acts were placed on the statute books. In descending order the leading half decades, in each of which over 300 acts were passed, were

1810–14	547 acts
1800–4	450
1805–9	430
1795–9	344
1775–9	321
1770–4	319

The temporal sequence can be demonstrated graphically, as in Figure 8 for the years 1750–1819, from which it clearly emerges that the Napoleonic war period was more important in gross numbers than any other lengthy period. In particular can be seen the growth in the annual number of acts, culminating in the two peaks of 1801 and 1811. As already indicated the first year coincides with both the 1801 General Enclosure Act and the 1801 crop returns. The fact that after this bumper year there followed, in the wake of several years of bad harvest, several good or at least average harvest years, has a parallel in some senses with the resurgence of enclosure activity after 1809 during a period of five years of annual harvest failure from 1809 to 1814. The implications of bad harvests and their effects on agricultural prices, and hence the possibility of their acting as a determinant of enclosure, will be considered in Chapter 5.

Having identified the main periods of activity, the broad chronology of parliamentary enclosure can be summarised, as in Table 11. Before 1793 there were 1,611 acts of enclosure which enclosed about 2·6 million acres, or in other words about 7·9 per cent of the total area of England. Divided into constituent parts this represented about 1·9 million acres of *mainly* open field arable and 0·7 million acres of *exclusively* common and waste, or 5·8 and 2·2 per cent respectively of England. This method of aggregation however hides the considerable county differences that existed and these will have to be discussed in due course. Also, as we have already established, before 1793 there was a pronounced concentration of activity in the 1760s and 1770s. In fact, of the 1,611 acts passed before 1793 no less than 1,133 were passed during those two decades, in other words over 70 per cent of all pre-1793 parliamentary enclosure. In comparison, during the French Revolutionary and Napoleonic wars there were 1,969 enclosure acts which accounted for about 2·9 million acres or 8·9 per cent of England. This was made up of 2 million acres of *mainly* open field arable and 0·9 million acres of *exclusively* common and waste, representing

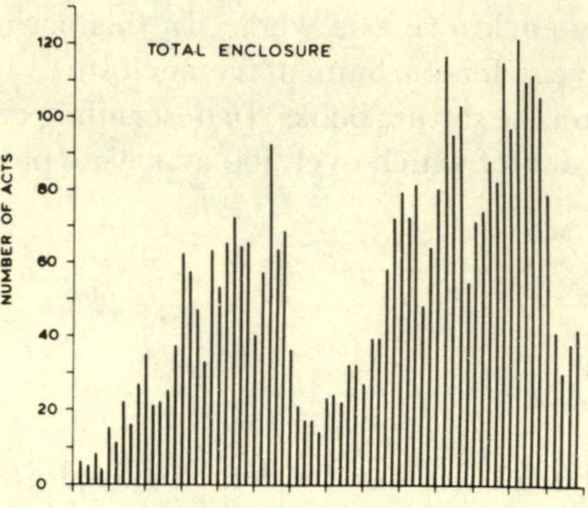

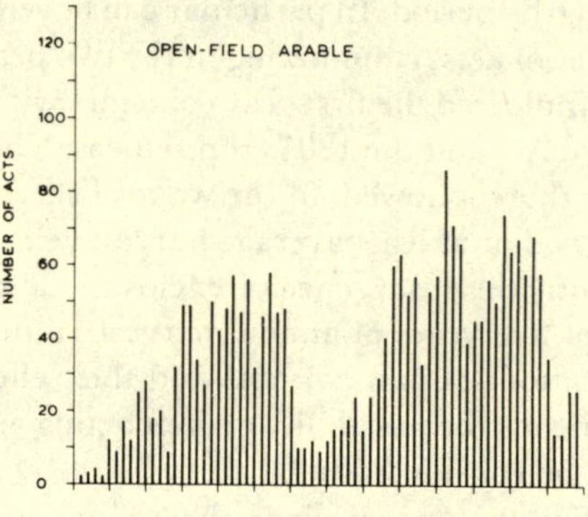

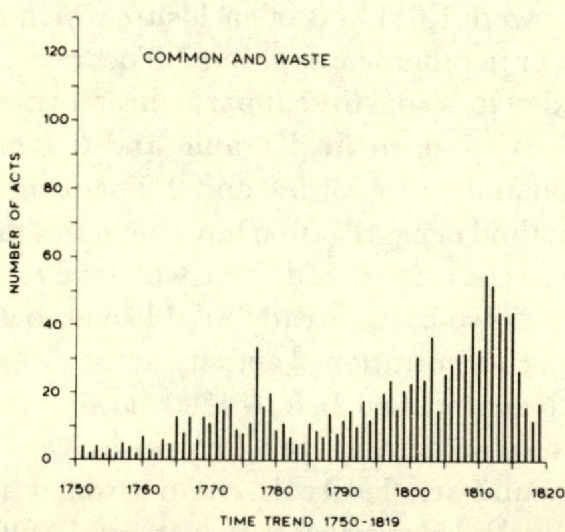

Fig. 8. Chronology of parliamentary enclosure in England, 1750–1819.
(a) Annual total enclosure
(b) Annual open field arable enclosure
(c) Annual common and waste enclosure

Table 11. CHRONOLOGY OF PARLIAMENTARY ENCLOSURE: A SUMMARY

Time periods	Total enclosure	Of which open field arable	Of which common and waste
		Acts	
Pre-1793	1,611	1,177	434
1793–1815	1,969	1,283	686
1816–29	365	184	181
Summary pre-1830	3,945	2,644	1,301
		Acres	
Pre-1793	2,562,660	1,853,567	709,093
1793–1815	2,892,137	1,986,888	905,249
1816–29	382,047	239,308	142,739
Summary pre-1830	5,836,844	4,079,763	1,757,081
		As percentage of England	
Pre-1793	7·9	5·7	2·2
1793–1815	8·9	6·1	2·8
1816–29	1·2[a]	0·7	0·4
Summary pre-1830	18·0	12·6	5·4

a. Subject to a rounding error.

6·1 per cent and 2·8 per cent respectively of the total area of England.[12] Table 12 is a useful summary of parliamentary enclosure, and shows that 85·9 per cent of all parliamentary enclosure by acreage occurred before 1830.

Table 12. SUMMARY OF PARLIAMENTARY ENCLOSURE

Time	Arable acreage as percentage of all parliamentary enclosure	Common and waste acreage as percentage of all parliamentary enclosure
pre-1793	27·3	10·4
1793–1815	29·2	13·3
1816–1829	3·5	2·1
	or 60% of all parliamentary enclosure	or 25·9% of all parliamentary enclosure

As a first conclusion therefore it can be said that the enclosure of *mainly* open field arable was at all times the more important, but that the relative importance of the enclosure of common and waste became greater in the period 1793–1815, during the wars. The increase in the enclosure of open field arable from 27·3 per cent before the wars to 29·2 per cent during the wars was less significant than the increase in enclosure of common and waste from 10·4 per cent to 13·3 per cent over the same period.

Enclosure before 1793

The differences in chronology of enclosure between the counties can be so striking that it is possible to some extent to classify the counties according to periods of heavy enclosure activity. Thus we can recognise war-enclosed counties and pre-war enclosed counties; and also it is possible to base the classification on whether it was enclosure *mainly* of open field arable or *exclusively* of common and waste. In a number of ways the two broad periods of greatest enclosure activity were not at all comparable; it was as if two distinct 'movements' had taken place, each one attended by different motives and different results. The first period of greatest enclosing activity in the 1760s and 1770s was *mainly* concerned with the enclosure of open field arable lands, especially those associated with the claylands of the midland counties. By a careful editing of the various appendixes this can be demonstrated. Table 13 shows those counties where over 50 per cent of all parliamentary enclosure was enacted before 1793, and there is also a reserve list of counties which claim a high percentage of parliamentary enclosure before this date. The counties in the first part of the list are situated geographically in a broad swath from Warwickshire in the west and extending in an easterly and north-easterly direction to

Table 13. COUNTIES FOR WHICH THE PERIOD BEFORE 1793 WAS MORE IMPORTANT THAN ANY OTHER FOR PARLIAMENTARY ENCLOSURE

County (in alphabetical order)	Percentage of parliamentary enclosure enacted before 1793	Of which open field arable	Of which common and waste
Durham	50·3	1·6	48·7
Leicestershire	78·1	78·0	0·13
Lincolnshire	51·0	43·2	7·8
Northamptonshire	61·9	61·7	0·2
Northumberland	58·6	4·7	53·9
Nottinghamshire	52·3	48·34	2·94
Warwickshire	67·3	65·1	2·2
Yorkshire, East	62·9	57·48	5·45
A reserve list of counties would contain the following:			
Buckinghamshire	35·3	35·3	—
Gloucestershire	37·8	36·1	1·7
Oxfordshire	38·5	37·9	0·6
Rutland	42·4	42·4	—
Worcestershire	49·2	39·4	9·8
Yorkshire, North	41·5	19·5	22·0
Yorkshire, West	38·7	17·44	21·21
The national average was:			
England	37·7	27·3	10·4

the East Riding of Yorkshire. In other words they comprise those counties already defined as open field England, in all of which open field arable enclosure was more important than the enclosure of common and waste. The exceptions in the main list are the two north-eastern counties of Durham and Northumberland in both of which less than 20 per cent of county area was enclosed by parliamentary act and also in which the pre-1793 period, or for that matter all periods, was dominated by the enclosure of common and waste. Leicestershire, Northamptonshire, Warwickshire, and the East Riding of Yorkshire however can be numbered among *the* counties of open field England in about 1750. Figure 9 (a)–(d) shows the chronologies of enclosure for these four counties summarised in half decades from 1730 to 1849. The pattern that emerges could be couched in a more explicitly diffusionist framework, as indeed employed to some extent by Butlin in his discussion of enclosures of pre-1750 vintage. He sees the counties of Leicestershire and Warwickshire as the heartland of the diffusion, where large amounts of open land were to be enclosed after 1750 but where also in both counties there was considerable enclosure before 1750.

> The obvious effectiveness of enclosure there in the seventeenth century paved the way both for a rapid diffusion of enclosure by agreement to neighbouring counties and for the rapid spread within Leicestershire and Warwickshire of enclosure by Act of Parliament. It is, in fact, tempting to see these 'heartland' midland counties as the centre of a distinctive enclosure movement which diffused outwards first to neighbouring areas and subsequently to more distant counties in the course of the seventeenth and eighteenth centuries.[13]

A summary of chronology of enclosure for all the English counties can be found in Appendixes 11–13. The first of these shows the chronology of enclosure of open field arable, the second of common and waste and the third is the aggregate of the two.

For Leicestershire, Hunt attributes the observable fluctuation in the chronology of enclosure to 'the varying response from parish to parish to the changing economic conditions in the second half of the eighteenth century'.[14] More specifically he sees the recovery of food prices in the 1750s and 1760s, after the relative depression of much of the second quarter of the century, as a sign that enclosure could bring about a greater return on capital expenditure than the depressed prices in the previous decades were able to achieve. The defeat of the cattle disease in the late 1750s he also sees as important, especially in cattle grazing counties (obviously) which Leicestershire in part became, because

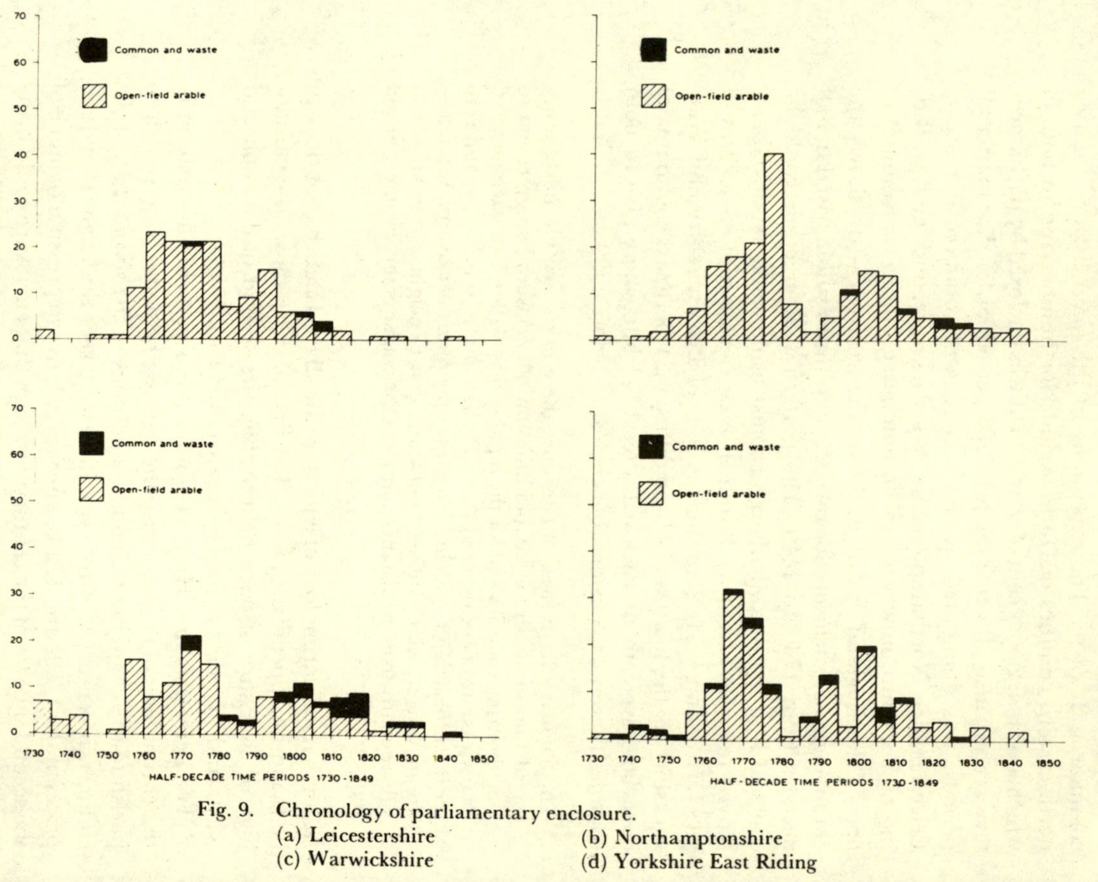

Fig. 9. Chronology of parliamentary enclosure.
(a) Leicestershire (b) Northamptonshire
(c) Warwickshire (d) Yorkshire East Riding

> most of the early Parliamentary enclosures in the county were promoted in order that arable land might be converted into permanent pasture,

or alternatively,

> a study of the influence of soil type on the chronology of enclosure in Leicestershire reveals a distinct tendency for lands unsuited to arable farming to be enclosed first

and

> in general enclosure took place first where a change in land use was imperative.[15]

This was a tendency which J. D. Chambers found also in the neighbouring county of Nottinghamshire.[16] Enclosure was only delayed in Leicestershire until the war period in those areas where

> the soil was thought to be too poor in quality to recompense its owners for the very high cost of enclosure before the steep rise in the price of provisions.[17]

The Nottinghamshire Vale of Belvoir before enclosure was a corn country, after enclosure it was pasture. This came about because of the enclosure of twelve parishes between 1766 and 1792 where

> their stiff lias clay soils were now proving most profitable under grass, while the light marlstone soils of the bordering upland were taking on a new value [as arable] with the agricultural advances of the time.

What was true of Belvoir was true of Leicestershire and what was true of Leicestershire was true of the midlands.[18] And this view is strongly supported by Hunt:

> Many parishes in the Melton Mowbray area where the soil is a strong heavy loam, often wet and cold in winter, were enclosed in the early phase of the eighteenth century movement. In the north west of the county where the soil is less suitable for a large extension of pasture farming, parliamentary enclosure came comparatively late.[19]

In Warwickshire some of the early enclosures, that is before about 1740, have been interpreted as a device by which freeholders sought to rescue themselves from the arable depression of the 1720s; they were enclosures on the heavy clays which were more suited to grassland.[20] In direct contrast, in the Kesteven division of Lincolnshire enclosure was generally a device to improve or extend arable farming.[21] The same can be said of the earlier enclosures of the East Riding of Yorkshire. However, it is true to say that 'much of England came to look greener than before'. In general the light soils were kept more in tillage (and in general, if not already enclosed remained in open fields until after about 1790 as over much of East Anglia and the East Midlands) and the strong heavy lands were generally laid down to permanent pasture.[22] By 1800 the leading arable county was Norfolk with two-thirds of its area under crops (containing large areas of light soils still much in open fields), and the leading grazing county was Leicestershire with three-quarters under grass (mainly enclosed in the preceding 40 years).[23]

The 1801 crop returns give support to the idea that the first wave of enclosure activity in the 1760s and 1770s, and indeed on into the 1790s, was followed by if not motivated by the conversion of arable to pasture. The counties of Leicestershire, Northamptonshire, Warwickshire, and Bedfordshire are well represented in this evidence.[24] The incumbent of Breedon on the Hill in Leicestershire made the following observation:

> Within the last 30 years almost all the country north-west of Leicester to the extremity of the county has been inclosed; by which means the land is become in a higher state of cultivation than formerly; but on account of a great proportion of it being converted into pasturage much less food is produced than when it was more generally in tillage.[25]

And the incumbent of Kegworth, also in Leicestershire, observed that 'the quantity of land under tillage is considerably diminished since the inclosure, which took place about 20 years ago'.[26] The Northamptonshire village of Welford was enclosed in 1778, 'since which time the greater part of it has been laid down in grass', and the parish of Wilbaston, also in Northamptonshire, was newly enclosed in 1798 and was already in 1801 in the process of being 'laid or laying down, for grazing'.[27] So the process of converting the heavy intractable clays of the midlands out of open field arable and into pastures continued even during the grain shortages of the 1790s. The following observation in 1801 from Wolvey in Warwickshire perhaps summarises the situation:

> Last spring it was six years since an inclosure took place here. It is thought that a greater number of acres of wheat was got last harvest than was got while our fields were open. But we expect the cultivation of it will decline apace, as the land comes to be laid down in grass, as has been pretty generally the case after inclosure.[28]

More evidence on the conversion of arable to pasture, both in the two centuries before the era of parliamentary enclosure and during the early parliamentary enclosures, will be forthcoming in the chapters which follow. Suffice it to say at this stage that such consequence of enclosure (which indeed may have been the cause) is supported by evidence from most of the midland counties.

Enclosures in wartime, 1793–1815

The second period of intensive parliamentary enclosure, during the French Revolutionary and Napoleonic wars, was characterised by a wider spatial distribution, both geographically and topographically. That is to say geographically because more counties, and topographically because more environments in more counties were involved. It has already been established that there was a pre-war dominance of parliamentary enclosure in the midland clays; now the wartime peak of activity witnessed the movement spreading to include the remaining clays and to invade the fens of East Anglia and Somerset, the gravel and sand soils of river valleys and heaths, the sandlands of Norfolk, and the poorer soils of the inhospitable and relatively remote areas of England, especially the Pennine counties. In Wales also, a country remembered for its upland ruggedness rather than its clay vales, there was a peak of enclosure activity during the war with 93 enactments compared with only 12 before 1793.[29] The war period is also characterised by the increasing, though still subordinate, enclosure of common and waste.

In some counties, where enclosure was mainly concentrated during the war, there was hardly any at all before the war. For example there were only 8 enactments in Cambridgeshire before 1793, and in Norfolk there were only 23 concerning open field arable compared with 140 during the war, and 20 concerning common and waste compared with 59 during the war. Figure 10 depicts the chronological history of parliamentary enclosure in Norfolk. In Somerset there were no acts concerned with open field arable before the war compared with 34 during the war. In Suffolk also there were few acts before 1793, and similarly in Devon, Essex, and Herefordshire.

It is now possible to appreciate just how varied this so-called 'enclosure movement' was, both spatially and temporally. As it was enacted in Warwickshire, Leicestershire, and Northamptonshire it had nearly run its course by 1793, but in Norfolk and Cambridgeshire it had hardly begun.

In some counties the spate of wartime enclosures was almost exclusively for the improvement of commons and wastes, as in Cheshire, Cornwall, Devon, Durham, Kent, Lancashire, Monmouthshire, and Westmorland, or predominantly so as in Cumberland, Northumberland, Salop, Staffordshire, and Yorkshire North Riding. What is more, nearly all these counties are located in that area of secondary enclosure activity previously described, secondary to the core of open fields in the English midlands. Table 14 summarises the

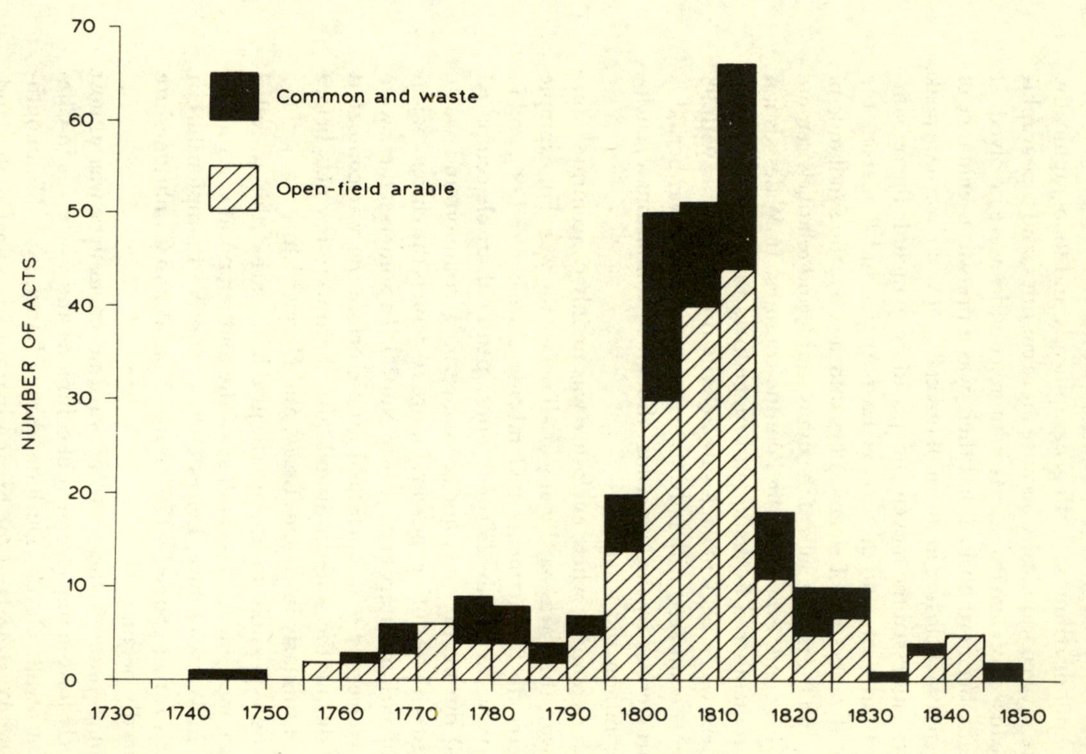

Fig. 10. Chronology of parliamentary enclosure in Norfolk.

importance of the war period as far as the enclosure movement in these counties was concerned, Figure 11 shows the chronology of enclosure for Cumberland, a county dominated by the enclosure of common and waste, and Figures 13 and 10 that for Cambridgeshire and Norfolk.

Table 14. COUNTIES FOR WHICH THE WAR PERIOD, 1793–1815, WAS MORE IMPORTANT THAN ANY OTHER FOR PARLIAMENTARY ENCLOSURE

County (in alphabetical order)	Percentage of enclosure enacted 1793–1815	Of which open field arable	Of which common and waste
Bedfordshire	65·2	64·7	0·5
Berkshire	57·4	55·3	2·1
Cambridgeshire	54·3	52·2	2·1
Cheshire	52·8	0·4	52·3
Cumberland	56·1	1·7	54·5
Isle of Wight	77·6	—	77·6
Hertfordshire	54·8	44·1	10·7
Huntingdonshire	57·9	57·4	0·4
Lancashire	53·6	—	53·6
Middlesex	65·4	60·7	4·7
Monmouthshire	75·1	—	75·1
Norfolk	65·9	52·4	13·5
Suffolk	72·5	54·4	18·1
Surrey	67·6	45·2	22·4
The national average was:			
England	42·5	29·2	13·3

A summary of the evidence so far presented in this chapter, in very broad terms, indicates or confirms our knowledge of the dominance of open field arable in the midland counties and their common and waste counterparts in the peripheral counties. The two types of enclosure were clearly more mixed during the Napoleonic war years (as in Table 14) than in the period before the war when open field arable enclosure was dominant (as in Table 13).

Two peaks in activity between 1760 and 1815

For some counties the Napoleonic war period marked a second peak in enclosure activity, a resurgence of activity of relatively equal importance to the earlier peak during the decades of the 1760s and 1770s, and with the characteristic trough in activity during the 1780s. Table 15 is a summary of the enclosure histories of these counties, while the chronologies of enclosure for Buckinghamshire, Gloucestershire, Lincolnshire, and Yorkshire West Riding, are shown in Figure 12 (a)–(d).

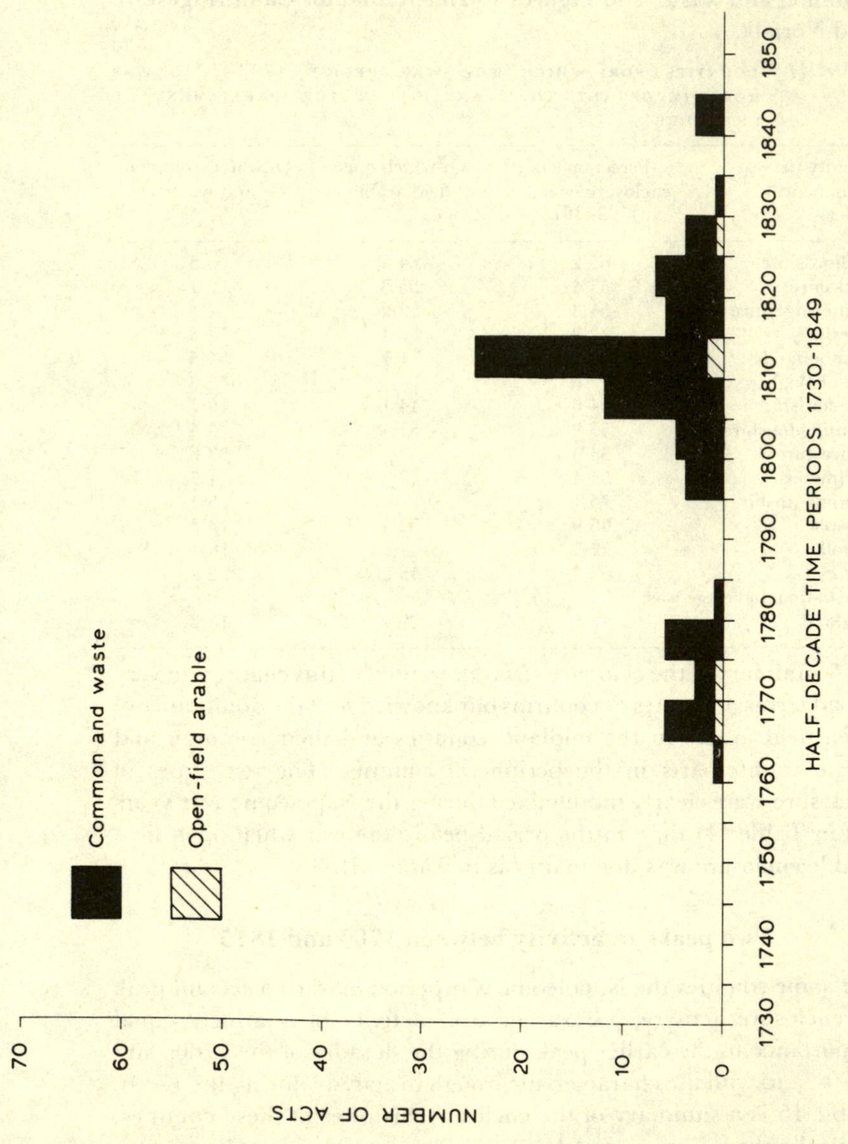

Fig. 11. Chronology of parliamentary enclosure in Cumberland.

Table 15. COUNTIES FOR WHICH THERE WERE TWO PERIODS WHEN PARLIAMENTARY ENCLOSURE WAS RELATIVELY EQUALLY IMPORTANT

County (in alphabetical order)	Percentage enclosed pre-1793	Of which open field arable	Of which common and waste	Percentage enclosed 1793–1815	Of which open field arable	Of which common and waste
Buckinghamshire	35·3	35·3	—	41·8	40·7	1·1
Derbyshire	42·6	25·4	17·2	45·5	38·7	6·8
Gloucestershire	37·8	36·1	1·7	44·2	41·7	2·5
Hampshire	29·7	24·1	5·6	38·8	19·7	19·0
Lincolnshire	51·0	43·2	7·8	41·9	28·4	13·4
Oxfordshire	38·5	37·9	0·6	33·7	31·8	1·9
Rutland	42·4	42·4	—	42·0	42·0	—
Somerset	35·1	—	35·1	46·1	18·6	27·5
Wiltshire	35·4	33·8	1·6	46·7	43·0	3·8
Worcestershire	49·2	39·4	9·7	37·1	31·0	6·1
Yorkshire, North	41·5	19·5	22·0	38·6	13·7	24·9
Yorkshire, West	38·7	17·4	21·2	35·6	21·8	13·8
The national average was:						
England	37·7	27·3	10·4	42·5	29·2	13·3

In those counties where open field arable enclosure predominated before 1793 it was also the most important form of enclosure during the war. In this category are Buckinghamshire, Gloucestershire, Oxfordshire, Rutland, Wiltshire, and Worcestershire. In two counties, where there was some common and waste enclosure before 1793 but which were nevertheless dominated by open field arable enclosure, there was a more rapid growth of common and waste enclosure during the war, namely in Hampshire and Lincolnshire. In those counties where common and waste enclosure was relatively very important before 1793, they remained as leading counties for this type of enclosure during the war. In this category there are Somerset and Yorkshire North Riding, and to a lesser extent Yorkshire West Riding; Derbyshire defies placement with any of these categories. At all times open field arable enclosure was the most important but before 1793 common and waste enclosure was also important. It ceased to be so during the war.

Cambridgeshire and Oxfordshire, two non-conformist counties

From the reserve list of counties in Table 13 the inclusion of Buckinghamshire (north and north-west of the Chilterns), Gloucestershire, Oxfordshire, Worcestershire, and Rutland extends in area the spatial definition of open field England. In the light of this definition the notable omissions from Table 15 are Bedfordshire, Huntingdonshire, and Cambridgeshire, all counties of mainly open field arable enclosure but all mainly enclosed after 1793, and furthermore all mainly in the lighter soiled region of the midlands.

Cambridgeshire was enclosed mainly during the war years but in addition there was a marked resurgence in this county of enclosure activity after the war and indeed after 1830. In fact only eight enclosures were enacted before 1793 in this, the second most densely enclosed county. The process of parliamentary enclosure, hardly begun by 1793, proceeded apace during the war years, especially after 1796, stopped abruptly with the end of the war in common with most other counties but, and this is the distinctive or even peculiar way in which Cambridgeshire differs, the 'movement' picked up again in the 1820s and continued well after the 1830s. This temporal history is depicted in Figure 13. In fact as a percentage of *all* Cambridgeshire parliamentary enclosure, 36·6 per cent took place after 1830. This proportion is exceeded by a number of other counties, Cornwall, Devon, Essex, Kent, Lancashire, Westmorland, and Sussex, but then these are counties in which parliamentary enclosure was never very

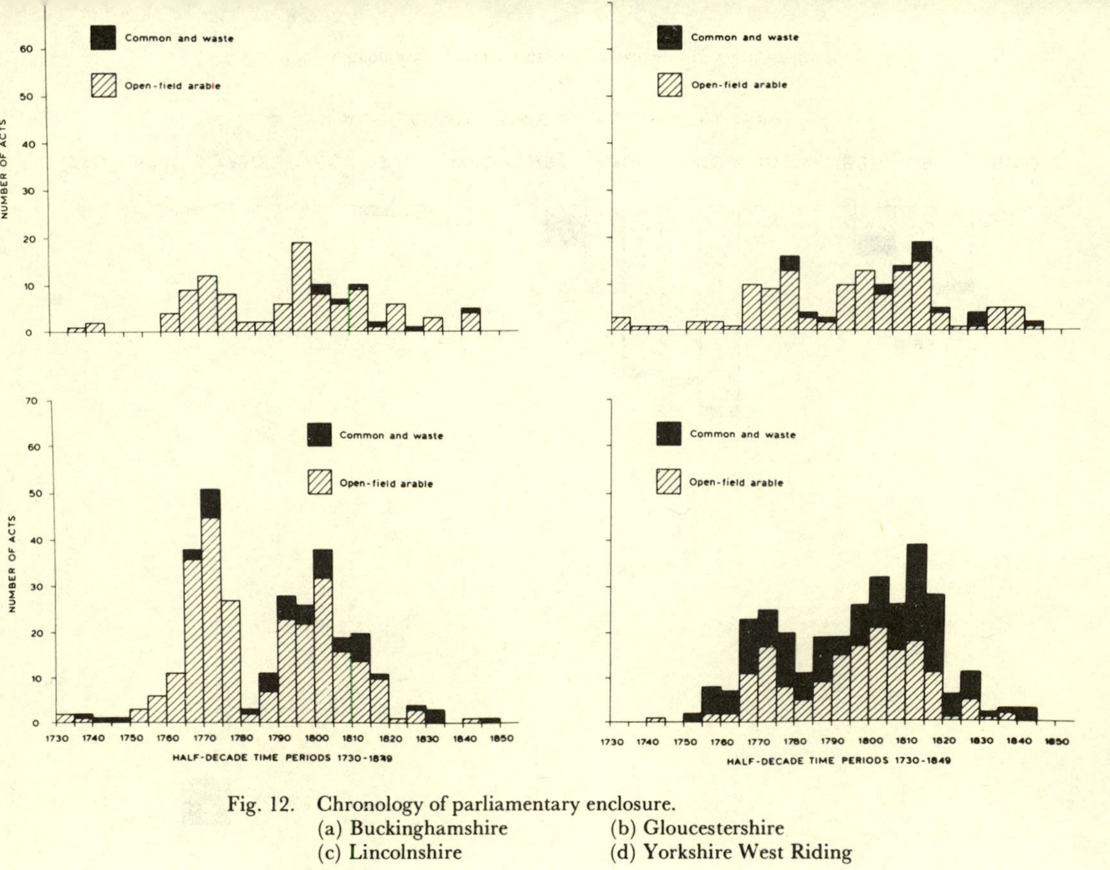

Fig. 12. Chronology of parliamentary enclosure.
(a) Buckinghamshire (b) Gloucestershire
(c) Lincolnshire (d) Yorkshire West Riding

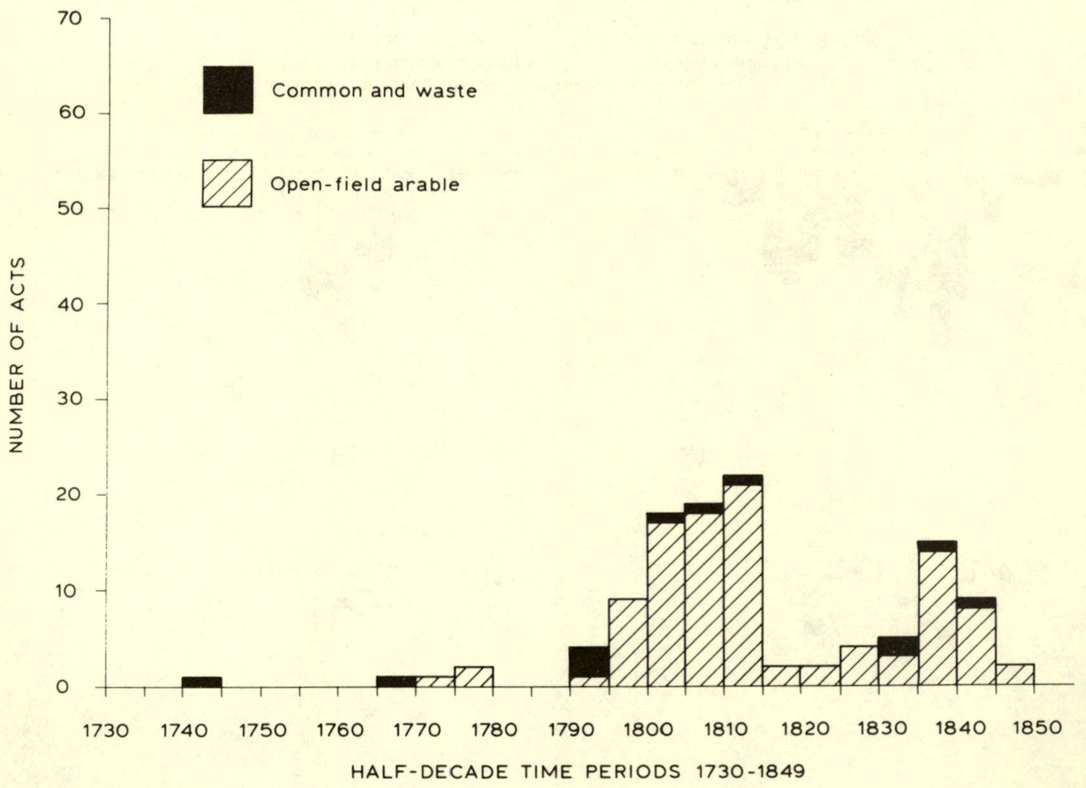

Fig. 13. Chronology of parliamentary enclosure in Cambridgeshire.

important in terms of acreage and density. Of the mainstream counties Cambridgeshire was clearly the peculiar one with such late enclosures: 19·6 per cent of it was enclosed after 1830, a statistic which easily distinguishes it from all other counties. Only Oxfordshire with 12·4 per cent of land area enclosed after 1830 is in double figures. Of the 19·6 per cent of Cambridgeshire as much as 14·6 per cent was open field arable, a remarkably late and extensive survival of the ancient open fields.

Perhaps a reason for such late enclosure of the open arable fields in Cambridgeshire, and to a lesser extent in the neighbouring counties of Huntingdonshire and Bedfordshire, was the intimate relationship all three counties had with the Great Ouse River, the fens, and the historical problems attached thereto with respect to periodic inundations of flood water, as well as their lighter soiled characteristics. The high wartime prices for agricultural produce may have encouraged the enclosure and drainage of these relatively marginal lands for the first time. The marginal returns at record arable prices were greater than the marginal cost of improvement, although an aggregated enclosure map of the counties along the Great Ouse does not establish this one way or the other. Certainly most enclosure in Cambridgeshire north of the City of Cambridge was along the Ouse and was partly the enclosure of common and waste (in this case the extensive fen enclosures such as Grunty Fen in 1857–61), and was partially at least associated also with drainage improvements, but it was also mainly enclosure carried out after the wars, or even after 1830, at times when agricultural prices had slumped relatively to the artificial levels associated with the wartime corn laws. In neighbouring Bedfordshire and Huntingdonshire, although there was much enclosure along the Ouse during the war it was not exclusively so, nor was it common and waste enclosure, in fact quite the contrary. There may still be some relationship in Cambridgeshire between chronology and soil and topography, but if there is it does not seem to be supported from the neighbouring counties of Bedfordshire, Huntingdonshire, Lincolnshire, Norfolk, or Suffolk. Cambridgeshire may remain truly a peculiar county.

In Oxfordshire there was temporally a more even history of parliamentary enclosure with three comparable peaks of activity: the pre-1793 period centred on the 1760s and 1770s; the war period; and the very late post-1830 peak of activity. During the first two periods 38·5 and 33·8 per cent respectively of all parliamentary enclosure was enacted in the county. Arthur Young in his 1813 *General View* of the county observed that enclosure

> has been the capital improvement of the county; for proportionately to the extent of it, more land has been enclosed since I first travelled in it which is about 40 years ago, I conceive, than in any county in England.[30]

It was clearly a very important county for parliamentary enclosure and indeed continued to be so with the enactment of 22·7 per cent of all parliamentary enclosure after 1830. Though this figure compares to some extent with Cambridgeshire (36·6 per cent), it does not compare at all with the other midland counties where the main period of enclosure was before the war. In Leicestershire, Northamptonshire, Nottinghamshire, and Warwickshire only 0·8, 5·6, 6·3 and 7·0 per cent respectively of all parliamentary enclosure was enacted after 1830. Figure 14 depicts the temporal history of enclosure in Oxfordshire.

Common and waste enclosure and the war, 1793–1815

There may be a topographical explanation behind the enclosure of common and waste during the war years. Spatially there was a pattern with the improvement of the heaths of Hampshire and those in the adjacent counties of Surrey and Dorset, the moors of Yorkshire North and West Ridings, and the fens of Lincolnshire and Somerset where drainage accompanied enclosure. These fens were formerly common and waste, that is they were under water or liable to water inundation, but they were probably converted to arable or dry pastures, though this has not yet been clearly established. In later chapters we will speculate a theory that this enclosure of heath, moor, and fen, as well as much of the open field arable enclosure, was stimulated by the effect of a combination of bad harvests, wartime disruptions and possibly population pressure, on the course of agricultural prices. Simply stated, on poor yielding soils and relatively costly maintained soils the returns to agriculture at a time of high prices may have outweighed the input costs (a) of improvement by costly enclosure; (b) high labour costs because of inhospitable location and intractable soils; (c) high density of seed required to improve on low yields; and any other costs which formerly dictated a land use more suited to waste or rough grazing for sheep or other animals. As Williams has said,

> The wastes were often marginal lands, both in their position and their productivity. They were brought into cultivation during a period of scarcity and rising prices.[31]

And these were two prerequisites which prevailed throughout much of the war period. Williams further observed that

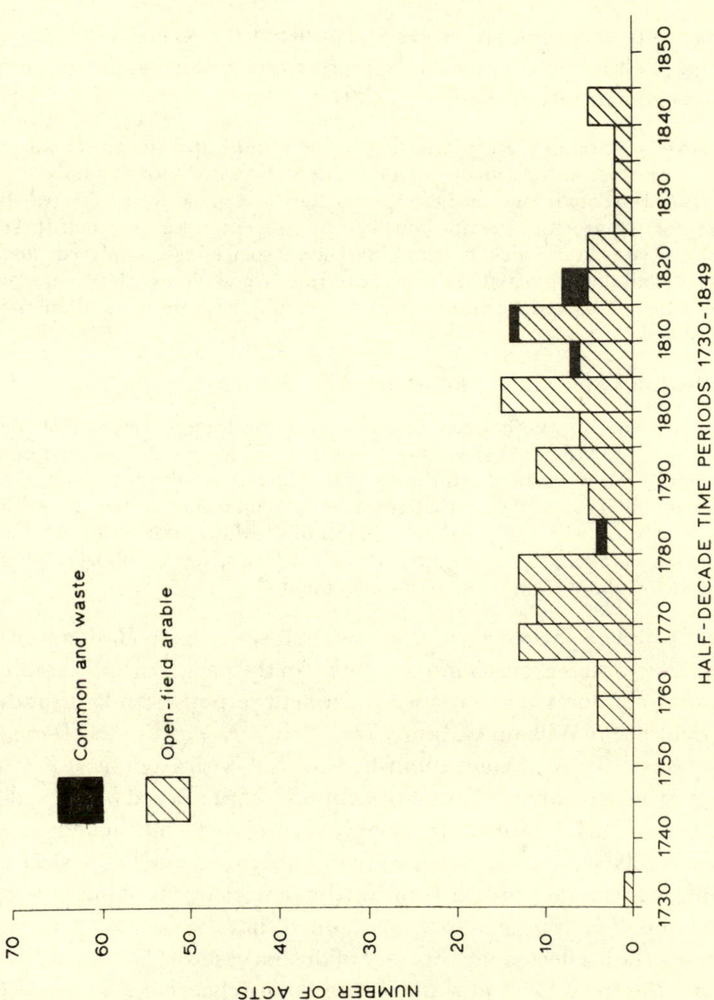

Fig. 14. Chronology of parliamentary enclosure in Oxfordshire.

> it was the wars with France between 1795 and 1815 that brought about an increased awareness of the value of the waste, and the conquest of the waste and the conquest of France became synonymous in some minds.

It became a 'desire to increase food production from these marginal lands' and the object was to see the wastes 'wave with luxuriant crops of grain'.[32]

Contemporary opinion strongly supported this general theme. J. Billingsley, himself a writer on Somerset agriculture and the west country, offered this generality in 1807:

> A general system of facilitating the division and improvement of waste lands and commons, is an object anxiously to be wished for, not only as a means of promoting general prosperity, but as a measure calculated to increase the growth of grain, and thereby prevent a recurrence of these years of scarcity, which not long ago were so feelingly deplored; and which, had they occurred at the present time (when almost all the foreign ports are shut against Great Britain), would have been fatal in the extreme.[33]

And Sir John Sinclair in 1803 said:

> We have begun another campaign against the foreign enemies of the country. . . . Why should we not attempt a campaign also against our domestic foe, I mean the hitherto unconquered sterility of so large a proportion of the surface of the Kingdom? . . . let us not be satisfied with the liberation of Egypt, or the subjugation of Malta, but let us subdue Finchley Common; let us conquer Hounslow Heath; let us compel Epping Forest to submit to the yoke of improvement.[34]

The problem facing agriculture with respect to food shortages during the war has aroused much interest in the past. See for example W. E. Minchinton's summary of government responses and attitudes to agriculture.[35] William Galpin's *The Grain Supply of England During the Napoleonic Period*, though published over 50 years ago, is still the authority on this subject. Citing the minutes of the Board of Agriculture he shows that in Yorkshire the only way to overcome the shortage of corn in 1800 was by extending the cultivable area, and in the House of Lords this was interpreted as the further enclosing of commons and waste lands.[36] Galpin therefore maintained that the General Enclosure Act of 1801 reflected the shortage of the harvests of 1800 and 1799, showing the need for a new and more comprehensive law, an Act which dealt chiefly with common lands. The exceptionally good harvests of 1801 and several successive adequate harvests up to 1808 rather took the wind out of the effectiveness of the 1801 Act. It is now generally regarded as merely a clauses Act only, that is to say an Act designed to simplify the presentation of bills to Parliament and render them less expensive rather than as a great enclosing device. The exceptional enclosure activity in the six years after 1808 has already been alluded to in Chapter 2 and in the early part of this chapter. It too seems to have been a response to bad harvests. Galpin sees the effectiveness and urgency of the wartime enclosures of commons and wastes, and the increase in acreage it brought about, as one of the solutions for the starving of Britain.[37]

Thus in a few passages we may have identified the reason behind the enclosure of commons and wastes during the war period: marginal land made less marginal because of scarcity and high prices, and ultimately ploughed up for grain. Certainly this theory is partially supported by J. Thirsk and J. Imray for parts of Suffolk, where in general, aside from any enclosure, a change took place out of dairying and into corn growing in response to the high grain prices during the war; where in sandy soiled regions these high prices brought marginal land under the plough; and where on the heavy clays there was a plough-up of dairy pastures in favour of the more profitable corn.[38] And for Staffordshire H. R. Thomas has spoken of 'the emergency area which was put under the plough to meet the need for an increased food supply during the French Wars.'[39] These are views confirmed by Postgate for the Breckland of Suffolk and Norfolk where wartime reclamation occurred.[40] I have mildly supported the theory in my investigation of Buckinghamshire enclosures, in particular as it applied to the gravel soils of the parishes in the Thames Valley where whatever parliamentary enclosure there was, was a wartime phenomenon. Here we see the enclosures of Wraysbury in 1799, Iver in 1800, Upton in 1808, Langley in 1809, Stoke Poges and Wexham in 1810, and Datchet in 1810, in all of which parishes there is evidence of the reclamation and improvement of lands which were formerly commons or wastes, wastes like Iver Heath. At the same time there is evidence of a wartime plough-up of clay grasslands in the north of the county.[41] In Oxfordshire also there was the wartime enclosure of parishes in the Thames sands and gravels.[42]

The theory expounded here is refuted by Chapman in his work on the parliamentary enclosures of the North Riding of Yorkshire. He found that the enclosure of common and waste in the region of the North York Moors was not concentrated during the war period, and contrary to much popular opinion, the high prices of the time did not induce land reclamation any more than in other periods and possibly even less. Perhaps Chapman is here highlighting the problems of using the county as a unit of study in the way that I have done. He was looking at a smaller area within a county, but for the county as a whole it certainly looks as if the theory still holds good because as Table 15 indicates the greatest *single* concentration of parliamentary enclosure in the North Riding was the enclosure of common and waste during the war. But at the same time Chapman's point has to be conceded because there was almost as much of this type of enclosure before the war as well.[43]

The 1801 crop returns are a good body of evidence to support the general claim that there was a lot of improvable wasteland, and that it was enclosed during the war. By 1801 in St Minver in Cornwall much wasteland had been brought into tillage cultivation 'and much more will in a few years be subject to the plough'.[44] In Cornwall in general according to the incumbent of Otterham, 'it would tend much to the improvement of agriculture and the raising the common necessaries of life if waste and common lands or downs . . . were all inclosed'.[45] The enclosure of commons and moors in 1797 and 1800 in the Somerset parishes of Holwell and Locking had already resulted in improved and extended arable cultivation by 1801.[46] The incumbent of the Westmorland parish of Morland was categorical about the use of the wastes, the plough-up of the wastes, and the relationship thereby with high prices. He wrote in 1801 that

> the late scarcity and dearness of grain has induced great numbers to plough and sow more land by one-fourth than is consistent with good husbandry in this parish and although the produce upon this increased quantity of ground has this season been very abundant and very well ripened and carried home without loss yet there is great reason to believe it would not be sufficient for the home consumption nor will it ever be possible to supply the manufacturing towns of (?) and Lancashire without foreign importation of grain or the enclosure of more commons in Westmorland. I'm very well assured that the lower classes of people in (?) must have died of want the last two years if they had not procured bread corn from some wastes lately cultivated in Cumberland.[47]

The wastes and commons that existed were, by the estimation of a number of incumbents in 1801, capable of producing an 'abundance of corn' if enclosed (quoting Wick in Worcestershire), and within five miles around Dalby in the North Riding there were 'considerably more than ten times the quantity of acres of land now converted into tillage than there were 40 years ago', and this was ascribed to enclosure.[48] In the Leicestershire parish of Sproxton 'much of the land on tillage was before the enclosure, heath and moor' and though it only yielded slender crops, 2 quarters of barley per acre as compared with a normal average for barley of 4 quarters, it was nevertheless a better crop than had been yielded heretofore.[49] J. Bailey and G. Culley in their *General View of the Agriculture of Cumberland* in 1794 estimated that there were 150,000 acres of improvable commons in the county which were capable of a yearly income of £227,000 as arable lands and improved sheep pastures.[50]

Table 16 lists some of the places mentioned in the 1801 crop returns in all of which there existed commons, wastes, or moors, and

Table 16. COMMON AND WASTELAND MENTIONED IN 1801 CROP RETURNS AS CAPABLE OF IMPROVEMENT

County	Parish or place	Area of common etc., mentioned in 1801 crop returns (acres)	Date of enclosure (act)	Area enclosed (acres)
Cheshire	Coppenhall	not mentioned	1814	157
Cumberland	Hesket in the Forest	see note [a]	1803	see note [b]
	Hutton in the Forest	see note [a]	1803	see note [b]
	Isell	not mentioned	1808	1,600
	Kirkbride	1,000 plus	1810	600
	Wetheral	see note [a]	1803	see note [b]
	Wigton	4,000–5,000	1811	3,205
	Workington	2,100	1809	1,000
Derbyshire	Alvaston and Boulton	not mentioned	1802	1,200[c]
Kent	Blean	100	see note [e]	
Middlesex	Finchley	600	1811	900
	Harlington	200	1819	820[c]
	Harmondsworth	1,300	1805	2,270[c]
Salop	Stapleton		see note [e]	
Somerset	Holwell	500	1797	500
	Locking	not mentioned	1800	161
Staffordshire	Penn	126	see note [e]	
Surrey	Beddington	500	1812	500[c]
Wiltshire	Tollard Royal	300–400	1828	?[d]
Worcestershire	Areley Kings	70	1846	60
	Salwarpe	340	1813	228
	Wick	250	1806	1,406[c]
Yorkshire	Ampleforth	1,200	1804	812
North Riding	Carlton	not mentioned	1808	2,114
	Fylingdales	7,000	1808	220
	Old Malton	1,000	1794	1,516[c]
Yorkshire	Mexborough	150	1859	90
West Riding	Ripponden	'many hundreds'	1814	750
	Wickersley	160	1814	500[c]

a. Part of Inglewood Forest, mentioned in 1801 crop returns as containing 25,000 acres.
b. Inglewood Forest enclosed 1803–19 and estimated to contain 28,000 acres.
c. All of these enclosures contained some open field arable as well as common and waste.
d. Part of the enclosure of Cranborne Chase.
e. I have been unable to trace the enclosures of these places.

Table 17. THE ANNUAL DECLINE OF THE STOCK OF ENCLOSABLE LAND, 1781–1819

Year	Number of acts passed		Stock of enclosable land remaining (measured as the number of acts yet to be passed)	
	1 Open field arable	2 Common and waste	3 Open field arable	4 Common and waste
1781	10	11	2,122	1,863
1782	10	7	2,112	1,852
1783	12	5	2,102	1,845
1784	9	5	2,090	1,840
1785	12	11	2,081	1,835
1786	15	9	2,069	1,824
1787	15	7	2,054	1,815
1788	18	14	2,039	1,808
1789	24	8	2,021	1,794
1790	15	12	1,997	1,786
1791	24	15	1,982	1,774
1792	29	10	1,958	1,759
1793	40	18	1,929	1,749
1794	60	12	1,889	1,731
1795	63	16	1,829	1,719
1796	52	20	1,766	1,703
1797	57	24	1,714	1,683
1798	33	15	1,657	1,659
1799	43	21	1,624	1,644
1800	57	23	1,581	1,623
1801	86	31	1,524	1,600
1802	71	24	1,438	1,569
1803	66	37	1,367	1,545
1804	39	15	1,301	1,508
1805	45	26	1,262	1,493
1806	45	29	1,217	1,467
1807	56	32	1,172	1,438
1808	50	32	1,116	1,406
1809	74	41	1,066	1,374
1810	64	33	992	1,333
1811	67	55	928	1,300
1812	58	52	861	1,245
1813	68	44	803	1,193
1814	58	48	735	1,149
1815	35	44	677	1,101
1816	14	27	642	1,057
1817	14	16	628	1,030
1818	26	12	614	1,014
1819	25	17	588	1,002

Note: This technique while used to illustrate more fully the significance of chronology can also be misapplied. For example, later in the nineteenth century when there is very little open land left to be enclosed, each act as a percentage of enclosable land may be allotted greater significance than it deserves simply because it could be expressed as a proportion of what has become a low total of acts. The technique is really an illustration that, for example, 72 acts passed in 1772 may be less significant than 72 acts passed in 1796 because by the latter date the supply of enclosable land has diminished.

in all of which the parish clergy made protestations as to the great benefit enclosure would bring to the arable acreage. Two of the places were enclosed before 1801, and all but three of the remainder were subsequently enclosed in the following 20 years.

Whatever determined enclosure during the war period, one point seems fairly certain: the enclosure of open field arable and common and waste resulted in either the continuation of arable or the extension of it into marginal areas, and not a conversion to pasture.[51] After the war it seems equally certain that there was some degree of reversion back to grass, especially on the heavier soils, and some reversion back to former conditions of moor or rough grazing.[52]

When the distinction is made between the enclosure of *mainly* open field arable and the enclosure *exclusively* of common and waste, at no time on a national basis was the importance of the latter ever greater than that of the former. But taking national aggregates in this way disguises the increasing importance of common and waste enclosure during the war, and in view of some of the analysis in later chapters it should be made abundantly clear how important the war was for this type of enclosure. From 1750 to 1829 1,301 acts were passed for the enclosure exclusively of common and waste. This totalled 1·8 million acres or 5·4 per cent of the area of England.[53] During the 22 years of the war there were 686 acts enclosing 0·9 million acres or 2·8 per cent of England.[54] Therefore in slightly more than a quarter of the time half of all common and waste enclosure before 1830 was so enclosed during the war. Table 17 demonstrates this importance of the war period. The method of compilation is that of the total of 5,265 enclosure acts comprising 3,093 for open field arable *mainly* and 2,172 for common and waste *exclusively*; by 1781 there were still 2,122 acts for the former and 1,863 for the latter still to come. In each subsequent year and with the passing of each act the stock of enclosable land was reduced. By the eve of war in 1793 the stock of enclosable arable land had been reduced by over 1,100 acts but the stock of enclosable common and waste by only a little over 400 acts. By 1798 the stocks of the two types of land were equal. Thereafter, although arable still dominated enclosure until later in the nineteenth century, the enclosure of common and waste competed more favourably so that by 1815, 1816, and 1817 there were more enclosures of commons and wastes than there were of open field arable.

4

The General Determinants of Enclosure

Introduction

It is now time to consider the question of why parliamentary enclosure occurred in such a short period over such a wide area. The preceding chapters have identified two main waves of parliamentary enclosure suggesting that each was exclusive in time and space, that not only were the temporal sequences different but that the type of enclosure was also different, and that this had a regional expression. The initial impression was that the first wave of enclosures was motivated in part by the desire to convert to pastures those lands which were unsuited to the plough in the prevailing economic conditions; and the second wave comprised lands increasingly of common and wastes, and lighter soiled regions of open fields, possibly motivated by the desire to expand arable production. These were *possibly the motives* but they were *probably the effects*. We must be careful not to confuse cause and effect, while also recognising that logically the effect of an action should reflect the causes for initiating it. Bearing this in mind we will search for the motives for initiating parliamentary enclosure.

Contemporary accounts

Oft-quoted reasons begin by pointing out the possibility of raising rents by absentee landlords after enclosure and of consolidating scattered holdings, and continue by debating the merits or otherwise of so-called capitalist agriculture. Whereas enclosure undoubtedly resulted in or was followed by improved rents, it is not sufficient in itself to explain the occurrence of enclosure. This is said in the full knowledge that many examples can be found showing open field and enclosed ground juxtaposed in which for the same land use, the latter yielded two, three, or even four times the rent of the former. Another explanation, related to improved rents, is that enclosure petitions, bills, and ultimately acts, complained of the unimprovable nature of the soil while the system of husbandry remained in open fields.[1] This however was a blanket paragraph to be found at the head of nearly every enclosure act in one form or another; it became a formality to preface the petitions, bills and acts in this way with the equal formality that the succeeding paragraphs explained who were the major interested parties in the enclosure, what tithe obligations there were, what provisions would be made for the construction of roads, footpaths, bridlepaths and so on. The statement of improvability *might* mean little more than the country solicitor using existing bills to frame succeeding petitions and it *should not necessarily* be assumed that this was the sole motive nor indeed the main motive for instigating enclosures.

The retarding qualities historically associated with open field husbandry have often been forwarded as motives for enclosure. This might be inextricably bound to the points already raised, that is the possibility of improving rents and the unimprovable nature of the open fields, but we now recognise that the open fields were not always so backward and inflexible. However, having said that, it is now possible to test the notion that open fields were less efficient than enclosures, by the use of contemporary grain yield data. 1793–1801 was a period of considerably divergent harvests; it was a period marked by more than one episode of severe harvest shortages, concomitant riots and subsequently government inquiries. It culminated in 1801 with the now famous crop returns, but the lesser known and comparatively little used inquiries of 1795 and 1800 give useful data on harvest yields.[2] Following is a summary of the recorded harvest yields for wheat as given in response to the 1795 inquiry for the county of Northamptonshire, a county which while predominantly enclosed in the first main wave of enclosure activity still had areas of open fields surviving.[3] The inquiry attempted to compare the yield of 1795 with that of 1794 and with that also of what they called a common average or a good average year. It is clear that this meant the mean harvest of the seven years before 1794. It was the desire of central government to attempt a measure of regional grain production both in response to the witnessed harvest failure of 1794 and to the needs and requirements of self-sufficiency at a time of war. I have extracted the information for wheat only but it is also available for the other grains, notably barley and oats.

Name of Hundred of Northamptonshire	Open field (wheat yield measured in bushels per acre)			Enclosed	
Willibroke Hundred	Average year	17¾	average of 4 parishes	18⅘	average of 9 parishes
	1794	15¾		17	
	1795	12½		16½	
Navisford Hundred	Average year		no open fields	20	average of 6 parishes
	1794			18½	
	1795			16⅗	
Polebrook Hundred	Average year	18⅗	average of 3 parishes	19⅘	average of 6 parishes
	1794	18		18½	
	1795	16⅗		17⅕	

Comparing like year with like year it is clear that wheat yields were greater in enclosed parishes than in open field ones, and a closer inspection of individual parishes reveals that they were consistently greater. Exactly the same conclusion can be made with respect to barley and oats. A similar pattern emerges for those parts of Warwickshire which can be treated in the same way. In the open fields and enclosures the following yields can be calculated for wheat:

	Open fields	Enclosures
Average year	16 bushels per acre	19 bushels per acre
1794	14½ bushels per acre	15 bushels per acre
1795	15 bushels per acre	16 bushels per acre

and a similar pattern emerges for the other grains.[4]

Even if the enclosure of open fields meant the conversion to pasture, there could occur the situation as described at Barton upon Humber in Lincolnshire: 'Although there is a decrease in the number of acres under plough since the inclosure in 1793, yet from a superior mode of cultivation, there is an increase of grain upon the whole.' This is a sentiment endorsed by the incumbents at other Lincolnshire parishes such as Firsby and Grasby.[5] Perhaps these are not startling conclusions, but they are demonstrable, and understandably could be offered as the motive for enclosure.

The last three Lincolnshire examples have been taken from the 1801 crop returns, and this source has further evidence, of a qualitative nature, expounding the extravagance and wastefulness of open field farming. Some of the incumbents talk of the losses occasioned in the open fields because of trespass, because of the wasteful fallow, and because of the unproductive nature of scattered peasant holdings. If the enclosure of land was not desirable then at least a rationalisation by the exchange of lands was essential. The loss of production on fallow fields in a course of two or three crops and a fallow was particularly felt by 1801 because of the recent history of dearth. Indeed in Landbeach in Cambridgeshire in 1801 the incumbent said, 'It is worthy of remark that some parts of the fallow fields have been sown with corn in this district during the high price, and probably so in other parts of the Kingdom'; and in Arkesden in Essex the fallows were planted out of turn in both 1800 and 1801 with potatoes as a preparation for an early sowing of wheat in response to the high price for wheat. In Standish in Gloucestershire the open fields were restricted by a course of two crops and a fallow whereas if enclosed 'they would not require a fallow oftener than once in six or seven years'. In Bosbury in Herefordshire in 1801 the common fields were 'highly injurious to agriculture, as they invariably lie fallow every third year', and in the Wiltshire parish of Latton they lay fallow every fourth year: 'This course of common field husbandry allows not of turnipping, nor of any other late and valuable improvements in agriculture.'[6]

The scattering of holdings in the open fields of Broughton Hackett in Worcestershire was described as the 'evil of bad cultivation', and earlier in the 1770s Arthur Young had many outspoken remarks to make on the same subject. In the Vale of Aylesbury the author of 'Goths and Vandals' described open field farming thus: 'The landlords have fourteen shillings where they might have thirty and the tenants reap bushels, where they ought to have quarters.' Improvements by enclosure he therefore saw under the joint heads of landlord and tenant.

> 'In no part of the Kingdom have I met with husbandry that requires greater amendment than this: such products are, their soil considered, contemptible. Improvement must be treated under two heads: first, the management while the land is in its present state, which is the farmer's business; and secondly, the inclosing it, which is the landlord's.'[7]

Without denying the great good that could come from enclosure by way of improved husbandry, Thomas Davis in his *General View of the Agriculture of Wiltshire* in 1811 recognised that there was also another important variable, namely the industry and effort of the farmer himself, 'though the common field husbandry doesn't make land better, it keeps it from becoming worse' or 'severalty makes a good farmer better, and a bad one worse'.[8] Thomas Stone pointed to the conservativeness of the open field farmer who through centuries of inheritance believed that he already farmed by best practice methods and who given a village and farms newly enclosed may well look out for another open field situation 'rather than subject himself to deviate in the least from the beaten track of his ancestors for the means of subsistence'.[9]

The literature denouncing the evils of open field farming and the virtues of enclosures was wide ranging both spatially and temporally, but then so also was the literature against enclosures. It was particularly vehement in respect of the loss of commons and commonable places which the landless used, and the great expense of enclosure, and the great injury this expense wrought on the smaller landowners. Contempoary poets waxed eloquent on this matter. John Clare in 1821 spoke of Lubin's Anguish,

Inclosure, thou'rt curse upon the land,
And tasteless was the wretch who thy existence planned.

And the anonymous Thornborough Lamentation passes judgement on the contemporary enclosure of that parish in 1798:

Ye Thornbro' youths bewail with me;
Ye shepherds lay your reeds aside,
No longer tune the merry glee,
For we are rob'd of all our pride.
The time alas will soon approach,
When we must all our pastime yield;
The wealthy on our rights encroach,
And will enclose our common field.[10]

Rent

Rent is often forwarded as a motive for enclosure, that is the opportunity enclosure gave to increase landlords' rent and thereby improve landlords' income. G. E. Mingay, for example, suggests that 'from the landlords' point of view enclosure was an investment in land which enabled them to raise rents', concluding that if post-enclosure rents were to double, which was by no means unusual, returns could be as high as 15–20 per cent, 'making enclosure one of the best investments of the age'. F. M. L. Thompson has supported this view and cites the enclosures on the Fitzwilliam estates which realised a 16 per cent return on the outlay, while T. W. Beastall estimates a 32 per cent per annum improvement on the rent roll of the Scarborough estates in Lincolnshire in the 1760s, attributable to enclosure.[11]

Contemporary observers provide much information on the question of rents, and certainly the difference between rents on old enclosures and those on open fields could be substantial.[12] In the Buckinghamshire village of Princes Risborough at the end of the eighteenth century old enclosed arable let for 18 shillings per acre and old enclosed pasture for up to 30 shillings whereas open field lands were let for only 14 shillings per acre. In mid-Buckinghamshire Arthur Young observed that in 1766–7 open field lands were let for 14 shillings per acre but upon enclosure could expect 28 shillings: 'This rise of rents on enclosing justifies by observation on the expediency of inclosing the Vale of Aylesbury.'[13] Examples abound which show this rise of rent upon enclosure, sometimes doubling, sometimes trebling.[14] The most recent evidence supporting the claim that post-enclosure rent increases motivated enclosures comes from J. Purdum. 'The hypothesis under investigation is that the parliamentary land enclosures on five Nottinghamshire manors during the period 1787 through 1796 were undertaken in response to the monetary benefits.'[15] This empirical study by Purdum seems to establish forcefully the notion that enclosure was easily financed out of post-enclosure improvements in rents.

However, we should also bear in mind that rent as a motive for enclosure will have been subject to the influence of other variables; it was certainly an effect of enclosure but whether it was a cause is another matter. Rent may have been influenced by the ability of the landowner to finance enclosure in which case we may look with profit at the loan market and ultimately at rates of interest, or rent may have been influenced by the ability of tenants to raise the extra rental in which case prices may have been influential; if not rising prices then at least stable prices such that the income to the tenant in severalty exceeded his income from the open fields by at least the increment in rent that would occur. Thus in Oxfordshire, 'Fringford has been improved greatly in rent *and* produce since the inclosure, at least trebled in both'.[16]

Diffusion

Perhaps one possible motive for enclosure which is often neglected, or at least does not seem to command very much attention, is the one that the individual encloser might have. He may have thought in terms of current prices, or the availability of funds to finance the work, or the rent increase he could exact after the work was done, or perhaps it was a whim which told him to enclose because current local 'fashion' was to enclose. There were 13 enclosures in Northamptonshire in 1778 alone and 13 also in Norfolk in 1801 and numerous others a few years before and after these dates. We may consider therefore a diffusion mechanism in operation because undoubtedly, apart from the initial wave of enclosing activity, there was considerable opportunity to witness it in operation. H. G. Hunt partially supports this idea for Leicestershire enclosures:

> The psychological influence of enclosure on neighbouring proprietors of open fields and common rights; when an enclosure proved successful it would overcome much conservatism and inertia in adjoining parishes and encourage the landowners there to take similar action.[17]

Seen in another way is the effect of local pamphleteers, improving farmers, and worthies on the decision to enclose.[18] It was landlords and large owner-occupiers who negotiated for enclosure, it was they who signed the petitions, who were mentioned in the acts, and who nominated at least one of the commissioners. They were the people with motives, and for an individual enclosure one petitioner may have been in a position to approach Parliament on his own, but all too often these people are an anonymous group about whom there is little surviving biography. They can be studied in other ways, however. For example, were early enclosures dominated by a few but large landowners and were later enclosures typified by less differentiation between the landowners, with smaller and medium sized landowning groups to dilute the distribution? Not a national nor even a part-national study of landownership distribution at enclosure is yet possible with the present state of completed research. A number of local studies do exist which analyse landownership patterns and these will be referred to in detail in a later chapter on the relationship between landownership and parliamentary enclosure.[19]

Some factors which may have determined enclosure

There are a number of plausible economic factors which we can cite in our search for the motives for enclosure, and indeed these have been lucidly summarised by Hunt as some of the *major factors usually considered.*[20]

> We are all clear that a growing population provided the market for a considerable increase in national food production; and it has been shown that enterprising farmers and landlords were encouraged to part with large sums of money to secure the right to farm in severalty by the expanding possibilities of commercialised agriculture. Further powerful stimuli came from substantially reduced overland transport costs which, by widening markets, weakened the power of farmers' local monopolies and increased the competitive nature of farming; and from wartime scarcities which sent prices soaring and made profitable the cultivation of much waste land. Recent research suggests also that periodic falls in the rate of interest facilitated the financing of enclosure.

Alternatively stated, and again from Hunt,[21]

> The causes of enclosure were often complex and perhaps not always explicable purely in terms of economic motive. . . . In Leicestershire the increase in population, rises in the price of provisions, the availability of comparatively cheap money, improvements in the means of communications, the nature of the soil and its potential value in relation to the costs of enclosure, the distribution of landownership and the example of agrarian change set in neighbouring parishes were clearly important factors influencing the chronology of parliamentary enclosure. But it is not possible to isolate one predominant cause of enclosure, or to determine which single combination of these factors was primarily responsible for the varying pace of the movement. Neither is it possible to distinguish clearly the 'prime cause' of enclosure from the 'favourable conditions' . . . enclosure was the result of a conjuncture of factors whose importance varied according to the particular case.

But this is all too neatly expounded and based on somewhat superficial observations rather than rigorous analysis. In addition and possibly just as important as what determined enclosure after about 1750 is to ask the question, why were conditions not right before 1750? On open field agriculture D. N. McCloskey says, 'So plain has the inefficiency [of the open fields] seemed that the question has been not why enclosure occurred when it did, but why it did not occur earlier.'[22] His subsequent work on the open fields, on strip farming and the disposition of strips within the open fields, and the idea of scattering as an insurance against agricultural failure suggests that there was every reason for the open fields to persist.[23] However, the open fields had been savagely eroded in the centuries before 1750, so while appreciating McCloskey's twist in the argument it is still pertinent to ask, recognising the persistence of the open fields thus far in some areas, why did they not continue to persist – which is the converse of asking why enclose?

The following exposition, while not attempting to exhaust all the possibilities, allows a start to be made. Suppose the timing of parliamentary enclosure was some function of factors like prices, money supply, population pressure, war, landownership, self-sufficiency, harvests, and the inadequacies of open field husbandry. The last factor will be debated in a later chapter, but my own feeling is that the predominance of clayland enclosure before 1780 was a response to a desire to change from arable to pasture farming, or at least to a greater flexibility of mixing animals with crops. The motive therefore was land shortage. Landownership is also considered later and my own proposition will be that the differentiation between the strata of peasantry in terms of landownership size groups influenced the timing of enclosure.

Of the factors which remain prices will be agricultural prices and money supply should correctly consider both the cost and financing of enclosure. If the cost of enclosure fell over time we should expect the rate of enclosure to increase, in theory. The financing of enclosure was a cost which needed prompt payment, it could not be deferred until several years' accumulated rents were available, unless such deferment took the form of a loan. In this sense enclosure might be sensitive to the cost of the loan and for this it may be proper to look at interest rates. The simple theory for involving population is that a rising population will demand a rising aggregate food supply to maintain a certain level of subsistence. A greater food supply may be accommodated by greater efficiency, greater acreage, or both. Enclosure could be considered as more efficient and it may have increased available acreage by eliminating part or all of the yearly fallow or by reclaiming land from common and waste.

Earlier chapters have established that there was a coincidence between the French Revolutionary and Napoleonic wars and a peak in enclosure activity. That war therefore may be considered as a factor. A serious problem arises here because the war may in turn have influenced the course of prices, interest rates, self-sufficiency, and other defined variables. Interest rates may have risen as a response to government pressure to attract funds into government war financing schemes or war-induced enterprises. The effect of wartime blockade may have been to reduce supply of food and hence increase price. This may also have effected self-sufficiency in that it may have prohibited the free trade in food supplies.[24] The self-sufficiency expliquand may be partly analogous with population pressure. If there was an increasing need to import food then consideration may have been given to finding a more efficient use of the land; perhaps a more intensive use for example by eliminating fallow land; or a more extensive use for example by the reclamation of commons and wastes. Enclosure may be seen therefore as a way of improving efficiency by increasing output by one or other of these two methods.

Another consideration of the self-sufficiency expliquand may be linked to the problems of the harvest, and greater consideration is given here to this factor because of the special chronology of bad harvests during the war years and the special relationship between harvests and price.

The wartime harvests and price responses

A bad harvest may simply result in importation and thus expose the frailty of self-sufficiency. Hitherto it was thought that the primary cause of the large rise in agricultural prices during the Napoleonic wars was an inordinate number of bad harvests. One scholar in recent times has disputed this function of bad harvests as a dominant cause of the shortfall in the supply of basic foods.[25] In so doing Glenn Hueckel almost certainly underestimates the effect the poor harvests had upon agricultural prices, and more specifically grain prices. His assessment of the effect of rising import freight charges on prices is not in dispute but any disruptions in trade were surely exacerbated by poor harvests, and may have been even more disruptive. In addition, but for an extensive and rapid enclosure movement, in particular of relatively marginal lands, the price of grain may have risen more than it did.

In any series of prices that are susceptible to the quality or quantity of the 'harvest' one bad harvest would produce shortages and the instigation of rationing through an increase in price. If subsequent harvests returned to normal then the price curve would show just one abnormal peak in the series. However, the important point about the Napoleonic war was not the number of bad harvests compared with an equivalent period either before or after the war, but rather the extremity and chronology of those bad harvests: 'The bad and indifferent years occurred in runs, so that in the absence of a reserve of supplies from the previous year conditions of great dearth ensued.'[26] Most of the harvests from 1794 to 1800 were bad, especially 1794, 1795, 1799, and 1800, as indeed were those from 1808 to 1812. Such bad runs had a lasting long-term effect on prices but perhaps they were insufficient on their own to account for all the observable price increase. In this respect Hueckel's points about wartime restrictions on trade are both inevitable and incontrovertible as part of the explanation.[27]

Wartime imports were *greater* than they had been before the war, but if home production of grain had been sufficient, high and rising prices would not have prevailed. But high and rising prices did prevail and this must have been due to causes other than insufficient imports. Poor successive harvests are therefore offered as the very material reason. The disruption of war impeded the importation of food but in no sense can these disruptions have caused the high prices, this was the province of insufficient home production. Even in 1810, the year of the highest wartime imports, overseas supplies of food represented only about nine weeks' consumption:[28] 'They only marginally supplemented home production. It was domestic farming which shouldered the main burden of wartime supplies, virtually as a response to market conditions.'[29]

Odd years of abundance could alleviate intermittent failure, but not recurrent failures. For example, even though the harvest of 1813–14 was relatively poor we learn that the harvest of the previous year was so good that 'the last of this crop was not consumed before the harvest of 1815'.[30] Conversely, the extreme deficiency of the 1799–1800 harvest is brought to light by an observation from Warwickshire in 1800–1:

> The Consumption of the New Crop began as soon as possible after the Harvest was in, and much of it was threshed out for immediate Use, the Stock of Old Corn being, comparatively speaking, none (the Case in most of the Midland Counties); in general there used to be enough to carry on the County for three months.[31]

The government tried to alleviate the deficiency of the 1795 harvest by sending supplies of foreign corn to various regions of the country, 'but though such action might mitigate, it could not entirely counteract, the effect of the bad harvest. Prices continued to rise and disaffection to spread'.[32] The government response to recurrent harvest shortages is well known and calendared by Minchinton, and culminated in the well-researched 1801 crop returns.[33] One thing that the majority of incumbents who acted as enumerators for the 1801 crop returns were certain about was that the harvest of that year was an excellent one for corn crops. In some cases the wheat was 'full as much as the two preceding years' and in places it was 'more productive than any known within the last seven years' and elsewhere it was such a fine crop that occupiers could 'at no time recollect finer crops'. It is clear that in many places the acreage under wheat was increased in the years immediately preceding 1801, at the expense of pastoral lands in some cases, and other grains elsewhere. This was done in order to forestall a further bad harvest because the record of the 1790s indicated a greater likelihood of a bad harvest than that which was actually reaped; the best crop for many years. The evidence for an increase in the wheat acreage in 1801 in the 1801 crop returns is large, but more important it is geographically widespread. A little under 200 individual returns make explicit reference to a changing acreage under wheat and for nearly all of them this is a reference to increasing the acreage under wheat both in respect to the plough-up of some pasture and the conversion of other grains to wheat production. For most of them this increased acreage under wheat refers to the preceding sowing season and was specifically in response to prevailing high prices and scarcity. In subsequent years, in Buckinghamshire for example, this trend towards increased wheat acreage continued until at least the time of the next major succession of poor harvests.[34]

During the period 1801–8 the price of grain, though never low, was much lower than in the crisis years of 1798–1800 and 1808–12. If this was a trend detectable in other counties then it was the supply of home grain which decided its price rather than the supply of foreign grain.

Even if not every county experienced the same conversion to tillage, for example clayland areas were never rightly suited to the plough until the advent of cheap underdrainage after 1840, there was a corresponding extensive enclosure of marginal lands during the war years as an aid to home supply. As we have already identified, this period was the most important for all parliamentary enclosure and more particularly for the enclosure of common wastes. Conversely, the extension of tillage was partly responsible for depressing prices at certain times. It has been suggested that the relatively depressed prices of 1804 and 1814 were caused by abundant harvests and a too great extension of tillage.[35]

Even though the harvest of 1801 was abundant there were fears that the price fall would not match the increased output. Many of the incumbents who submitted the 1801 crop returns accused farmers, corn dealers, and millers of the nefarious practice of forestalling, regratting, monopolising, and badging. This was an attempt to produce only a trickle of grain to the markets and thereby create the illusion of continued scarcity in order to maintain the high profit margins of the middle and late 1790s. There is abundant evidence, or at least suspicion, of this practice, both in the 1801 returns and in all the related Home Office papers of the period. The evidence is too great to condense in this study save to mention that it was not geographically specific, but rather was typical nationally.

Thus, the state of the harvest considerably influenced the prices of agricultural produce and therefore there are serious doubts surrounding the simultaneous analysis of such factors as harvests, self-sufficiency, and price. Nevertheless there are a number of factors which the remaining chapters of this book will investigate.

5
The Economic Determinants of Enclosure

Prices and money supply

Figure 15(a) is a time trend of a wheat price index for the period 1731–1819. It is a familiar enough trend reproduced in one form or another in many works. It shows quite clearly the depression in prices in the early 1740s and thereafter a steady rise in price which, when the occasional peaks and troughs are smoothed out, will give a progressive increase in the price of wheat from about 1750 until the early 1790s.[1] The price trend thereafter changes dramatically, I would say primarily in response to bad harvests, with wild fluctuations in some years and a resulting rate of price increase which was much faster than before 1790. The coincidence of this price history with the incidence of enclosure is apparently now complete. The permanent turning-point in the price series about 1740–50 coincided with the emergence of active parliamentary enclosure, and the major peak in activity during the Napoleonic wars coincided with a 300–500 per cent increase in wheat prices compared with the 1730s. Hunt, in his work on Leicestershire, certainly found the price theory attractive, at least for the period before 1795.[2] There is comparatively little enclosure in Leicestershire after this date but Hunt does further suggest a relationship between the high wartime prices and the enclosure of common and waste: 'A large part of the nineteenth century movement in many other Midland counties, especially in Staffordshire, consisted of the enclosure of rough common and waste land.'[3] No doubt he also had in mind Shropshire and Derbyshire. For Somerset Williams accepts without reservation the price theory as seen during the war, and the lower prices after the war he sees as explaining the fall-off in enclosure activity.[4] J. A. Yelling refers to the 'greatest amount of

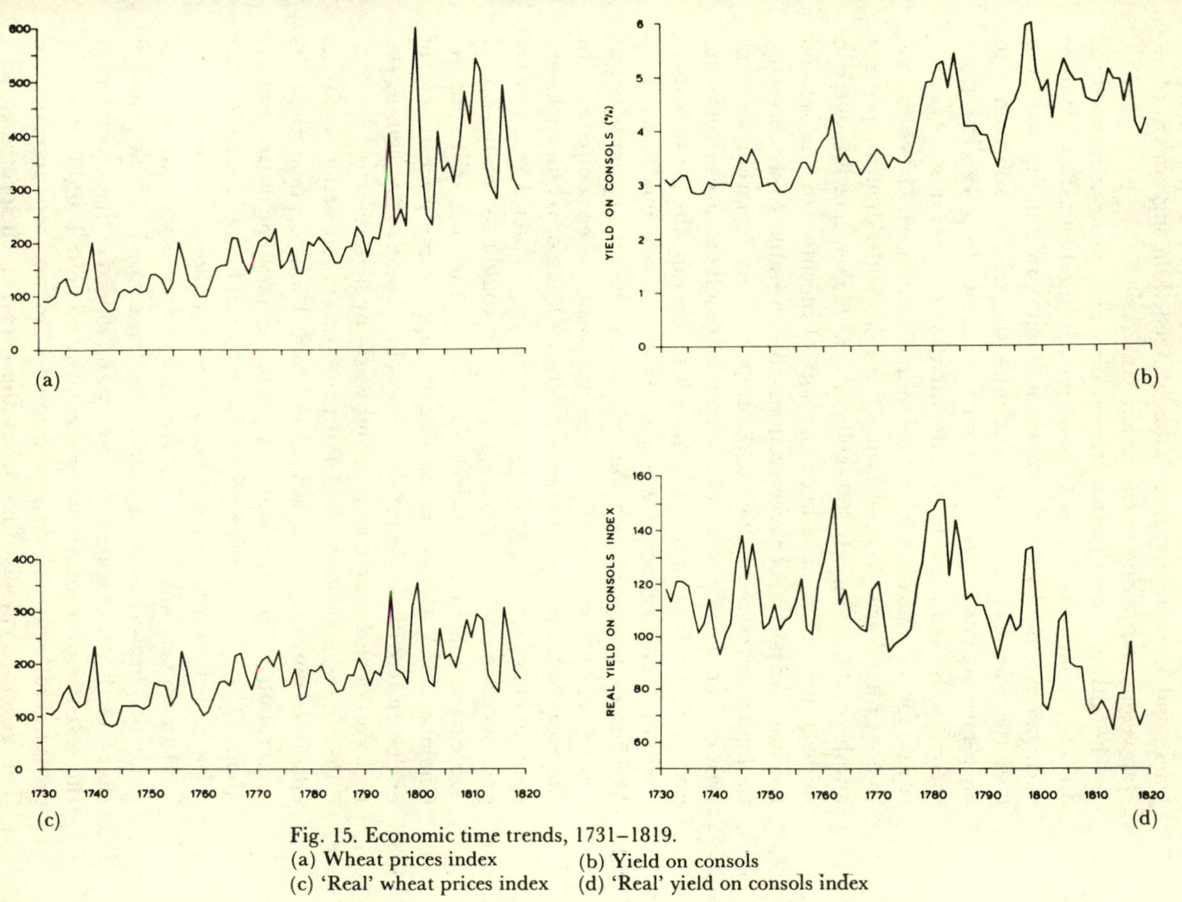

Fig. 15. Economic time trends, 1731–1819.
(a) Wheat prices index (b) Yield on consols
(c) 'Real' wheat prices index (d) 'Real' yield on consols index

enclosure' which 'of course coincided with the great upsurge in the price of agricultural products which occurred during the French wars', and for more marginal lands 'it needed the high prices of the Napoleonic war period to encourage conversion'.[5]

The attractiveness of the price theory and enclosure activity is obvious, though the first peak in activity in the 1770s does not have such an obvious 'observable correlation' with prices in the same way that the war enclosures do. Nor does the relative subsidence in enclosure activity in the 1780s seem to relate to price. The price theory is also attractive in that the inflation of the war years gives a reason for the added enclosure of common and waste. If we assume that such land was poor in terms of arable yields, then the price of arable products at levels 300–500 per cent higher than they were in mid-century might have been the sort of incentive to enclose and reclaim, and possibly convert from pasture to arable. More correctly, the higher prices even at low yields might have given marginal returns greater than the marginal return if left as rough pasture or common, and may also have been high enough to warrant the great costs of enclosure. This certainly was part of the theory put forward by McCloskey, though he also pointed out that the rise in price of wheat during the Napoleonic wars was less impressive when compared with the rise in 'other prices'.[6] Other prices he took as a proxy for enclosure costs and in general I corroborate later in this chapter that the cost of enclosure was so high as to suggest that it would take many years of aggregated inflationary prices to counter the cost of enclosure. Chambers and Mingay in particular support the price theory of enclosure activity and Hunt mentions it in relation to overcoming the high cost of enclosing common and waste by high returns.[7]

While superficially I find the price theory attractive as far as enclosure during the war was concerned, I am sceptical about its application to the first wave of parliamentary enclosure activity, about 1750–80. In a succeeding chapter I put forward a theory that these earlier enclosures were a device which allowed the user of the land to convert arable to pasture and hence increase his stock of animals. This was as a response to the depression in arable prices in the first half of the eighteenth century and indeed in the second half of the seventeenth century, not necessarily to lay all arable down to grass but rather to allow a greater freedom to mix crops and animals. The geographical distribution of these earlier enclosures in part supports this theory, that is the enclosure of the heavier clay vales of the midland counties like Warwickshire, Leicestershire, and Northamptonshire. In this respect therefore we should be looking for relative increases in the returns (prices) of animals and animal products in the period 1750–80 rather than the modest rise in grain prices outlined above. Indeed, according to this theory a decrease in grain prices would be preferred. However, a comparable series of animal and animal product prices is not available for the period before 1790, or at least not to compare with the series of grain prices. Therefore if my theory in the first case study below is to withstand analysis, the statistical tests presented in this chapter will ideally negate the price theory. We shall see.

The money supply theory has also had its champions, but none more so than T. S. Ashton. In the absence of a more reliable series he took the yield on consols as the most sensitive indicator of money demand and supply. Figure 15(b) is a time trend of the yield. Ashton pointed out that an observable relationship seemed to exist between it and the incidence of enclosure, or rather it did for the first peak in enclosure activity in the 1760s and 1770s when there were relatively stable or declining interest rates. Conversely, the high interest rates of the 1780s coincided with a decline in the incidence of enclosure.[8] Enclosures before 1790 therefore seemed to be associated with the ease or difficulty of borrowing money, low interest rates in the 1760s and 1770s allowing money to be borrowed cheaply but high interest rates in the late 1770s and early 1780s attracting funds away from agriculture and into financing the American wars. The theory quite clearly falls down for the 1790s and 1800s when interest rates reached record heights but so also did the incidence of enclosure. Ashton also pointed out this flaw in his argument.

No great originality is claimed over the methods and most of the sources employed in the following analysis and investigation of both the price theory and money supply theory. McCloskey aired his views a number of years ago and also suggested the possibility of a relationship between the chronology of enclosure and a number of variables.[9] N. F. R. Crafts circulated a paper in 1974, when I was conducting my own experiments, and his work has subsequently been published in modified form.[10] Even so, by employing subtle twists, and some not so subtle, it is possible that different interpretations can be put on and applied to the same phenomena.

That there was approaching one hundred years of almost continuous parliamentary enclosure activity might reasonably lead to the conclusion that there was no single factor which determined the timing of enclosure. Indeed it is further reasonable to suppose that there were many factors, some ephemeral and some omnipresent. The analysis of these factors should begin in the mid-eighteenth century for it was from this time that parliamentary enclosure superseded all other methods of enclosure, though there had been enclosure acts before this date. In Leicestershire for example there were three acts in the 1730s, though they all confirmed existing agreements; so too did the five Lincolnshire acts of the 1740s and 1750s. Perhaps therefore they were more closely related to the seventeenth-century enclosures by agreement. The early acts for Berkshire, Gloucestershire, Hampshire, and other counties also confirmed existing agreements. Indeed a high proportion of pre-1750 acts, about 34 per cent, seemed to be less for approaching Parliament to authorise enclosure for the first time than for seeking ratification of existing agreements. In consequence, the reasons, motives, determinants of or for these early parliamentary enclosures were more closely related to the reasons, motives, determinants of or for the enclosures by agreement of the sixteenth and seventeenth centuries. As Beresford remarks,

> Many acts simply ratified decrees, and even where there was no decree, the early acts were more akin to instruments for registering agreements among local proprietors rather than for overriding the obstinate opponents of Improvement.[11]

In the following analysis therefore a starting date in the 1750s is chosen since from about that date parliamentary enclosure began in earnest, as distinct from parliamentary ratification of existing agreements. The precise start in 1755 is somewhat arbitrary though after this date there were at least ten enclosure enactments every year. The terminal date of 1819 is even more arbitrary, but since over 80 per cent of all parliamentary enclosure was enacted from 1755 to 1819 *the period cannot be said not to represent the parliamentary enclosure movement.* A terminal date sometime in the 1820s would have been necessary anyway because the price series used in the study ended then. 1815–19 was therefore the last half decade for which information was complete.[12]

The analysis

Consider the model,

Enclosure was some function of (Xi + Xii + Xiii + ...Xn),

where Xi to Xn are the independent variables we will use in the analysis. The model is defined as having a linear form as follows,

Enclosure = A + BXi + CXii .... NXn + E,

where A, B, C....N are the coefficients we wish to estimate for the model, representing the constant term and the independent variables, and E is the random error term.[13] The reason for this last term is that 'exact models do not account for the observations, and discrepancies between observations and the predictions of exact theory are accounted for by the error term. This is taken to represent the influence of omitted variables (those that cannot be measured or observed or identified) on the dependent variable'.[14] In other words it is standard practice to account for the error term in this way though the regression will not compute an estimate for it.

Enclosure quite obviously is the dependent variable and for present purposes the annual number of enclosure acts is taken as a proxy for enclosure. Accuracy would not be greatly enhanced if annual acreage was substituted since the physical size of enclosures did not differ significantly over time. In one sense only does it matter and this because in general enclosure of common and waste was smaller in acreage than enclosure of open field arable. Also, the date of the act is taken as the moment of the decision to enclose. This of course is not correct since one, two or more years were usually needed before the enclosure petition was in a fit state to present to parliament. The precise moment when this decision was taken cannot be ascertained except for a very small sample of all enclosures, though it is hoped that the application of lagged variables might negate this error. The date of the act is preferred to the date of the award since the date of the act is closer to the *decision* to enclose than is the date of the award, which may in fact be many years after the act. This is another reason for using the annual number of acts in preference to the amount enclosed. A matrix of variables is given in Table 18 with a brief explanation as to origin.

Total enclosure, 1755–1819

The model was considered for all enclosures for the years 1755–1819 with money wheat prices and the yield on consols as the independent or explanatory variables, and the annual number of enclosure acts as the dependent variable. It yielded the first regression estimate in Table 19. The only significant variable is that for wheat price which has the correct *predicted* (positive) sign and is significant at the 99 per cent level of significance. The Durbin–Watson statistic (hereafter referred to as DW), however, suggests problems of autocorrelation. This is a common enough problem when using time subscripted data,

Table 18. VARIABLES FOR AN ANALYSIS OF THE DETERMINANTS OF PARLIAMENTARY ENCLOSURE

Date	1	2	3	4	5	6	7	8	9	10	11	12
1755	1	12	3	15	0	122·24	88	3·14	92	2374·7	3021	2122
	2	9	2	11	0	200·72	89	3·37	92	1027·5	3009	2119
	3	17	5	22	0	169·36	92	3·39	109	−1300·2	3000	2117
	4	12	4	16	0	125·61	94	3·21	106	− 111·2	2983	2112
	5	25	2	27	0	116·61	96	3·59	100	2274·8	2971	2108
1760	6	28	7	35	0	98·87	97	3·77	98	3936·1	2946	2106
	7	18	3	21	0	98·87	91	3·90	94	4419·6	2918	2099
	8	20	2	22	0	122·80	90	4·29	94	2953·3	2900	2096
	9	9	6	15	0	152·51	92	3·37	100	4294·7	2880	2094
	10	32	5	37	0	157·30	94	3·61	102	3968·6	2871	2088
1765	11	49	13	62	0	154·20	97	3·41	106	625·8	2839	2083
	12	49	8	57	0	207·48	96	3·39	107	1539·2	2790	2070
	13	34	13	47	0	206·92	93	3·17	109	−4928·3	2741	2062
	14	27	6	33	0	163·73	92	3·31	108	−3418·4	2707	2049
	15	50	13	63	0	140·73	92	3·47	99	455·1	2680	2043
1770	16	42	11	53	0	174·39	92	3·64	100	754·2	2630	2030
	17	48	17	65	0	200·20	96	3·55	107	75·8	2588	2019
	18	57	15	72	0	220·91	103	3·30	117	−185·2	2540	2002
	19	47	17	64	0	198·51	102	3·47	119	−492·2	2483	1987
	20	56	9	65	0	226·54	101	3·43	116	−2732·2	2436	1970
1775	21	32	8	40	0	150·26	96	3·39	113	−4699·5	2380	1961
	22	46	11	57	0	164·01	102	3·51	114	1900·9	2348	1953
	23	58	34	92	0	187·13	99	3·85	108	−1456·4	2302	1942
	24	47	16	63	0	139·20	106	4·51	117	346·8	2244	1908
	25	48	20	68	0	138·08	102	4·88	111	2172·2	2197	1892
1780	26	27	9	36	0	200·16	106	4·88	110	2201·4	2149	1872
	27	10	11	21	0	193·29	105	5·22	115	−568·5	2122	1863
	28	10	7	17	0	208·00	106	5·26	116	644·6	2112	1852
	29	12	5	17	0	195·38	113	4·76	129	−5322·4	2102	1845
	30	9	5	14	0	178·73	111	5·41	126	−1276·6	2090	1840
1785	31	12	11	23	0	159·07	109	4·76	120	218·2	2081	1835
	32	15	9	24	0	158·50	106	4·06	119	1540·0	2069	1824
	33	15	7	22	0	188·02	106	4·08	117	612·0	2054	1815
	34	18	14	32	0	193·53	111	4·06	121	−657·4	2039	1808
	35	24	8	32	0	227·10	108	3·92	117	273·6	2021	1794
1790	36	15	12	27	0	210·41	112	3·90	124	−1916·7	1997	1786
	[illegible]	[illegible]	[illegible]	[illegible]	0	169·76	109	3·58	121	−3984·3	1982	1774

	38	29	10	39	0	208·48	113	3·33	122	2778·6	1958	1755
	39	40	18	58	1	205·75	117	3·96	129	−4135·3	1929	1749
	40	60	12	72	1	253·64	121	4·40	136	−1728·5	1889	1731
1795	41	63	16	79	1	401·41	119	4·52	147	−2949·5	1829	1719
	42	52	20	72	1	230·20	122	4·80	154	−8545·2	1766	1703
	43	57	24	81	1	260·35	142	5·90	148	−4072·4	1714	1683
	44	33	15	48	1	228·51	142	5·94	148	−3369·4	1657	1659
	45	43	21	64	1	450·34	146	5·07	160	−4238·2	1624	1644
1800	46	57	23	80	1	597·10	168	4·71	212	−12425·1	1581	1623
	47	86	31	117	1	336·75	166	4·92	228	−13963·6	1524	1600
	48	71	24	95	1	248·29	149	4·23	174	−4983·6	1438	1569
	49	66	37	103	1	229·35	148	4·99	156	−2971·5	1367	1545
	50	39	15	54	1	404·10	151	5·30	161	−3980·7	1301	1508
1805	51	45	26	71	1	331·72	158	5·04	187	−8428·8	1262	1493
	52	45	29	74	1	346·64	159	4·87	184	−2807·8	1217	1467
	53	56	32	88	1	307·60	159	4·92	186	−3798·3	1172	1438
	54	50	32	82	1	386·01	167	4·55	204	131·2	1116	1406
	55	74	41	115	1	478·49	169	4·49	212	−4247·1	1066	1374
1810	56	64	33	97	1	420·18	169	4·47	207	−14913·4	992	1333
	57	67	55	122	1	540·81	183	4·67	206	−2383·7	928	1300
	58	58	52	110	1	515·68	181	5·08	237	−2443·9	861	1245
	59	68	44	112	1	338·08	190	4·92	243	−4818·0	803	1193
	60	58	48	106	1	301·57	189	4·92	209	−7410·9	735	1149
1815	61	35	44	79	1	277·44	190	4·48	191	−1565·3	677	1101
	62	14	27	41	0	490·55	160	5·02	172	−2108·8	642	1057
	63	14	16	30	0	386·01	155	4·10	189	−7723·3	628	1030
	64	26	12	38	0	315·80	170	3·87	194	−16355·9	614	1014
1819	65	25	17	42	0	296·30	174	4·17	192	−5809·5	588	1002

1 Time trend 1755–1819 inclusive.
2 Number of acts passed in corresponding year for open field arable.
3 Number of acts passed in corresponding year for common and waste.
4 Number of acts passed in corresponding year for all enclosures, i.e. 2 + 3.
5 Napoleonic war dummy variable, 1793–1815 inclusive equals 1 and all other years equal O.
6 Wheat Prices Index, adapted from B. R. Mitchell, *Abstract of British Historical Statistics* (1962), 486–7.
7 Price Index of goods other than cereals, taken from ibid., 468–9.
8 Money yield on Consols, taken from S. Homer, *A History of Interest Rates* (1963), 161 and 195.
9 Price Index of consumer goods, taken from B. R. Mitchell, *Abstract*, 468–9.
10 Deficit or surplus on wheat imports and exports in quarters multiplied by 10^{-2}, taken from D. Barnes, *A History of the English Corn Laws* (1930), 299–300.
11 Stock of enclosable arable taken as the number of acts of enclosure still remaining to be passed in the specified year and thereafter.
12 Stock of enclosable common and waste taken as the number of acts of enclosure still remaining to be passed in the specified year and thereafter.

Columns 13, 14, and 15 are not printed here but are generated in the computer to stand for:

13 Price index of column 8.
14 Real wheat price index taken as (Column 6 × 100)/Column 7.
15 Real interest rate index taken as (Column 13 × 100)/Column 9.

Table 19. REGRESSION ESTIMATES FOR TOTAL ENCLOSURE, 1755–1819, USING 'MONEY' VARIABLES

	Const.	Money wheat price	Money interest price	WAR	R^2	DW	F
1	5·84	0·148	2·991		0·365	0·818	17·795*
No lag	(0·318)	(4·907)*	(0·619)				
2	61·91	0·054	−8·624	46·83	0·610	0·878	31·76*
No lag	(3·621)*	(1·901)**	(2·029)**	(6·188)*			
3	28·54	0·181	−4·108		0·434	0·880	23·357*
1 year lag	(1·656)***	(6·374)*	(0·906)				
4	74·27	0·0897	−13·28	44·04	0·677	1·010	41·942*
1 year lag	(5·026)*	(3·501)*	(3·579)*	(6·726)*			
5	36·09	0·189	−6·098		0·462	0·8696	25·805*
2 year lag	(2·160)**	(6·827)*	(1·385)***				
6	69·47	0·105	−12·53	39·66	0·691	1·12	44·047*
2 year lag	(5·060)*	(4·278)*	(3·579)*	(6·615)*			
7	34·85	0·1666	−4·294		0·368	0·73	17·191*
3 year lag	(1·924)**	(5·47)*	(0·896)				
8	62·67	0·078	−9·298	40·65	0·627	0·969	32·444*
3 year lag	(4·259)*	(2·831)*	(2·448)*	(6·336)*			

Levels of significance
* 99%
** 95%
*** 90%
't' values in brackets

which is the case here demonstrated, but is deserving of some explanation. A full consideration is beyond the scope of this book. It is not an easy concept to convey to others, less so if one is a historian employing statistical and econometric methods as distinct from an econometrician whose data happen to have a time subscripted base, but very simply, in the linear form considered above,

$$E_t = A_t + BX_t + CX_t + \ldots\ldots\ldots\ldots\ldots\ldots E_t$$

A, B, and C are the coefficients identifiable with our constant term and explanatory variables, E is the disturbance or error term and the subscript $_t$ refers to a time period. To suspect autocorrelation is to suggest that the error term at any time t is correlated with one or more of its previous values (E_{t-1}, E_{t-2} etc).[15] Thus the error term no longer satisfies a necessary assumption of independence.[16] The model must be rewritten or transformed, or we must consider the possibility that there is something missing from the model, perhaps one or more variables. In other words it might be an error of specification, because the error term after all can pick up the influence of variables which exist but which the model has ignored in specification. The DW statistic which is automatically computed by standard regression packages is an indication of the problem of autocorrelation. The theory behind it and its application and interpretation is readily explained in most econometrics texts.

In order more closely to identify the source of the autocorrelation a number of adjustments have been made to the original model. One recommended method of counteracting the problem of autocorrelation is to take 'first differences'. If the modei holds true for time t then it also holds true for time t−1.[17] By subtracting the observations in one time period from the observations in a former time period and repeating for all time periods, a new set of observations will be generated which measure the changes between time periods and therefore attempt to explain the increasing or decreasing progress of enclosure by changes in the explanatory variables. However, such a new regression based on first differences did not solve the problem of autocorrelation. The insertion of a time trend also did not improve the autocorrelation.[18] It may be therefore that the problem is less one of a time-related autocorrelation but rather one of a mis-specified model with the error term picking up the influence of one or more omitted explanatory variables.

The chronology under study, 1755–1819, encompassed the years of the Napoleonic wars but this is in no way accounted for in the model except that it might have influenced the levels of wheat prices and interest rates; in the latter case it almost certainly did so. The application of a dummy variable, to equal nought for times of non-war and unity for times of war, improved the coefficients and statistics as in Table 19, number 2.[19] The sign on the interest rate coefficient is negative, which is predictable from Ashton's theory, that is high interest rates attracting funds into non-agricultural uses and low interest rates promoting agricultural investment. However, though the autocorrelation improves it is still present.

Perhaps the easiest criticism of the model is that it could hardly be expected that this year's prices and interest rates could influence the decision to enclose this year. Enclosure was a lengthy process involving negotiations at the parish level and in parliament and therefore there would be a time lag between the decision to enclose and the successful passing of an act. The explanatory variables were lagged by one, two, and three years with the new regression estimates numbers 3–8 in Table 19. With a war dummy also as in numbers 4, 6, and 8 the significance of the estimates has improved in every way, even with respect to autocorrelation.

The use of variables expressed in 'real' money terms

It may be incorrect to consider pure money prices, perhaps there should be some consideration in terms of opportunity costs. The money price of wheat may be rising or falling faster or slower than the prices of other goods. If the *real price* of wheat is rising faster than the *real prices* of other goods there may be expected either (a) a change to arable production or rather wheat production out of less rewarding areas, or (b) a change in consumer preference to cheaper food. The former affects supply and the latter demand, but in the absence of a fully commercialised agricultural system the producers rather than the consumers might have had the greatest determining powers. It may have been therefore a question of supply adjustment. Figure 15(c) is a time trend of real wheat prices formed by deflating the wheat prices index with respect to an index of the price of goods other than cereals. Compare it to Figure 15(a) and it will become clear that up to about 1780 the real price of wheat was comparable to its money price in terms of trend, but that after 1780 it was always rising at a slower rate than its money price. Interest rates also should be considered in terms of opportunity costs and Figure 15(d) illustrates the reason why. It is the corresponding trend of real rates of interest formed by deflating the money rate index with respect to an index of consumer goods prices; that is, comparing the price of money with the price of goods. With *minor* exceptions the trend of the real price of money was mostly moving diametrically opposite to the trend in the money rate of interest, and in particular the disparity widened during the Napoleonic wars. Thus at a time of record interest rates the real cost of borrowing was less than the real cost of purchasing consumer goods. Therefore it was a cheap money period, and perhaps here is the resolution of Ashton's interest rate argument.[20]

Perhaps a rise in the price of consols from 3 to 5 per cent would not have had much effect on the decision to borrow. Although enclosure was costly, even at 5 per cent the repayment of say £1,000 borrowed would only be £1,050 and an investigation of the *leading* enclosure promoters suggests that the availability of funds was no great worry to them. It would only be significant if other debts had been incurred, for example if estates were already mortgaged. Undeniably many small landowners went to the wall, but then these were not the promoters of enclosures in general. Besides, the usury laws kept interest rates within certain limits, they were not allowed to fluctuate wildly and therefore it was more likely that *real* interest rates would affect the decision to improve, agriculture being viewed as a better prospect in real terms than other enterprises especially during the Napoleonic wars. On the other hand, money wheat prices may have influenced the decision to enclose; the marginal efficiency of land may have improved as the returns from the land improved, for example as common and waste and other marginal lands became for the first time agriculturally viable at such high and rising product prices as prevailed for long periods between 1790 and 1815. The everyday world of two centuries ago may have reacted to the sensitivity of food prices on the one hand and the different uses of capital on the other, that is, to money wheat prices and the real price of capital.

Table 20. REGRESSION ESTIMATES FOR TOTAL ENCLOSURE, 1755–1819, USING 'REAL' VARIABLES

	Const.	Real wheat price	Real interest price	WAR	R^2	DW	F
1	106·9	0·099	−0·671		0·364	0·706	17·775*
No lag	(4·375)*	(1·519)***	(4·477)*				
2	82·28	0·0007	−0·387	38·76	0·632	0·881	34·956*
No lag	(4·310)*	(0·014)	(3·16)*	(6·665)*			
3	110·2	0·1303	−0·751		0·493	0·698	29·625*
1 year lag	(4·928)*	(2·223)**	(5·487)*				
4	89·61	0·0406	−0·506	33·43	0·692	0·887	44·894*
1 year lag	(5·012)*	(0·841)	(4·418)*	(6·226)*			
5	87·593	0·1897	−0·636		0·497	0·798	29·656*
2 year lag	(3·845)*	(3·249)*	(4·555)*				
6	65·948	0·107	−0·392	32·063	0·685	0·974	42·843*
2 year lag	(3·558)*	(2·203)**	(3·304)*	(5.·942)*			
7	74·05	0·189	−0·499		0·370	0·805	17·316*
3 year lag	(2·899)*	(2·901)*	(3·162)*				
8	55·9	0·078	−0·255	36·32	0·614	0·947	30·769*
3 year lag	(2·742)*	(1·435)***	(1·950)**	(6·059)*			

Levels of significance
* 99%
** 95%
*** 90%
't' values in brackets

The estimates reported in Table 20 repeat the earlier regression but using real wheat prices and real rates of interest. Without a lag the significance of the variables except real wheat is encouraging, as is the negative sign attached to the real interest rate coefficient. This accords well with the theory of cheap money encouraging enclosure. The two-year lag is clearly the best result but it is still a long way short of an explanation especially since the autocorrelation is still present, and the transformation to first differences does not help. The preceding paragraph explained the efficacy of considering money wheat prices in association with real interest rates. Such regression estimates are reported in Table 21 and show the same problem.

Working under the assumption that the theories hold good but that something else is hindering an explanation, an obvious conclusion is that maybe the model has been mis-specified. One obvious reason for this might be that enclosure is being considered as an unchanging movement from 1755 to 1819 whereas Chapters 2 and 3 earlier emphasised that spatially and temporally there may have been two distinct movements. Could a mis-specification of this nature generate the autocorrelation effect so far encountered?

Table 21. REGRESSION ESTIMATES FOR TOTAL ENCLOSURE, 1755–1819, USING 'MONEY' AND 'REAL' VARIABLES

	Const.	Money wheat price	Real interest price	WAR	R^2	DW	F
1	77·27	0·1006	−0·445		0·427	0·785	23·056*
No lag	(3·235)*	(3·045)*	(2·667)*				
2	81·81	0·00151	−0·385	38·61	0·632	0·88	34·96*
No lag	(4·239)*	(0·0477)	(2·847)*	(5·842)*			
3	92·35	0·09696	−0·5702		0·533	0·717	34·81*
1 year lag	(4·235)*	(3·260)*	(3·738)*				
4	93·09	0·0161	0·5007	33·04	0·690	0·861	44·48*
1 year lag	(5·195)*	(0·5646)	(3·973)*	(5·508)*			
5	80·02	0·1112	−0·4762		0·519	0·763	32·324*
2 year lag	(3·567)*	(3·703)*	(3·025)*				
6	75·97	0·04094	−0·3835	31·37	0·671	0·9334	40·12*
2 year lag	(4·059)*	(1·441)***	(2·897)*	(5·229)*			

Levels of significance
* 99%
** 95%
*** 90%
't' values in brackets

Periodisation

If the two identifiable movements are linearly related with time but with a shift in the plane of relationship, periodisation may result, as in Figure 16. Such structural breaks have been identified in other studies. For example, D. A. Wilton in his study of the Canadian automobile industry identified a structural shift in the import of United States produced automobiles from 1951 to 1973 in the context of the Canada–USA Automotive Agreement of 1965 which permitted controlled free trade. In his case he was able to identify exactly the structural transition. As he pointed out,

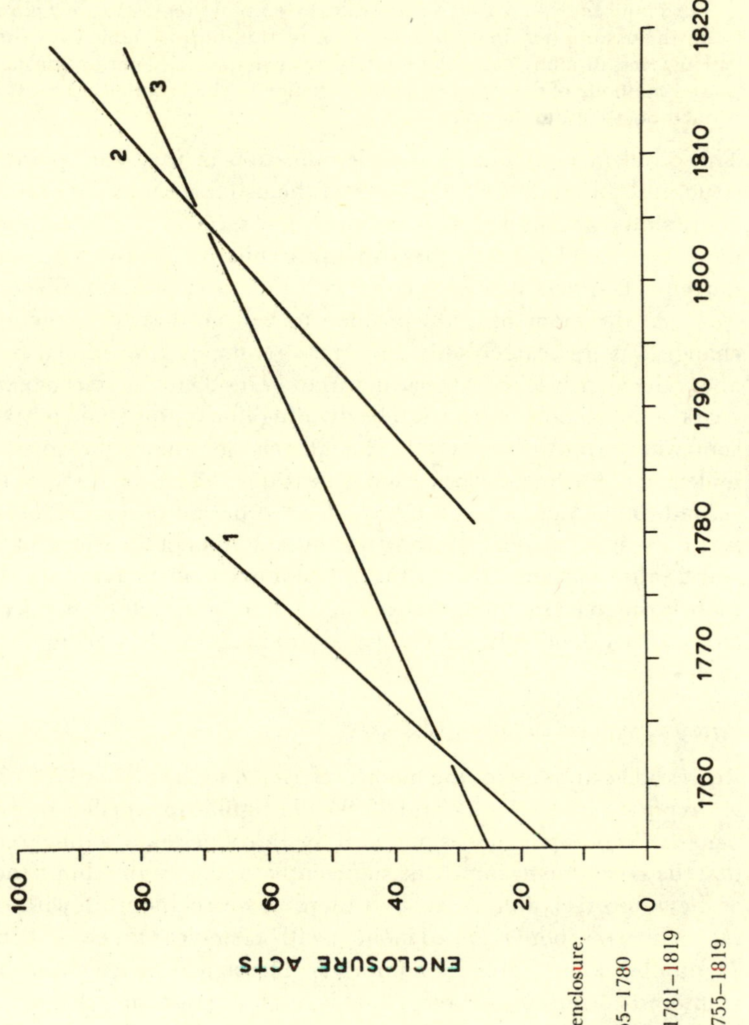

Fig. 16. Periodisation of parliamentary enclosure.

1 Regression line for the first period 1755–1780
E = 14·87 Constant + 2·198 Time

2 Regression line for the second period 1781–1819
E = 27·81 Constant + 1·734 Time

3 Regression line for the whole period 1755–1819
E = 25·19 Constant + 0·9 Time

> Economic analysis of time series typically employs regression techniques on the assumption that an underlying relationship is stable over time. However, in many cases the underlying structure may not be constant, and methods of detecting structural change in the relationship must be incorporated into the analysis.[21]

The problem thereafter is the identification of the exact point of structural shift and the acceptance of the usual assumption that the entire shift is accomplished in one interval of time. It would be a brave man who could identify the structural shift in the two enclosure movements unless it was equated with the onset of the Napoleonic wars. At the moment I am inclined to believe that the structural change was less cataclysmic and more genuinely transitional from about the middle of the American war of 1776–83 to the start or early years of the Napoleonic wars. The dividing line in this study is taken somewhat arbitrarily at 1780. Though this does mark the approximate end of the first enclosure movement it is clearly too early for the second, but it does allow a clearly defined period of non-European war to be studied, thus allowing the investigation of the effects of the war dummy variable. Now is the moment to sound a caveat because there is the constant thought in my mind that the structural break has already been identified precisely by the introduction of the war dummy.

Periodisation, total enclosure, 1755–80

Regression estimates for the model, restricted to the period 1755–80, are reported in Tables 22 and 23. While significant coefficient estimates were obtained it was not until the introduction of a time trend that the DW statistic improved sufficiently to suggest the elimination of the autocorrelation. At its best there was a relationship with the rate of interest (both real and money) with a one-year time lag (Table 22, number 4 and Table 23, number 4). The sign attached to the rate of interest coefficient is correct, that is, high interest rates discouraging but low *real* interest rates encouraging enclosure, but the sign attached to the wheat price variable is incorrect and should be positive to indicate rising money or real wheat prices encouraging enclosure. No matter, as the coefficients are not significant anyway. The two-year time lag also gives the same sort of results. In all cases the improvement of the DW and the F statistic is encouraging because it suggests that the model may be more correctly specified. The fact that the time trend is producing these encouraging results may be indicative of a diffusion process at work, but this will be considered separately in due course.

Table 22. REGRESSION ESTIMATES FOR TOTAL ENCLOSURE, 1755–1780, USING 'MONEY' VARIABLES

	Const.	Money wheat price	Money interest price	Time	R^2	DW	F
1	−50·24	0·2998	12·56		0·283	1·072	45·397*
No lag	(1·334)***	(2·833)*	(1·513)***				
2	47·21	0·0343	−11·45	2·48	0·643	1·792	13·237*
No lag	(1·384)***	(0·362)	(1·457)***	(4·716)*			
3	−23·06	0·2599	7·425		0·178	1·174	2·378
1 year lag	(0·4698)	(2·18)**	(0·689)				
4	103·7	−0·0714	−24·01	2·862	0·682	1·902	15·002*
1 year lag	(2·714)*	(0·7499)	(2·74)*	(5·768)*			
5	11·95	0·226	−0·427		0·170	1·085	2·153
2 year lag	(0·2064)	(1·94)**	(0·0312)				
6	120·0	−0·0725	−27·8	2·594	0·636	1·653	11·637*
2 year lag	(2·683)*	(0·735)	(2·59)*	(5·057)*			
7	−76·89	0·306	21·39		0·294	1·088	4·161**
3 year lag	(1·188)	(2·859)*	(1·326)***				
8	−27·16	0·118	8·755	1·687	0·496	1·365	
3 year lag	(0·4607)	(1·028)	0·595)	(2·760)*			6·232*

Levels of significance
* 99%
** 95%
*** 90%
't' values in brackets

Table 23. REGRESSION ESTIMATES FOR TOTAL ENCLOSURE, 1755–1780, USING 'REAL' VARIABLES

	Const.	Real wheat price	Real interest price	Time	R^2	DW	F
1	19·83	0·183	−0·055		0·108	0·757	1·392
No lag	(0·401)	(1·381)***	(0·184)				
2	41·43	0·029	−0·271	2·19	0·636	1·794	12·831*
No lag	(1·275)	(0·317)	(1·364)***	(5·653)*			
3	85·07	0·065	−0·44		0·150	0·767	1·937
1 year lag	(1·554)***	(0·476)	(1·318)***				
4	77·39	−0·036	−0·483	2·119	0·648	1·673	12·876*
1 year lag	(2·145)**	(0·394)	(2·194)**	(5·45)*			
5	75·15	0·119	−0·427		0·198	0·904	2·592***
2 year lag	(1·393)***	(0·929)	(1·247)				
6	42·946	0·045	−0·268	1·854	0·552	1·534	8·224*
2 year lag	(1·021)	(0·448)	(1·010)	(3·978)*			
7	−1·05	0·259	0·0429		0·210	0·905	2·658***
3 year lag	(0·0198)	(2·037)**	(0·126)				
8	−39·57	0·159	0·281	1·932	0·529	1·45	
3 year lag	(0·912)	(1·519)***	(1·012)	(3·585)*			7·107*

Levels of significance
* 99%
** 95%
*** 90%
't' values in brackets

Periodisation, total enclosure, 1781–1819

Regression estimates for the second period are reported in Tables 24 and 25. The introduction of a war dummy variable improves the results to the extent that the autocorrelation is eliminated, the R squared is doubled and the F statistic is quadrupled, and it produces significant variables with the correct (predicted) signs (see especially Table 24, number 4 with a one-year time lag and Table 25, number 4, also with a one-year time lag). I do not think that the inclusion of the war dummy is acting in the same way as the time trend did for the period 1755–80 because the substitution of a genuine time trend in place of war does not improve the estimate at all and even the time trend itself is not significant. I think therefore that there is less of a diffusion process at work and more of a relationship with exogenous explanatory variables, not least of all the war. A new combined relationship between money wheat prices and real interest rates with a war dummy also might be the closest specification of the model yet achieved. Such a model produced the following regression estimates, with a one-year time lag.

$$\text{Encl.} = 67{\cdot}75\ \text{Const.} + 0{\cdot}04762\ \text{Mon. Wh.} - 0{\cdot}448\ \text{Real Int.} + 4{\cdot}229\ \text{War}$$
$$(4{\cdot}511)^{*} \qquad (2{\cdot}211)^{**} \qquad (4{\cdot}402)^{*} \qquad (9{\cdot}582)^{*}$$

R squared = 0·887
DW = 1·8969
F = 88·81*
* = Significant at the 99 per cent level
** = Significant at the 95 per cent level

This one-year time lag accords well with the known facts, not least the immediacy of the war, periodic runs of very poor harvests, and *possibly* the passing of the 1801 General Enclosure Act which hastened the parliamentary procedures. A two-year lag of the above produced the following estimates:

$$\text{Encl.} = 28{\cdot}19\ \text{Const.} + 0{\cdot}08772\ \text{Mon. Wh.} - 0{\cdot}171\ \text{Real Int.} + 43{\cdot}22\ \text{War}$$
$$(1{\cdot}56)^{***} \qquad (3{\cdot}622)^{*} \qquad (1{\cdot}402)^{***} \qquad (8{\cdot}548)^{*}$$

R squared = 0·850
DW = 1·817
F = 62·23*
* = Significant at the 99 per cent level
*** = Significant at the 90 per cent level

Table 24. REGRESSION ESTIMATES FOR TOTAL ENCLOSURE, 1781–1819, USING 'MONEY' VARIABLES

	Const.	Money wheat price	Money interest price	WAR	R^2	DW	F
1	−15·9	0·1617	6·256		0·360	0·93	10·117*
No lag	(0·4464)	(4·176)*	(0·8107)				
2	53·15	0·0624	−9·057	54·38	0·793	1·55	44·75*
No lag	(2·41)**	(2·485)*	(1·889)**	(8·564)*			
3	14·15	0·1897	−0·184		0·456	0·93	14·667*
1 year lag	(0·4294)	(5·354)*	(0·2586)				
4	51·33	0·1023	−10·49	48·89	0·854	1·985	66·4*
1 year lag	(2·895)*	(4·943)*	(2·727)*	(9·637)*			
5	15·39	0·1854	−1·539		0·462	0·836	14·57*
2 year lag	(0·4635)	(5.322)*	(0·2145)				
6	18·81	0·1096	−3·335	45·11	0·844	1·897	59·63*
2 year lag	(1·037)	(5·267)*	(0·85)	(9·005)*			

Levels of significance
* 99%
** 95%
*** 90%
't' values in brackets

Table 25. REGRESSION ESTIMATES FOR TOTAL ENCLOSURE, 1781–1819, USING 'REAL' VARIABLES

	Const.	Real wheat price	Real interest price	WAR	R^2	DW	F
1	12·57	0·07987	−0·8135		0·425	0·68	13·31*
No lag	(4·425)*	(1·011)	(4·458)*				
2	85·43	−0·0123	−0·4968	48·13	0·845	1·797	63·38*
No lag	(5·493)*	(0·2868)	(4·889)*	(9·717)*			
3	112·9	0·1528	−0·8232		0·548	0·639	21·22*
1 year lag	(4·343)*	(2·161)**	(4·99)*				
4	75·43	0·0673	−0·529	43·36	0·882	1·841	84·38*
1 year lag	(5·376)*	(1·781)**	(5·822)*	(9·786)*			
5	85·35	0·2078	−0·645		0·493	0·779	16·54*
2 year lag	(3·014)*	(2·773)*	(3·608)*				
6	41·49	0·134	−0·3236	43·8	0·836	1·69	56·00*
2 year lag	(2·413)**	(3·03)*	(2·932)*	(8·300)*			

Levels of significance
* 99%
** 95%
*** 90%
't' values in brackets

The following tentative conclusions are now possible. A one-year time lag produces the best estimates; the combination of money wheat prices, real interest rates and war offers the best *statistical* explanation; but war seems to be the most significant expliquand. Crafts found that for two sub-periods 1767–92 and 1793–1815 money variables generally provided the best estimates. He also found that the relative importance of wheat prices and interest rates was different between the two sub-periods: 'Periodisation thus seems to be important'.[22] At all times he found that the money variable was best but that interest rates worked better in the first sub-period than in the second. My own results suggest that if anything interest rates were best but that in the second time period interest rates combined with wheat prices provided good estimates.

Some reservations

It is still possible to question whether the model remains mis-specified; is the use of acts of Parliament the correct measurement of the demand for enclosure? It is undoubtedly a measure of supply, but even in this it is questionable whether it is an accurate measure. One criticism against the use of acts is that it implies that 72 acts passed in 1772 had the same significance as 72 acts passed in 1797. This does not account for the observable fact that the stock of enclosable land was being reduced yearly. Thus in 1772 there were still 4,542 acts to be passed in the future whereas in 1797 there were only 2,469 acts to come. It may be more accurate therefore to consider the annual acts in terms of the proportion of the stock of enclosable land. Thus in 1772 the 72 acts passed that year represented (72 × 100)/4542 per cent of the stock of enclosable land and in 1797, 72 acts represented (72 × 100)/2469 per cent of the stock of enclosable land. The implication therefore is that 72 acts passed in 1797 were more important than 72 acts passed in 1772. The results of a duplicate analysis but substituting the stock of enclosable land instead of acts for the whole period 1755–1819 produced significant variables but at no time could the problem of autocorrelation be solved. For the first sub-period 1755–1780 money interest rates in association with a time trend and a one- or two-year time lag offered the best explanation with the autocorrelation also solved. Similarly, good results were obtained with real interest and a time trend. On the whole the results tend to confirm Ashton's belief that interest rates were the most sensitive indicator of the decision to enclose. Alternatively, by using a measure of self-sufficiency such as the balance of trade on wheat, a new combined relationship between real or money interest rates, wheat trade balance and time suggests a possible causal link with enclosure. For the second sub-period 1781–1819, although significant coefficients were obtained the main problem remained one of autocorrelation.

There is another obvious source of mis-specification. Thus far the analysis has looked at total enclosure though it may be more realistic to look at the two different types of enclosure, the open fields as distinct from the common and waste. It may be that as economic conditions changed through time they may have affected the future viability of arable lands and common and waste in different ways. For example, in its simplest form and at first sight a possible explanation for the increasing enclosure of common and waste during the Napoleonic wars may have been a combination of bad harvests and/ or the wartime disruption of trade causing a decrease in the supply of basic food which therefore encouraged the plough-up of otherwise non-arable lands. This may not have been possible without enclosure. At the same time the inflationary prices may have encouraged a diversion of land use into arable production. Common and waste by its nature may have been of low yielding quality but at the high prices that prevailed the returns to arable, even at low yields, may have outweighed the returns from other uses. At the same time the high returns may have compensated for the high cost of enclosure. This then is one simple theory. Following the same procedure the regression model was repeated for open field arable enclosure and common and waste enclosure separately for the two sub-periods and in terms of the stock of enclosable land. Without recording every estimate of every regression the most encouraging results can be summarised as follows.

For *open field arable enclosure from 1755 to 1780* there appeared to be a relationship involving real or money interest rates and the incidence of enclosure, as Ashton theorised, but it was only applicable in the presence of a time trend and a one- or two-year time lag. For *open field arable enclosure from 1781 to 1819* there were good *statistical* results with seemingly a very good relationship involving the rate of interest, wheat prices, and war with the incidence of enclosure. With a *one-year time lag* the following estimates were obtained:

In *money* terms

$$\text{Encl.} = \underset{(3{\cdot}637)^{*}}{43{\cdot}15\ \text{Const.}} + \underset{(3{\cdot}722)^{*}}{0{\cdot}05157\ \text{Wh.}} - \underset{(3{\cdot}32)^{*}}{8{\cdot}549\ \text{Int.}} + \underset{(10{\cdot}146)^{*}}{35{\cdot}5\ \text{War}}$$

R squared = 0·852
DW = 2·046
F = 65·167*
* = Significant at the 99% level

In *real* terms

$$\text{Encl.} = \underset{(3{\cdot}089)^{*}}{32{\cdot}59\ \text{Const.}} + \underset{(2{\cdot}148)^{**}}{0{\cdot}06101\ \text{Wh.}} - \underset{(3{\cdot}484)^{*}}{0{\cdot}238\ \text{Int.}} + \underset{(9{\cdot}325)^{*}}{31{\cdot}08\ \text{War}}$$

R squared = 0·848

DW = 1·8
F = 63·225*
* = Significant at the 99% level
** = Significant at the 95% level

Such estimates were only obtained with a one-year time lag. This accords well with the known facts, namely the war and disruptions of trade causing fears over self-sufficiency; rocketing wheat prices; declining real interest rates and cheap money conditions; and *possibly* the 1801 General Enclosure Act which it could be argued hastened the passage of bills through Parliament.

For *common and waste enclosure in both sub-periods* there were no regression estimates from which to draw positive conclusions, and similarly with the two types of enclosure considered as a percentage of the stock of enclosable land.

Diffusion, self-sufficiency, and population pressure

Diffusion has been mentioned a number of times as a possible expliquand of enclosure and perhaps it is pertinent to give it an airing. It is a very attractive explanation. One way in which it can be tested is to redefine the model to take into account the observable fact that enclosure itself may have been a variable. In this sense enclosure could act as a proxy for diffusion, in order to explain subsequent enclosure. To incorporate it into the existing model requires enclosure to become a right-hand side variable. Furthermore, to act as a diffusion expliquand it must appear as a lagged variable. The whole range of regression estimates thus far computed were repeated. The results for total enclosure 1755–1819, arable enclosure 1755–1819, and common and waste enclosure 1755–1819 are reported in Tables 26 and 27. As far as total enclosure was concerned, money wheat prices, money or real interest rates, the incidence of war and diffusion, all gave coefficient estimates which were significant, with the correct predicted signs. The equations moreover were good predictors with R squared values in the 70–80 per cent range. These conclusions are true also for arable enclosure, but less so and in part only for common and waste enclosure. However, this test needs to be treated with considerable caution because although the autocorrelation which has bedevilled the whole experiment has apparently been eliminated with the DW statistic at all times close to the value 2, the DW test 'is designed for use in regression equations with exogenous explanatory variables. In the presence of the lagged dependent variable, the statistic is biased towards 2, and hence gives overoptimistic answers'.[23]

Table 26. REGRESSION ESTIMATES FOR TOTAL ENCLOSURE, 1755–1819, USING 'REAL' AND 'MONEY' VARIABLES AND ENCLOSURE ITSELF AS A PROXY FOR 'DIFFUSION'

	Const.	Money wheat price	Money interest price	Real wheat price	Real interest price	War	Enclosure	R^2	DW	F
(1) Total one year lag	50·8 (4·093)*	0·0534 (2·507)*	−10·68 (3·573)*			24·64 (4·006)*	0·5107 (5·957)*	0·798	2·192	58·408 *
(1a) Total one year lag	45·28 (2·597)*			0·0445 (1·095)	−0·2861 (2·703)*	17·05 (3·063)*	0·4716 (5·052)*	0·785	1·953	53·81 *
(2) Arable one year lag	42·16 (4·293)*	0·0302 (1·987)**	−0·876 (3·865)*			15·77 (3·341)*	0·5278 (5·859)*	0·746	1·978	43·267 *
(2a) Arable one year lag	22·48 (1·762)**			0·0376 (1·209)	−0·145 (1·881)**	7·034 (1·713)**	0·5601 (5·763)*	0·710	1·796	36·08 *
(3) Common and waste one year lag	7·869 (1·404)***	0·022 (2·030)**	−1·833 (1·299)***			8·226 (3·181)*	0·5271 (5·571)*	0·754	2·478	45·1 *
(3a) Common and waste one year lag	17·26 (2·252)**			0·0077 (0·4174)	−0·1168 (2·396)*	7·828 (3·356)*	0·4863 (5·262)*	0·76	2·394	46·74 *

Levels of significance: *99% **95% ***90% 't' values in brackets

Table 27. REGRESSION ESTIMATES FOR TOTAL ENCLOSURE, 1755–1819, IN TERMS OF ENCLOSURE ACTS AS PERCENTAGE OF ENCLOSABLE LAND, USING 'MONEY' AND 'REAL' VARIABLES AND ENCLOSURE ITSELF AS PROXY FOR 'DIFFUSION'

	Const.	Money wheat price	Money interest price	Real wheat price	Real interest price	War	Enclosure	R^2	DW	F
(1) Total one year lag	0·8596 (2·164)**	0·00288 (3·681)*	−0·2688 (2·694)*			0·6868 (3·572)*	0·6442 (9·846)*	0·899	2·319	131·119 *
(1a) Total one year lag	1·598 (2·684)*			0·00187 (1·412)***	−0·0133 (3·479)*	0·6347 (3·554)*	0·589 (8·385)*	0·900	2·084	132·09 *
(2) Arable one year lag	1·142 (1·915)**	0·00549 (4·792)*	−0·4101 (2·739)*			0·9036 (3·003)*	0·5909 (8·487)*	0·889	2·113	118·63 *
(2a) Arable one year lag	2·251 (2·411)*			0·00446 (2·204)**	−0·0210 (3·515)*	0·8764 (3·07)*	0·542 (6·797)*	0·887	1·84	115·99 *
(3) Common and waste one year lag	0·4318 (1·119)	0·00127 (1·664)**	−0·1302 (1·354)***			0·5055 (2·956)*	0·6971 (9·137)*	0·837	2·482	76·00 *
(3a) Common and waste one year lag	1·085 (2·069)			0·00014 (1·1126)	−0·00804 (2·355)**	0·4667 (3·077)*	0·6518 (8·816)*	0·842	2·402	78·83 *

Levels of significance: *99% **95% ***90% 't' values in brackets

It is possible that there are other variables thus far not considered, indeed the introductory paragraphs of this chapter considered *population change* and *self-sufficiency* as well. As far as the latter is concerned, as Figure 17 shows, if it is measured as the net importation of basic grain, then from about 1767 the country was almost continually in net deficit. Ordinarily this wheat balance situation would have had an effect on price but it could be that it is a more apposite variable, more directly related than price to the supply side. The analysis of wheat balance in a regression model however goes no further in offering an explanation than has already been obtained. Merely as a substitute for wheat prices it confirms the interest rate theory.

As far as *population pressure* was concerned it is known that between 1700 and 1850 there was about a 300 per cent increase in the English population, an increase which was particularly marked after 1780. The main problem concerned in studying this population change is that there are insufficient data, and certainly not on a yearly basis. Regardless of the causes of population change which may or may not have been related to, or acted as a stimulus upon enclosure, there are some reasons why population change should be considered as a variable in determining enclosure.

(1) The growth of the urban population outstripped rural population growth, which for present purposes meant that there was an increasing proportion of the population engaged in non-primary food production and therefore dependent on a declining proportion of primary producers.

(2) Enclosure in part meant an increase in agricultural acreage because (a) of reclamation of some common and waste, (b) it allowed either the complete elimination of the fallow or at least a more economical use of the fallow, and (c) regardless of those who defend open field agriculture and who claim that it was less restrictive than earlier scholars believed, the maximum freedom of land-use choice after enclosure could result in a better attempt to cater for consumer demand.

Population increase presumably meant an increase in consumer demand in aggregate terms for basic foodstuffs, and the argument continues that this was met, at least in part, by enclosure. It may be of course that this population change has already been included as a partial or major determinant of the price variable. B. R. Mitchell gives some estimates of population for the eighteenth century and from 1801 there is the decadal census.[24] From these estimates a half decade population series can be constructed from 1730 to 1820, giving a total of eighteen observations. Data for all the other variables can

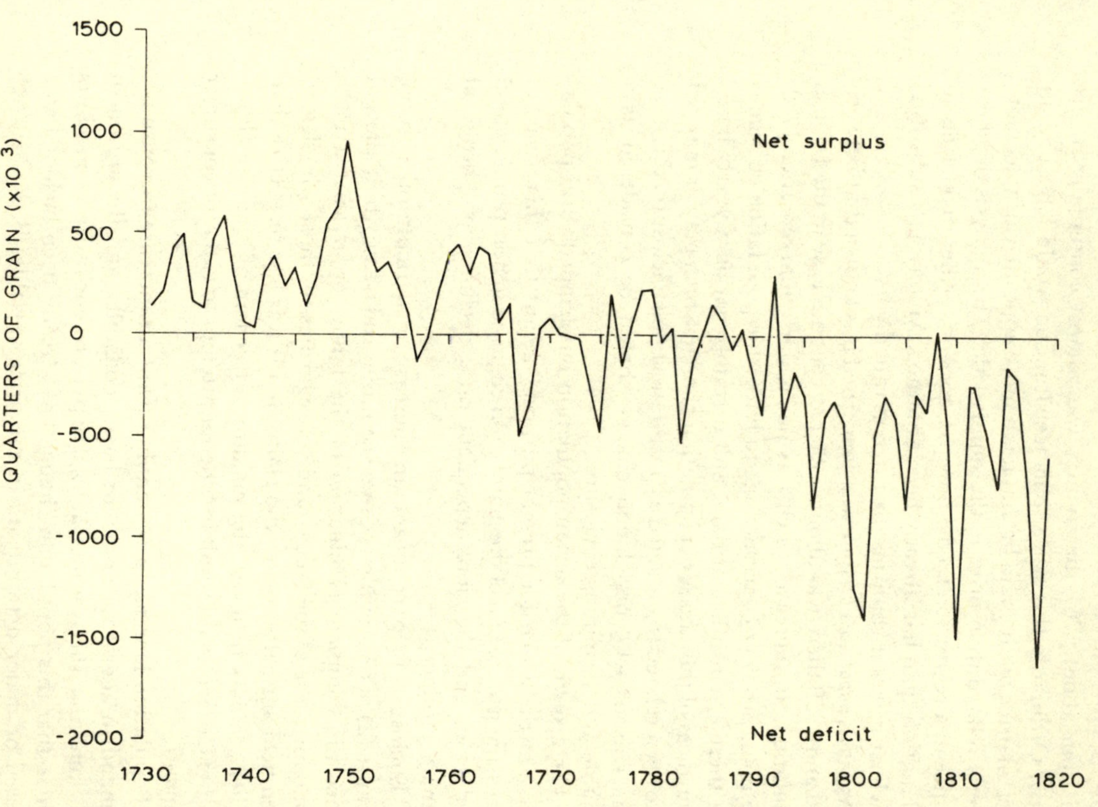

Fig. 17. Time trend of the 'wheat balance', 1731–1819 (i.e. the net import–export position)

also be presented in terms of aggregate half decades and so also can the acts of enclosure. The regression estimates from such a model however in no way suggested that population was a significant explanatory variable. Indeed the only consistent result obtained in this limited experiment with only eighteen observations was the significance of the wheat prices variable. In a bi-variate regression the following was obtained:

No time lag Enclosure = −420·6 Const + 3·567 Real Wheat Price
(4·78)* (7·303)*

R squared = 0·769
DW = 2·379
F = 53·339*
* = Significant at the 99% level

and with a one time period time lag (the aggregate of five years)

Enclosure = −311·0 Const + 2·817 Real Wheat Price
(4·258)* (7·344)*

R squared = 0·771
DW = 2·064
F = 53·934*
* = Significant at the 99% level

These are results which further complicate the entire analysis, which if anything was leaning towards the interest rate theory.

The cost of enclosure

In the foregoing analysis there has been at least one important omission. The returns to agriculture have been discussed in terms of prices and the returns to investment in terms of the rate of interest, but there has been no discussion of the cost of enclosure as a variable. Ordinarily it might be supposed that an increase in the cost of enclosure might deter further investment and conversely a decrease in costs might act as an inducement to further investment. This must remain speculative in the face of insufficient data on enclosure costs. Yearly data certainly do not exist and the survival of enclosure accounts as a proportion of all enclosures is relatively poor. The best available aggregate data are those produced by B. A. Holderness.[25] On a decadal basis he has aggregated the average cost per acre from 326 sets of enclosure accounts. Readers familiar with my earlier work will recall that I consider the cost of enclosure heretofore has been underestimated. This conclusion was based on a study of accounts for the county of Buckinghamshire, though I made my assertion from evidence which almost certainly would not be confined to that county alone. I was making a general point that estimates of enclosure costs need to be revised in an upward direction.[26] My Buckinghamshire figures and the Holderness national estimates are printed in Table 28, together with decadal wheat prices, interest rates, and the consumer goods index which heretofore has been used to deflate the money interest rates. These figures have been converted into index numbers using the 1760s as the base 100 decade (in brackets).

At all times one or other of the costs of enclosure produces the highest index and quite clearly if enclosure costs were deflated against any of the other indexes the real cost of enclosure would still be the highest cost.[27] A comparison of the ratio of enclosure costs to all other prices indicates analogously that the 'terms of trade' move away from enclosure as time proceeds. There is support for this from one of McCloskey's most telling points, 'The rise in the price of wheat during the Napoleonic wars, which is sometimes considered sufficiently by itself to explain the spurt of enclosures, is less impressive when compared with the rise in the other prices', and 'other prices are meant here to stand as a rough proxy for the costs of enclosure'.[28] Such a situation begs even more the question, why did enclosure take place? We *may* approach an answer by relating the price of produce per acre to the cost of improvement per acre. By the early nineteenth century with a wheat price at all times more than 58 shillings a quarter and yields for argument's sake between 1 and 2 quarters per acre, then the cost of enclosure could be met in one harvest year.[29] This assumes, quite wrongly, that all the produce of the land is surplus over and above other costs such as land tax, seed, labour, and personal consumption needs. In addition, the costs itemised so far are only the *general* enclosure costs assessed by the commissioners. They certainly do not cover the extra cost of fencing and other capital improvements. Ring or outward fencing, the fences which make the divisions between the plots of the individual landowners, was ordered to be completed in a relatively short period, perhaps 3, 6, or 9 months. It was therefore a cost which could be as high as the general costs. Effectively therefore the cost of enclosure as given in Table 28 should be doubled to represent the *final* cost of enclosure. There is some doubt over the size of crop yields in the eighteenth and nineteenth centuries but at least the lower half of the range of 2½–4½ quarters per acre of P. Deane does not conflict with the evidence from the Home Office Papers of 1793–1801, where it is clear that the total cost of enclosure could not be met in less time than two or more harvests.[30]

Table 28. COST OF PARLIAMENTARY ENCLOSURE

Decade	Wheat price index	Other foods price index	Money interest rate	Consumer goods index	Cost of enclosure Holderness (shillings per acre)	Cost of enclosure Turner (shillings per acre)
1755–9	146·908 (97·72)	91·8 (98·29)	3·34 (93·58)	99·8 (98·13)	10·5 (82·68)	— —
1760s	150·341 (100)	93·4 (100)	3·569 (100)	101·7 (100)	12·7 (100)	16·9 (100)
1770s	189·923 (126·33)	99·9 (106·96)	3·753 (105·16)	112·2 (110·32)	19·3 (151·97)	21·2 (125·44)
1780s	190·178 (126·5)	108·1 (115·74)	4·641 (130·04)	119·0 (117·01)	19·2 (151·18)	24·1 (142·6)
1790s	261·885 (174·19)	124·3 (133·08)	4·540 (127·21)	138·9 (136·58)	31·0 (244·09)	39·2 (231·95)
1800s	336·605 (223·89)	159·4 (170·66)	4·782 (133·99)	190·4 (187·22)	1800–1815 42·8 (337·01)	83·975 (496·89)
1810s	388·242 (258·24)	176·1 (188·54)	4·57 (128·05)	204·0 (200·59)		79·2 (468·64)

So enclosure could not be deferred with less than several years' accrued wheat prices. What if prices fell, as they did in the seven years after 1801? The cost of enclosing a parish in 1800 became fixed once the enclosure was completed but if it was intended to pay for the investment with a series of inflated wheat prices then some difficulties would be met after 1801. Wheat prices, though remaining high compared with the pre-war level, did not reach new inflationary heights again until the bad harvest period of 1808–13, and of course bad harvests meant poor yields. I wonder if the superficial evidence suggests that the prospect of high prices and hence high returns as an intended method of defraying enclosure costs was a mirage.[31]

Where much of the analysis falls down is in the implied assumption that the determinants of enclosure acted equally upon all landowning and occupying groups in the parishes. This is false because a relatively small number of owners, if sufficiently large in aggregate landowning strength, could successfully petition Parliament and obtain an act. In the words of the Hammonds 'the suffrages were not counted but weighed'.[32] One landowner could hold sufficient land to determine the timing of enclosure provided he had the support of the tithe owner and the lord of the manor. The implications of this will be discussed in a later chapter. Suffice it to say at this stage that perhaps we should really be trying to examine the motives of the individual while always recognising that his thoughts *might be* influenced by prevailing prices, money supply and the state of the harvest. It may be that the individual promoter of an enclosure was sufficiently wealthy to treat enclosure as an unbiased investment, the timing of which was not necessarily crucial, having little or nothing to do with the use of the land, and undertaken in a situation where it was possible for him to wait several years for the investment to produce a return. In this way it may be possible to understand why common and waste was enclosed and improved at a time of high returns in terms of agricultural prices and at a time of cheap money. These implications might also explain the positive role played by smaller landowners, at one stage blocking enclosure and at other times promoting enclosure.

The foregoing analysis must be treated with considerable caution both with respect to methodology and the data used. The debate over motive will continue until a great many contemporary observations are uncovered in which the promoters of enclosure air their views. At this stage my own conclusions tend to support the role of money as the major determinant while crafts tends to support agricultural prices. It is perhaps a healthy sign that we differ because with so little empirical research to be apparently diametrically opposed may encourage others.[33]

6

Open Field Inflexibility and Shortage of Pasture

Introduction

Professor M. W. Beresford sees the seventeenth century as a

> period between the Tudor statutes which sought to preserve tillage and houses of husbandry, and the Hanoverian statutes which offered the majority of proprietors in a village who wanted enclosure a means whereby they could override the conservative minority who were averse to Improvement.

In short, 'it is the period of Enclosure by Agreement'.[1] Embodied in this opening paragraph of Beresford's memorable article on enclosure by agreement there are some important words and phrases which may go a long way towards answering the 'Why' question with which this part of the book is concerned:

(1) The Tudor statutes *sought to preserve tillage and houses of husbandry*,
(2) The Hanoverian statutes offered the *majority* of proprietors etc. . . . but not necessarily all of them, and therefore,
(3) There was a conservative *minority* who were averse to Improvement.

The second and third aspects will be the main concern of the next chapter but the first part is directly relevant to the present one.

Beresford refutes the 'slander' that enclosure had to imply the conversion of arable to pasture, depopulation, and the decay of houses of husbandry, expressed in the aphorism, 'horn and thorn shall make England forlorn'; that enclosure agreements conceded 'to the realities of variety in local agrarian practice; an aspect of faith in the market mechanism and a distrust of regulation'.[2] The legislative process that occurred in the late sixteenth century and throughout the seventeenth century, first to impose restrictions on the erosion of tillage and then slowly to endorse enclosure by agreement, is superbly summarised by Beresford. It remains only to accept his authority on the subject in order to pose other questions and examine other problems. The desire to exercise local agricultural specialisation, to take advantage, or at least minimise the disadvantage, of the vagaries of topography, soil, drainage, and the market seem not wholly reprehensible aims to pursue (as some late sixteenth and early seventeenth-century pamphleteers and legislators would have had us believe). It may be true to say that had there not been a history of conversion to sheep pasture with its related depopulations, many of whose deserted sites or decayed villages were freshly to be seen in the midland counties at the time of the tillage acts, that enclosure in order to exercise comparative advantage over land use would not have been so long delayed as the middle to late eighteenth century. So can we see in this long held desire for pasture, if not wholly for grazing purposes but maybe for mixed farming purposes, a reason for the wave of parliamentary enclosures which began in the reign of Queen Anne and proceeded apace through the reigns of the first two Georges and ran amok through the reign of George III? I think there is some evidence for this suggestion though it should be strongly noted that enclosure is not put forward here as an *excuse* to convert to pasture. There was the continuation of tillage in many areas. Rather it is the exercise of comparative advantage which is important. As Beresford duly remarks of one early seventeenth-century observer, 'enclosure was not [necessarily] the first step towards a change in land use but a means to more efficient arable production',[3] and it became subject to local variations in land use so that the countryside could now be 'a Barne' and now 'a Dayrie house' in response to market forces.[4]

Consider pre-1760 enclosures, that is predominantly enclosures other than by act of Parliament. An analysis of stinting agreements suggests an alternative motive for enclosure, not in general for the period 1760–1840, but for the first great wave of enclosing activity between about 1760 and 1790. This alternative motive to be tested is one of land shortage for the temporary or permanent grazing of stock. It should be stressed at the outset that this can only be applied to areas like the traditional open fields of the midland counties, where little or no marginal land or waste existed by the mid-eighteenth century from which additional grazing could be reclaimed in times of shortage. But this area is also where most pre-1790 parliamentary enclosure occurred, which should add weight to any conclusions formed.

In the midland counties parliamentary enclosure was the single most effective method of enclosing, involving the greatest area in the shortest period. However, this should not be overstressed to the point of forgetting the contributions of medieval intakes, enclosures of the fourteenth to sixteenth centuries and the enclosure agreements of the seventeenth century and thereafter. Also, to consider parliamentary enclosure as the method used in the final dissolution of the open fields is to suggest that these open fields had an inflexibility that could only be changed in this way. Clearly it was the final act but in many cases it was a trivial finale to what had been a continuous process. In some parishes mere vestiges of the open fields remained to be enclosed by the eighteenth and nineteenth centuries; and very few had been left completely untouched by earlier piecemeal enclosure. It is also worth noting at this point that the open fields have been for long undeservedly regarded as a complete barrier to agricultural change. The retarding qualities historically attached to them have been refuted, for example by M. Havinden in Oxfordshire and by W. G. Hoskins and E. Kerridge elsewhere, and in some measure I can also establish this for Buckinghamshire.[5] Havinden has studied parish agreements which regulated the working of the open fields, and similar agreements exist elsewhere. They are characterised as much as anything by the regulation of that very important element of open field agriculture, common stinting and grazing, and should not be confused with enclosure agreements.

Therefore two important developments occurred before the period of parliamentary enclosure: a continuous history of enclosure, albeit piecemeal in time and space, and a continuous adaptation of rules and regulations to supervise the existing open fields. Both these developments seemed to have very close connections with the search for additional grazing lands and perhaps the eventual emergence of large-scale parliamentary enclosure.

Pre-parliamentary enclosure

The mere fact that many parishes enclosed by act of Parliament contained only vestiges of a once more extensive open field practice is evidence of non-parliamentary enclosure.[6] More evidence comes from the field plans of villages. Predominantly the villages of the midland clays were nucleated settlements but by the time of the parliamentary enclosures many had become more dispersed as a result of the spread of gardens and more extensive home closes. These were essentially old enclosures but were more distinctive because of their close proximity to the village (Figure 18 gives some Buckinghamshire examples). The spread of these old enclosures appeared in form somewhat like concentric rings of growth radiating from the village nucleus, encroaching on the open fields.[7] Much of it was very piecemeal. The vestiges of deserted village sites also conjure an image of extensive enclosures, though these desertions are now known to have been caused as much by other factors as by depopulating enclosures.[8] As T. H. Swales found for Lindsey, by the time of parliamentary enclosure, 'scarcely a single parish was exempt from some old enclosure'.[9]

There is in fact a mass of information available to show that there was a long intermittent history of enclosure.[10] In Buckinghamshire for example the Inclosure Inquisition of 1517–19, investigating the period after 1485, found that nearly 10,000 acres had been enclosed, which was 2 per cent of the county.[11] In the period 1555–66, as stated in the incomplete Inclosure Inquiry of 1566, a further 4,065 ½ acres were enclosed. The 1607 Inquiry found that another 7,000 acres had been enclosed since 1578.[12] The prelude to parliamentary enclosure was a period of sustained enclosure activity, however piecemeal.[13] Darby's lucid summary of the magnitude of pre-parliamentary enclosure should not be forgotten, and it is the very piecemeal nature of it which enhances the argument here being considered.[14]

Enclosure by agreement was common in the seventeenth century and in many ways it resembled the later enclosures by act of Parliament, though without the great expenses of obtaining an act. It was common but it is not yet possible to aggregate its effects. In the light of some of the densities of enclosure by parliamentary act illustrated in the chapters above, and considering that a certain percentage of each parish was occupied by settlements, highways, and water, the question is open to some debate. Certainly there may have been a great number of these agreements but in most cases they may have referred only to small proportions of parishes. Until a catalogue of these agreements is made the aggregate effect they had in acreage terms can only be guessed at. If in fact it is found that they dealt with only small proportions of parishes, so much the better as far as the argument in the present chapter is concerned. The agreements were valid in law and sometimes this validity was registered by enrolling the deed of enclosure at the Courts of Chancery or Exchequer, or on the Close Rolls. G. N. Clark has transcribed one of these agreements for an Oxfordshire parish.[15] The Buckinghamshire parish of Leckhamstead was enclosed by such an agreement in 1624, and the neighbouring parish of Foscott was enclosed in the same deed.[16] However, glebe

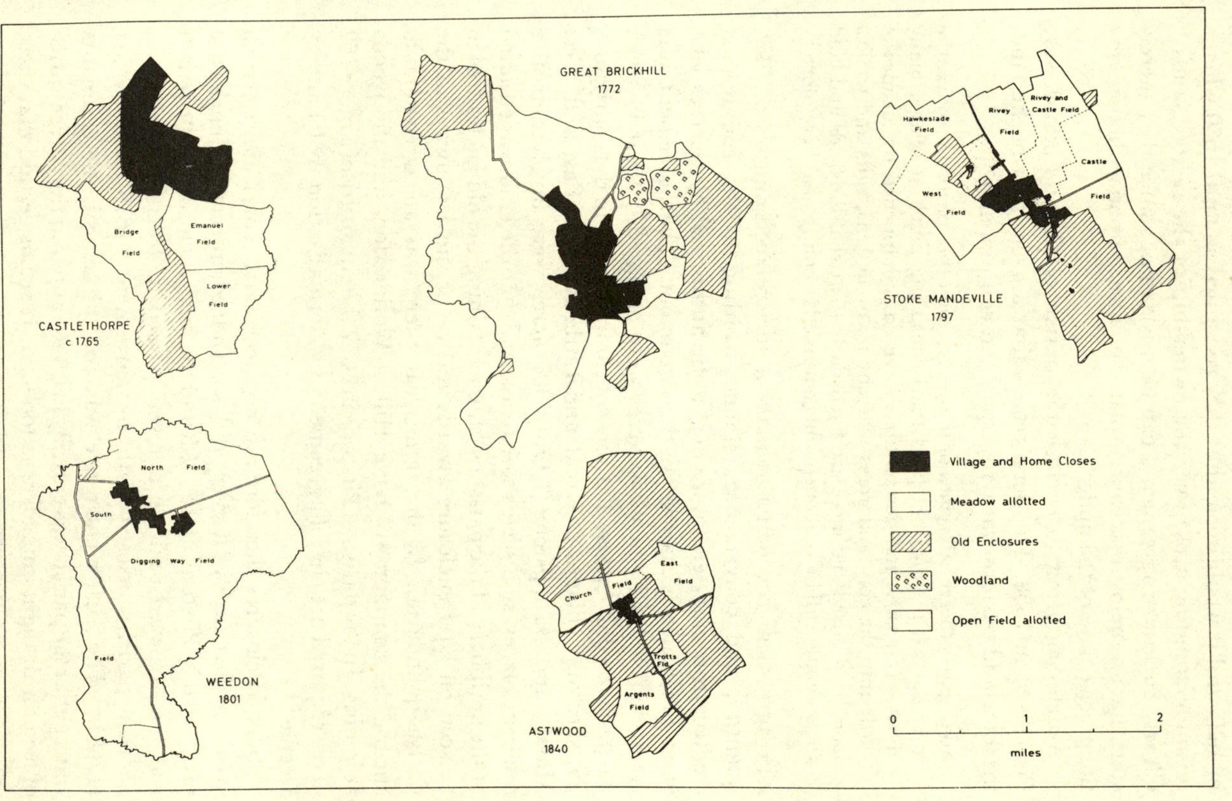

Fig. 18. Five Buckinghamshire villages at enclosure; the distribution of old enclosures and home closes.

terriers show that both of these parishes still had open fields surviving in 1625 and it would seem that they remained so until 1630 when a misunderstanding arose over the ownership of the rectory lands.[17] Clearly enclosure agreements can be misleading, since they merely state that an enclosure is contemplated or agreed upon without giving the precise date of the undertaking.

Articles agreeing to enclose the parish of Great Linford were formalised in 1658. The deed recites that a great part of the land, meadow and pasture was lying open and commonable:

> Some parts thereof all tymes of the yeare, and other parts thereof yearlie after harvest is inned . . . [and that] consisting much of tillage, many spoils, trespasses and destructions have daily happened by escapes of cattle into the corn and grass whereby many actions, suits and trialles have been raised and more are likely daily to arise if the fields and land there should still be kept open and continued in common as heretofore.[18]

The agreement covenants to make a survey according to quality, quantity, and convenience (similar wording to the counterpart eighteenth-century enclosure act) to be authorised by referees who were subsequently named in the document. The agreement was confirmed in 1662 when 250 acres were enclosed.[19] In 1669 seven parties agreed to enclose 300 acres of common field in the contiguous parishes and villages of Great and Little Kimble, East and West Marsh, and Bishopstone.[20] Only 300 acres were involved in five different places, so it seems safe to assume that the land was situated at the periphery of the parishes, thus explaining the old enclosures to be seen on later enclosure awards and maps, nearly always at the parish boundaries. In the same year there was an agreement to enclose the common at Oving Hill in Waddesdon, and the woods adjoining. In the parish of Pitstone in 1672 the enclosure of a mere 162 acres required articles of agreement and formalisation by Chancery Decree.[21]

Such enclosures therefore did not necessarily cover entire parish areas, in fact rarely, if ever, did so. Indeed, piecemeal enclosure proceeded in Pitstone up to 1795 and the final enclosure of the parish was not achieved until an act was passed in 1853.[22] Loughton is another parish enclosed both by agreement (1619) and by act (1768).[23] The earlier enclosure was only piecemeal, the claimants stating that the parish was entirely in tillage and that the current price of feed for draught animals was too high. It seems certain that there was little or no pasture ground for grazing these animals. It was agreed and made lawful for the tenants to enclose for personal use a piece of ground, 'to be taken at the outside of the field or else adjoining toe the towne'. This kind of agreement goes a long way towards explaining the growth of home closes and the extensive areas of old enclosures found at the periphery of parishes by the mid-eighteenth century. Certainly this was the case with the outlying enclosures of Steeple Claydon. The 1558 presentment at court asked the jury if any injury would be sustained if the lord were to enclose and hold in severalty part of the waste adjoining the parish of Addington. The jury replied that no one would suffer by such an enclosure and the land was duly marked off and enclosed.[24]

Such piecemeal enclosure was common, was spread over many years, and involved from as little as one to eight acres each time.[25] At Dorton in 1687 only three acres were enclosed but even an allotment that small still required a formal written agreement.[26] On other occasions however, formal agreements were not necessary. It may have become the custom of the manor to encroach on the edge of the open fields, or enclosure may have proceeded unchallenged because little land was enclosed each time with little inconvenience.[27] An agreement of 1687 for the parish of Dinton left such piecemeal enclosure entirely at the discretion of the individual; on the one hand it maintained the sovereignty of the open fields, and on the other it allowed enclosure. The lord of the manor and his heirs would assist in preventing any person from enclosing any lands in the common fields of Dinton, on pain of compensation to be paid by such persons enclosing for the loss of common of the ground.[28] Piecemeal enclosure of this nature must have been a slow process because by 1802 when Dinton was enclosed by act of Parliament there were still 950 acres to be allotted, which was 24 per cent of the parish.

This was not an uncommon method of piecemeal enclosure provided that it was the peripheral parts of the fields that were enclosed first.[29] There were cases of litigation against people, tenants rather than owners, who attempted to enclose lands situated in the middle of open fields.[30] Clearly there would be objections to too much of this kind of enclosure though one or two acres at the edge of a parish would not be missed.

Great Woolstone is another parish like Dinton for which there was a seventeenth-century agreement as well as a subsequent act of Parliament. The agreement covers the year 1674 but by the time of the act in 1796, 47 per cent of the parish still remained to be enclosed.[31] At Iver in 1776 there was an agreement in which the churchwardens allowed a certain John Main, who was 'desirous to inclose and shut up several *small parcels* of common field land and lammas grounds lying and being in or *near* several common fields' to enclose the land (three pieces totalling nearly seven acres) for the consideration of £60 to be invested in government securities, the interest therefrom to go to the poor for ever.[32]

One possible explanation for this very limited enclosure or encroachment was the severe land shortage felt in the seventeenth and early eighteenth centuries. Thirsk has also seen a connection between pasture resources and very early piecemeal enclosure and Yelling for the county of Worcestershire maintains that the closes, what I have termed home closes, were formed mainly for the conversion of tillage to pasture.[33] This land shortage was nowhere more severely felt than in a parish like Loughton (cited above) where there was little or no pasture or grazing land. Similarly in the village of Nash in the parish of Whaddon in 1702 the proprietors had 'no ground to putt their cattle into when the common fields are done except their orchards' and they were obliged 'to continue their cattle too long in the said common fields by which means they doe suffer frequent and great losses in their said cattle by rotting, and other casualties, which might be prevented by inclosing and keeping in severalty some of their said lands now lying in the said common fields for the relief of their said cattle during the winter season'. This situation at Nash was relieved by an agreement permitting the enclosure of four acres for every yardland that was owned.[34] Such land shortage had been felt since at least Tudor times when an increasing population meant that there was less waste from which to create new lands. Hoskins recalls the land problem of the early seventeenth century and attributes it to population increase combined with the engrossment of farms. Simply, 'land was no longer plentiful in England'.[35]

In counties like Lancashire and Shropshire encroachments proceeded throughout the sixteenth and seventeenth centuries on an amicable and peaceful basis, a reflection that land was still relatively abundant in these counties. In lowland England, however, these encroachments met with considerable opposition, reflecting the land shortage for common grazing.[36] In Westmorland Thirsk remarks that meadow and pasture was plentiful, but in the midlands the commons from which to develop pasture at times of shortage had become a 'somewhat rare commodity'.[37] In Somerset the overstocking of commons was a problem in the eighteenth century, even in the upland areas.[38] The distinction between the pressure on the commons in the highland and lowland zones of Britain is succinctly summarised by Stamp and Hoskins.[39]

In the Holland or Fenland division of Lincolnshire Holderness refers to the 'forage crisis',[40] and Thirsk says that the 'finding of adequate pasture and commons' was one of the problems familiar in the midlands and was 'brought to the surface in Holland' as early as the sixteenth century, but that this 'shortage of grazing was in no sense as serious as that which existed in Leicestershire, and in the more densely settled parishes at the foot of the Lincolnshire wolds, where the villages had no reserves of wastes to draw upon'.[41] These wold villages were crowded together and in the sixteenth century they suffered from an acute shortage of land: 'Overpopulation was also reflected in a serious shortage of common pasture'. This was because the wastes were converted to arable to meet the needs of population pressure and of course the wastes were formerly the common grazings; hence common grazing was lost.[42] These views are corroborated by E. M. Leonard in her memorable work of 1905 drawing evidence from Leicestershire and Northamptonshire in particular, and the midlands in general, where there was so little waste available for reclamation that any agricultural adjustments had to affect open field land almost exclusively.[43] Hoskins maintains that the enclosure and conversion to pasture in Leicestershire received a boost from 1660 onwards with a movement towards large-scale grazing, and in the same county Hunt, paraphrasing Hoskins, says that

> the grazier was able to overcome the shortage of pasture by turning his strips in the open fields into leys. Nevertheless the existence of fallow, rights of common and customary methods of farming were obstacles to the most efficient use of land, and were particularly irksome where the heaviness of the clay made advisable a change from arable or mixed farming to permanent pasture.[44]

In Northamptonshire the shortage of land was less severe because the villages of the royal forest of Wychwood could offer grazing rights to those open field parishes that were short of waste and common pasture, and this was a forest which crossed the border into north Oxfordshire with the same effect on local parishes, and it was not disafforested until 1852.[45] In Buckinghamshire the counterpart royal forest of Bernwood had provided a similar facility to the surrounding villages of Boarstall, Oakley, Brill and others but it was disafforested in 1623 at a time of land shortage and near famine prices.[46]

There are many instances of illegal enclosures and encroachments, not least of all in the south midlands. In Aylesbury the reaction of the freeholders to the illegal encroachment of John Packington on certain furlongs was to sue an agreement for compensation.[47] The waste of Hughenden was illegally enclosed in 1752 and at Shipton Lee there was a legal action over disputed rights of common in which the plaintiff alleged wrongful enclosure (1614–20).[48] The inhabitants of Stony Stratford took action against unlawful enclosure of commons and pasture and decried the diminution of their sheep pastures from as early as 1580:

> By reason of which enclosures . . . whereas the inhabitants did in times past yearly pasture and feed two hundred beasts and did keep one thousand sheep, for which they had yearly sufficient pasture and food, they do now not keep, neither are able to keep, above fifty beasts at the uppermost and four hundred sheep, neither are they able to keep the third horse which they did or might have kept before the said enclosure.

Their common rights were eventually protected from enclosure and encroachment by a series of orders issued at the manor court.[49]

One interesting feature of these piecemeal enclosures, emphasising the problems of land shortage, is that when they resulted in litigation the offending party was often styled as a 'yeoman'. It may be a feature of the period that small owner-occupiers were slowly building their estates. By 1607 in Leicestershire the peasants, so styled, as the initiators of enclosure were responsible for 19 per cent of the enclosures that had taken place in the previous 57 years and they continued so to initiate up to mid-century.[50]

It is clear that even where the so-called depopulating enclosures took place, resulting in village desertions, they did not always involve entire parish areas. Northamptonshire was one of the counties most affected by these depopulating enclosures, and with Bedfordshire, Buckinghamshire, Huntingdonshire, Leicestershire, Lincolnshire, and Warwickshire, was investigated by the Inquisition of 1607, yet it remained one of the classic open field counties with a high incidence of parliamentary enclosure; in fact over 50 per cent of its area was enclosed by act. Indeed parts or all of these seven counties were heavily enclosed by act of Parliament a long time after the 1607 Inquiry. Depopulating enclosures therefore may have gained a worse reputation than they deserve, though we can surmise with some assurance about the very piecemeal nature of enclosure in the 150–200 years before the era of parliamentary enclosure. In compiling his history of the village of Sherington, Professor A. C. Chibnall has detailed this piecemeal nature of pre-parliamentary enclosure for the parish and the neighbouring district.[51] Sherington, Emberton, and Lathbury were surrounded by a ring of villages in which the traditional pattern of open field farming had gradually been replaced by enclosed arable fields. In Sherington itself there were encroachments and illegal enclosures, and the surrounding villages of Tyringham, Filgrave, Chicheley, Weston Underwood, Hardmead, and

Ekeney cum Petsoe were all partially or totally enclosed in stages, dating from the unsuccessful attempt to enclose 30 acres in Filgrave in 1526 and continuing through the sixteenth and seventeenth centuries.[52] It was clearly a piecemeal enclosure movement, with slow but uninterrupted progress. Even the enclosure of as much as 480 acres in Tyringham in 1562 was not followed by the enclosure of the remainder of the parish until many years afterwards.[53]

Much of the midland clays suffered from an inadequacy of grazing. Land shortages were acute and called for at least partial enclosure in order to maintain a high standard of arable farming, by allowing a positive divorce of the animal population from encroachment and spoliation on the arable fields. At times of low corn prices, that is, plentiful supply of corn, illegal enclosures and other unlawful encroachments were pardoned and the offenders allowed to retain their newly acquired pastures. At times of corn scarcity Parliament was more concerned and ordered the removal of all new enclosures.

Land shortage

Accompanying the piecemeal enclosure was the emergence of strict rules and regulations governing the practice of open field agriculture. Initially these were the manorial bye-laws, rules which were introduced at the court leet to govern the cropping and harvesting and subsequent intercommonage of the open fields.[54] These bye-laws were of great antiquity and survived well into the eighteenth century. It was not until 1773 that the administration of the open fields passed from the manor court to the collective decision of the majority of freeholders.[55] However, these bye-laws should not be confused with other rules which developed which are of greater concern to us, and these were essentially agreements concerning the stinting and pasturing of the open fields when laid common. Such agreements seem to date from the sixteenth century and became more common in the seventeenth and eighteenth centuries.[56] Like much of the piecemeal enclosure, these agreements seem to reflect the land shortage of the period, the shortage of grazing and pasture land, albeit temporary grazing. They invariably state in the preamble that the open fields and commons of the parish had suffered from neglect and overstocking. At Cheddington in Buckinghamshire the agreement of 1719 recites that certain people had kept a greater number of cattle than they had right of common for, 'to the great damage and prejudice of other persons having right of common', and in neighbouring Ivinghoe Aston in 1772 an agreement was drawn up, 'because the common fields, common greens and commonable places are overstocked'. The preamble to the Wingrave agreement of 1777, also in Buckinghamshire, states that 'there have been much disorder within the said parish of Wingrave and Hamlet of Rowsham by overstocking the commons and otherwise which is at this time and hath been to the great prejudice and disadvantage of the inhabitants'. And at Sherington in 1722 there was not 'sufficient pasturage in the common fields for so many sheep as are necessary to be kept [and] there is nott a fitt quantity of grass to keep a sufficient stock of horses and cows as are necessary to be kept and fed upon the several farms'. The parish of Chearsley in the Vale of Aylesbury also suffered from overstocking, in this case as early as the seventeenth century.[57]

In Lincolnshire the shortage of commons in the Holland division prompted the idea of introducing stints in the reign of Queen Elizabeth. Overstocking continued in the seventeenth century and population pressure is claimed as the reason. The increase in the number of commoners that such population pressure would produce was problem enough, but there was also a tendency for the commoners to stock more animals in summer than they owned land for in winter: 'The old egalitarian principle that no one should keep more stock on the commons in summer than he could feed on his own land in winter' was abused.[58]

Expressive of this shortage of pasture was the case of the North Crawley tenants in Buckinghamshire in 1742. There was no stint whatsoever in the common fields of this parish; instead, after harvest, the sheep and cattle of the parish were allowed to graze on the stubble without any regulation. On the other hand there was a great deal of old enclosed pasture in the parish. The owners of this pasture, regardless of whether they possessed any common field land or not, would turn their stock onto the common fields after harvest, thereby saving their own pasture and thus exacerbating an already acute shortage of grazing land for those who owned or tenanted open field land only. A stint was suggested in proportion to the open field land possessed, according to the normal practice elsewhere.[59] This was clearly not adopted because in 1772, the year of the North Crawley enclosure, a witness stated,

> I am clearly of opinion that the reason why they follow the present course of husbandry in North Crawley field is because they have no stint of common, if they had a stint they would certainly lay down some part of the field with grass.[60]

A similar situation existed in the north Buckinghamshire parish of Shenley in 1739 except that on this occasion definite proposals were made to improve the commons with a stint, to alleviate as much as possible the pressure on the available grazing grounds. One-tenth of the arable was to be laid to grass and a stint imposed of three sheep per acre of fallow, and six sheep per acre of new or old pasture. The regulations for converting some of the arable to pasture were very precise:

> There shall be baulks laid down at least two feet wide between the lands of different owners and there shall not be three lands throughout the fields adjoining together without a baulk one foot wide . . . [the baulks] . . . shall continue unploughed for the space of twenty one years . . . and all joynts in the common fields shall be two poles wide . . . and laid down for grass.

There next followed strict regulations regarding the cropping and management of the fields.[61]

Thirsk traces the problem and the solution back to the sixteenth century when the shortage of land was 'the' outstanding problem of midland village husbandry. She cites Lincolnshire examples in explaining that the solution was to crop the fallow, and, as in the Shenley example above, increase the amount of pasture by introducing strips of ley into the open fields.[62] In Warwickshire a number of eighteenth-century enclosure awards showed clear evidence of cow pastures which were introduced into the common fields as part of an extended rotation, in the form of temporary grass leys.[63] Agreements between neighbouring villages to extend intercommoning rights was also a method of alleviating shortage of commons.[64]

The stinting agreement formed by the parishioners of Dunton in the Vale of Aylesbury in 1652 contained 28 restricting covenants. Only 10 lambs and 20 sheep per yardland could be stinted, and the cow pasture was not to be used until Michaelmas.[65] The orders were repeated in 1691 and 1699, though by the latter date the stint for lambs had been reduced by half. The orders were repeated for a third time in 1711. The restricting stints of the sixteenth century in the north Buckinghamshire parishes of Great Horwood and Newton Longville are recorded on the manorial court rolls.[66] The Newton Longville sheep stint was 30 per yardland in 1550 but the animals were not to be depastured in the stubble field until a fortnight after harvest. By 1600 the stint was still 30 sheep per yardland but a relaxation in the rules also allowed six beasts per yardland and depasturing was allowed just one week after harvest. Soon after, in 1608, the stint was reduced to 20 sheep and 4 beasts per yardland and furthermore, no commoner was to let or sell his land except to some other commoner or inhabitant of the village; there were to be 'no fforiners or strangers'. The shortage of grazing was beginning to be felt.[67] At the manor court for Grendon Underwood in the Vale of Aylesbury in 1678 a similar stinting agreement was proposed:

> No person shall keepe above three horses and thirty sheepe to a yardland in the Mill field and forty two sheeps att Michaelmas and soe to continue for the other two fields, and that noe man shall keepe above eighteene lambs to a yardland.[68]

The orders were repeated in 1692 and an action against one of the commoners for overstinting was presented in 1694.[69] The court roll of the Mercers Company for the manor of Wooton and Ham in Buckinghamshire in 1668 regulated the stinting thus: for every 35 ridges of land 1 horse, for every 12 ridges 1 cow and for every 4 ridges 12 sheep.[70] It seems that the sole purpose of the court leet for the south Buckinghamshire parish of Iver between 1781 and 1801 was to recite each year the rules for regulating the stinting and pasturing of the open fields.[71]

As the quoted examples show, the stints varied from place to place. In 1550 the stint of 40 sheep, 10 cows, and 10 beasts per yardland at Great Horwood was greater than the 30 sheep per yardland at Newton Longville. In the Warwickshire parish of Ufton the stints in 1641 were much smaller than similar ones in Buckinghamshire in the mid-seventeenth century – only 16 sheep, three beasts, and three horses per yardland, though there were also articles in the field orders preserving tracts of greensward between adjacent properties.[72] The size of the stints varied according to the pressure on the land; the greater the number of commoners the smaller would be the stint, and the greater the area of common and waste the greater would be the stint. Thus at Iver at the end of the eighteenth century the stint was as much as two sheep per acre (which for an average Buckinghamshire yardland would be from 50 to 80 sheep per yardland) because in this parish there was the extensive waste and common of Iver Heath.[73]

For Sherington the reduction of stint from 1682 to 1722 has been ascribed to the increased population of the parish, which resulted in the overstinting of the common and other commonable places. Even though the new cottages would not legally have a common grazing right, it was no doubt impossible to police the commons thoroughly or deny each cottage family an allowance of one or two grazing animals. Therefore in time the cow pasture and fallow field became overstocked. In due course the manorial court orders of 1682 limited the number of cows, sheep, and horses on the cow pasture, stubble, and fallow, and these orders were revised in 1722.[74]

That the pressure upon the grazing land continued throughout the eighteenth century is demonstrated by the gradual reduction in the size of the stints. In the Oxfordshire parish of Great Tew for example, in the three years 1756, 1759, and 1761, the sheep stint was reduced from 18 to 16 and finally to 12.[75] Evidence also comes from Warwickshire.[76] In Wingrave in the Vale of Aylesbury it was the custom 'time out of mind' for the stint to be 7 beasts or cow cattle per yardland, 6 cows per cottage and 40 sheep per yardland. The agreement of 1777 reduced the stint to 6 beasts and 32 sheep per yardland and 2 cows per cottage common.[77] The overstocking of the common at Walton, a hamlet in Aylesbury, was met with an order in 1781 for every occupier to reduce his stint by 'at least one full fifth part'. The hamlet was finally enclosed in 1799.[78] In Stony Stratford the problem of land shortage was felt a century earlier, in 1682. The manor court ordered that all encroachments on the roads and ways were to be removed and a new set of 'orders' were adopted to regulate the use of the common fields and common lands. Although encroachments continued up to 1850 it seems that the fines for violating the 'orders' acted effectively, both as a deterrent to overstinting and as a means of redress.[79] In 1656 the stint was 6 horses, 100 sheep and 12 beasts or bullocks per yardland, and 6 sheep and 2 beasts or bullocks per cottage common, but by the eighteenth century the pressure of overstinting had forced the court to issue new orders:

> Whereas too great numbers of horses have been kept within this manor by order of former courts it is hereby ordered and agreed that no person shall sell or let or dispose of any large commons in any case whatsoever . . . and that the four great farms shall keep but nine horses each.[80]

A number of the agreements preceded parliamentary enclosure by only a few years. Swanbourne (agreement of 1748) was enclosed by an act of 1762. Similarly Padbury (1779) was enclosed in 1794, Wingrave (1777) in 1799, Shalstone (1750) in 1767, Walton (1781) in 1799 and Shenley (1739) in 1762.[81] At least two explanations can be suggested. The agreements may not have been successful, the rules may not have been maintained, and overstinting may have remained a problem.[82] Inevitably perhaps a full enclosure would follow, not necessarily motivated by the need for farming in severalty but rather to allow the individual the choice of setting aside specific pieces of land for pasture. Alternatively these agreements may have been very successful, providing adequate grazing, and, more important, achieving co-operation. In that case the experience of arbitration would have been useful for the later enclosure negotiations.

Conclusion

The practice of revising field rules, reducing stints, and perhaps converting some arable strips to pasture in the seventeenth century and later, may have acted as a delaying mechanism for the more drastic and final act of enclosure.[83]

> If obstacles to the development of farming methods could be overcome without resort to a general enclosure of the open fields then this could postpone the application for a private act until well into the eighteenth century.[84]

Enclosure was therefore a consideration which in many places could be and was postponed for many years.[85] The piecemeal enclosures may have had the same effect.

In many respects the emergence of stinting agreements in the seventeenth century, and certainly those in the eighteenth century, came too late. It seems likely that in the century and a half before 1750 there was an accumulation of capital in the shape of livestock which became so large that the laws enforced by the manorial courts failed to prevent the overstocking of the common waste, common pasture and other commonable places.[86] Land shortage and the consequent shortage of grazing was a critical issue in the Tudor period when the expedient became piecemeal enclosure.[87] In the same way we may have shown that there were similar land shortages in the seventeenth and eighteenth centuries. This shortage was reflected in the search for grazing lands and was partially met in one direction by small piecemeal enclosures and numerous encroachments on the open fields, and in another by belated attempts, having mixed success, at reducing grazing stints and the pressures upon pasturage.

It seems therefore that the land shortage may have been an underlying cause, perhaps as important as many others, for the eventual emergence of enclosure on a large scale by act of Parliament. At the very least, the attempted solutions to the problem of land shortage should be viewed alongside other techniques considered in the past (such as the development of convertible husbandry with the introduction of new grasses and other fodder crops) as a positive measure to increase agricultural output in the late seventeenth and early eighteenth centuries. But clearly this had a limited geographical expression. The public outcry that enclosure resulted in a conversion to pasture and the concomitant reduction in employment that this would bring, was offered in the eighteenth century as a reason for objecting to enclosure. But it applies more, if not exclusively, to the enclosures which preceded the Napoleonic wars, and in particular to the first great wave of enclosing activity of the period 1750–80 such as was experienced in Warwickshire, Leicestershire, and Northamptonshire. These were counties dominated by heavy clays where the persistence of arable production in the face of declining profitability was a major problem. It was in these counties that enclosure had almost run its course by 1790. It was in these counties and in the midlands in general that the so-called agricultural depression of 1730–50 gave the most convincing argument for practising mixed or animal husbandry in clayland districts.[88]

However this is viewed, as a singularly economic reaction or as Butlin suggests a diffusionist process related to the midland economy, is at this stage perhaps less important than the identification of the enclosures of the period before 1790 as exclusive in most respects from those of the Napoleonic war period.[89]

7

Landownership and the Chronology of Enclosure

Introduction

In the words of the Hammonds, enclosure was a process in which 'the suffrages were not counted but weighed'.[1] This is a reference to the fact that it was landownership strength measured in acres rather than the number of landowners that was important in the decision to enclose. Assuming that the presentation of an enclosure bill to Parliament met with the approval of the tithe owners (both clerical and lay) and the lord of the manor (because of his special interest in the rights of the soil), theoretically a single landowner could decide upon the enclosure of a parish regardless of the opinions of all other landowners. He could do this if as signatory to the bill he could muster about two-thirds to four-fifths of all the lands proposed for enclosure.[2] There were clearly instances where such a situation did exist, where a single landowner was such a substantial freeholder as to own 70 or 80 per cent of the lands proposed for enclosure. Hunt itemises two Leicestershire examples where the leading landowner possessed 81 and 79 per cent respectively of the lands under consideration for enclosure and in Buckinghamshire quite a number of the earlier enclosures exhibit this feature.[3] Indeed, such a distorted picture of landownership distribution is a feature of many enclosures of the first main wave of activity before 1780, and Hunt, Martin for Warwickshire and I have likened some of these earlier enclosures to the alternative enclosure by private agreement.[4] If the lesser landowners, collectively or individually, objected to enclosure then it was up to them to present a counter-petition to Parliament to amend the bill or throw it out altogether. There were instances where such action occurred.[5] It was just as likely however that the landownership situation in a parish might require the approval of the majority of freeholders to gain 70 or 80 per cent of the landownership strength. Thus we have the two extremes of the landownership spectrum. In the one instance there might have been one substantial landowner and a number of smaller ones and in the second instance there might have been a number of landowners of almost equal strength and no substantial owners. The question to ask is whether this landownership situation was at all related to the chronology of enclosure. In the sense that successful objections to enclosure might delay it, the question of landownership differentiation and the relationship with landownership pressure groups might be important or at the very least deserving of some consideration as a determinant of enclosure.

A case study from Buckinghamshire

The enclosure award is a very good catalogue of landownership structure over those parts of the parish which were enclosed and it is cross-sectional in one particular year. Table 29 represents a summary of landownership in 81 Buckinghamshire parishes which were enclosed in the six decades after 1760.[6]

In the first decade of study, the 1760s, for eleven enclosures, owners of estates of over 500 acres were awarded 31·6 per cent of all the lands to be enclosed, but only five owners came into this category. At the opposite extreme 117 owners possessing fewer than ten acres each were awarded only 2·9 per cent of all the lands to be enclosed. On aggregate it seemed to be a situation of a small number of very large landowners dominating these parishes of early parliamentary enclosure. Similarly in Warwickshire where in 12 parishes enclosed from 1720 to 1749, 50 per cent of the land was allotted to estates of more than 500 acres and from 1750 to 1769, 30 per cent was allotted to estates of more than 500 acres.[7] The Buckinghamshire distribution, however, was not quite so straightforward because there was an intermediate group possessing up to 200 acres. They were strong both in numbers and in the proportion of land they owned. These parishes seem to confirm Ashton's contention that 'the process [enclosure] was closely associated with the concentration of ownership into fewer hands'.[8] The owners possessing from 10 to 200 acres were awarded 42·7 per cent of all the lands that were enclosed, and since normally those possessing from two-thirds to four-fifths would need to agree on enclosure to petition successfully, such intermediate landowners could have exercised considerable bargaining power and possibly

Table 29. ANALYSIS OF LANDOWNERSHIP DISTRIBUTION FROM 81 BUCKINGHAMSHIRE ENCLOSURES, 1760–1819

Decade	Church acreage (as percentage)	> 500 acres No. acreage (as percentage)	300–500 acres No. acreage (as percentage)	200–300 acres No. acreage (as percentage)	100–200 acres No. acreage (as percentage)
1760s 11 awards	1,060 (7·8)	5 4,293 (31·6)	3 1,228 (9·1)	2 451 (3·3)	13 1,793 (13·2)
1770s 19 awards	4,793 (16·1)	7 6,343 (21·3)	7 2,867 (9·7)	11 2,784 (9·4)	22 3,129 (10·5)
1780s 4 awards	644 (11·1)	1 1,110 (19·1)	3 1,207 (20·8)	1 212 (3·7)	3 373 (6·4)
1790s 25 awards	3,525 (10·9)	2 2,379 (7·4)	9 3,696 (11·5)	14 3,267 (10·1)	58 8,078 (25·1)
1800s 15 awards	2,245 (9·9)	8 5,539 (24·4)	9 3,776 (16·6)	6 1,428 (6·3)	16 2,312 (10·2)
1810s 7 awards	2,587 (19·1)	3 1,882 (13·9)	5 1,887 (13·9)	1 268 (2·0)	16 2,101 (15·5)

Decade	50–100 acres No. acreage (as percentage)	10–50 acres No. acreage (as percentage)	< 10 acres No. acreage (as percentage)	Other No. acreage (as percentage)
1760s 11 awards	26 1,946 (14·3)	93 2,068 (15·2)	117 389 (2·9)	22 354 (2·6)
1770s 19 awards	52 3,770 (12·7)	174 4,139 (13·9)	322 1,000 (3·4)	45 899 (3·0)
1780s 4 awards	11 828 (14·2)	27 691 (11·9)	69 227 (3·9)	14 550 (9·5)
1790s 25 awards	71 4,970 (15·4)	169 4,222 (13·1)	374 1,063 (3·3)	80 1,048 (3·2)
1800s 15 awards	43 3,063 (13·5)	101 2,479 (10·9)	411 765 (3·4)	68 1,094 (4·8)
1810s 7 awards	27 1,929 (14·3)	83 1,872 (13·8)	242 612 (4·5)	43 404 (3·0)

Source: Enclosure awards, *Buckinghamshire County Record Office.*

opposition, but they did not. In actual fact on only three occasions was this group of intermediate landowners of sufficient size and number to influence the enclosures, and therefore the inclusion of these three parishes in aggregating landownership distribution in the 1760s distorts the more general feature I am describing. Of the 30 enclosures enacted in the 1760s and 1770s landowners with estates larger than 500 acres owned 21·3 per cent of the allottable areas, a pattern repeated in Warwickshire where owners of estates greater than 300 acres received 44 per cent of the land allotted.[9]

For individual parishes in the 1760s and 1770s the leading landowner might receive 60 or 70 per cent of the land allotted in the award, as at Westbury in 1764–5, Winslow in 1766–7 and Olney in 1767–8, and at Shalstone in 1767–8 George Purefoy was allotted 87 per cent of all the lands that were enclosed. It is quite understandable therefore that these early enclosures proceeded through Parliament with haste and quite unmolested. Analogously to 'bell shaped' distributions, the landownership pattern was highly skewed towards the larger owners and there was a small range, that is there were relatively few allottees per parish (less than 30). There is some support for these findings from other counties but unfortunately the monograph historians of enclosure have not in all respects reported their findings in a comparable way. In Leicestershire Hunt found that the aristocracy, in association with the clergy and all those owners possessing more than 200 acres, controlled 48 per cent of the land allotted before 1780, and if we include landowners of greater than 100 acres the proportion rises to 62 per cent. Martin's evidence from Warwickshire has already been cited above,[10] and support also comes from the East Riding of Yorkshire.[11]

Over time the distribution of landownership and its apparent relationship with the chronology of enclosure changed somewhat. The parishes were less and less dominated by a few large landowners and the awards were much longer as there were more allottees to satisfy. By the second main wave of enclosure activity in the late 1790s as many as 60 or 70 persons per enclosure were receiving allotments and it might take as many as 10 per cent of them to hold the majority of land in a parish, compared with the one or two owners in the 1760s, and it might take many more to hold the two-thirds or four-fifths majority. The 1790s was the most active decade in Buckinghamshire enclosure history; for 25 enclosures only two landowners possessed more than 500 acres and they received only 7·4 per cent of the open fields that were enclosed. The largest single landowning group was intermediate, medium to large freeholders of 1–200 acres who received 25·1 per cent of the open fields. A broader group possessing from 0–200 acres, very much like V. M. Lavrovsky's so-called 'peasant' groups, received 56·9 per cent of the open fields. Indeed in Lavrovsky's study of eleven Suffolk parishes enclosed between 1797 and 1814 one of his main conclusions was the identification of a numerical predominance of a smaller type of peasant (judged by his definition to have fewer than 25 acres) and the emergence of a small group of middle and well-to-do peasantry (up to 150 acres)[12] and richer ones (over 150 acres) who were approaching capitalist proportions.[13]

With such a strong 'peasantry' in those parishes enclosed in the 1790s special influences might be considered to explain this chronology of enclosure, and here reference must be made to the influence of inflationary wartime prices on both land values and the produce of the land. The suggestion is, and it was under discussion in Chapter 5 above, that the cost of enclosure to these smaller, intermediate estates was, for the first time, outweighed by the short-run expected returns on the improved lands; the amortisation period on the enclosure investment was thereby shortened.[14]

The war period saw the only significant enclosure activity in the south of Buckinghamshire, recognising the wastes and extensive commons as potential arable lands. Some opposition was experienced in these parishes, in which, rather than being dominated by large landowners the balance of power lay in the hands of the lesser landowners possessing fewer than 200 acres each. Most of the parishes were genuinely controlled by these lesser landowners. For example at Wraysbury, enclosed in 1799–1803, there were three such owners, each with between 1 and 200 acres which accounted for 55 per cent of the lands that were allotted; similarly at Upton in 1808–19 where landowners of between 1 and 300 acres were the largest group. Some of these enclosures were accompanied by opposition at Westminster and it is suggested that the petitioners were anxious to capitalise on the prevailing high and inflationary prices and to bring otherwise marginal commons and wastes into cultivation for the first time.[15] At the same time there were landowners of comparable size who were not fully convinced of the efficacy of enclosure and it was they who presented counter-petitions. The situation seemed to call for a grouping of those landowners who were marginal in size between large and small to initiate enclosure proceedings, a grouping that formerly might have been divided in opinions in parishes where no single landowner was dominant.

A number of Buckinghamshire enclosures during the war years

were first proposed for enclosure in the earlier wave of enclosure activity, but they were successfully defeated by parliamentary counter-petitions or without ever reaching Parliament at all. Notably the enclosures of Stewkley and Iver were delayed until 1811 and 1801 respectively. Sheila Lambert has said that on a national basis 14 per cent of all enclosure bills presented to Parliament before 1774 failed.[16] It seems that the balance of power lay in the hands not of the smallest landownership groups but in the hands of those who possessed from 25 to 100 or 50 to 150 acres each. Parishes, which apparently in all other respects of geography and contemporary economics were the same as those parishes enclosed in the 1760s and 1770s, were not enclosed until the war years and it was these middling landownership groups which decided the timing of the process. It was they who blocked enclosure in the early period with the plea of high costs, but it was they who actively supported enclosure in the later period and even instigated enclosure proceedings.

In the traditional open fields of clayland Buckinghamshire the early history of parliamentary enclosure was mainly concentrated in the parishes in the north of the county. Here a substantial influence was exercised by the larger landowners. The largest, those possessing over 300 acres, received over 40 per cent of all lands that were enclosed before 1790, but in the 1790s there was a decline in their influence which persisted into the nineteenth century, The smaller or intermediate owners possessing between 1 and 200 acres became the most dominant group. During the war years they were both numerically and proportionately very strong in those parishes undergoing enclosure. The implication is that the economic conditions which prevailed in these years was the prime motivating force behind the decision to enclose. Formerly these landowners would have and did resist enclosure, and with the support of the very smallest proprietors they held enclosure in abeyance in many parishes.

It may be a feature of the chronology of enclosure in the Vale of Aylesbury (where traditionally the land was of the greatest value), that the more regular and evenly spread differentiation of landownership groups helped delay enclosure. The substantial peasant was therefore extremely important in decisions to enclose here and his importance increased during the war years. The largest landowners, in possession of over 500 acres, were allotted only 19 per cent of all lands which were enclosed,[17] whereas the group possessing from 50 to 200 acres was allotted nearly 36 per cent. The reason why these parishes did not remain open longer than they did may be bound up with the intervention of the war or more correctly with the high wartime prices. It may be that this was a period during which there was a betrayal within the ranks of the peasantry, many of whom perhaps were encouraged by more favourable financial and economic circumstances to support a 'land reform' that they had formerly resisted. The importance of a peasant class well into the nineteenth century seems to be an antithesis of Marxist interpretation and also of the Habakkuk model of landownership history before 1740.[18]

A class of peasant or lesser freeholder therefore became the promoters of enclosure in the war years. Formerly they had sufficient landowning strength in the parishes to hold enclosure in abeyance. As in the earlier period the smallest landowning group in the 1790s received very little of the land allotted, in this case only 3·3 per cent of the open fields. The size of this group and the proportion of land they owned did not change. The landownership distribution in the 1790s therefore was less skewed but broader based; statistically it was closer to a normal, bell-shaped distribution.

Patterns of landownership can be represented in a number of ways but in general the tabular form has been the most common. It may aid the explanation of the point being made about landownership differentiation and chronology of enclosure if the tabular figures are resubmitted in pictorial form. The Lorenz curve seems tailor-made for this purpose, though it is more usually used in demonstrating the distribution of national income.[19] The method in fact has a visual usefulness and also a numerical resolution since the area between the 45 degrees and the curve, known as Gini's coefficient, is calculable.[20] For the present purposes however it is sufficient to note the visual differences, illustrated in the seven examples of landownership distribution in Table 30. The Lorenz curves for two of these distributions are given, in Figure 19, for the parishes of Winslow and Padbury enclosed in 1766 and 1795 respectively and demonstrating the two poles of the landownership distribution. Table 31 is a summary of landownership distribution for 30 enclosures, comparing the 1760s with the 1770s and the war period. Figure 20 compares the Lorenz curve for the 1760s with that for the war period. The differences in landownership distribution between the parishes enclosed in the early decades and those enclosed in the war is not necessarily very dramatic but it is consistent between parishes and clearly visible.

Table 32 summarises the pattern of landownership from the Buckinghamshire enclosure awards into four broad groups. The differentiation in the 1760s is the recognised feature of a few large owners dominating early parliamentary enclosure. In the 1770s there was a convergence in the relative strengths of the landowning groups but

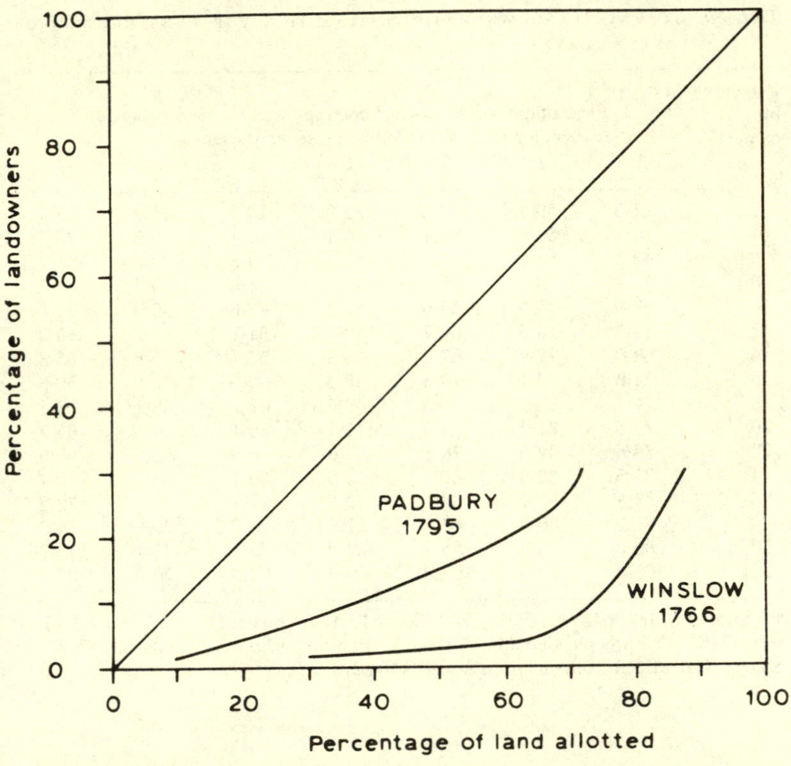

Fig. 19. Lorenz curves of landownership distribution for the parishes of Winslow (1766) and Padbury (1795).

still the power lay in the hands of estates of over 150 acres. The 1790s saw the reversal in these relative strengths and the suggestion that favourable wartime conditions, for both the farmer and the landowner, prompted the promotion of enclosure by that intermediate group of landowners who were formerly strong enough to resist pressures to enclose. The period 1800–9 was perhaps the most crucial decade, the period of closest convergence. On the one hand the largest landowners were allotted one-quarter of all lands that were enclosed but then so also were the other ownership groups, those possessing from 2 to 500 and from 50 to 200 acres respectively. This period in Buckinghamshire was characterised by much opposition to enclosure, possibly as a result of this clash and convergence of the landowning groups. It might well have been that the intermediate sized owners were divided in their reactions to the high prices and greater profitability of enclosure during the war years.

Table 30. DATA ON LANDOWNERSHIP DISTRIBUTION FOR CONSTRUCTION OF LORENZ CURVES

Percentage of owners	Percentage of land owned corresponding to percentage of owners for each of the following seven parishes						
	1	2	3	4	5	6	7
2	24·3	30·4	23·2	22·9	10·1	11·0	13·4
4	38·7	60·8	37·1	34·4	20·1	16·5	26·7
6	48·6	68·9	47·1	45·0	39·5	22·0	31·7
8	55·4	70·9	52·6	50·2	43·6	30·3	36·7
10	59·8	72·9	57·6	55·3	47·6	38·0	41·7
12	64·1	76·6	62·7	59·8	54·1	41·7	48·8
14	68·0	77·9	67·2	64·3	57·1	45·3	55·8
16	71·8	79·1	70·4	66·2	60·0	52·0	59·3
18	74·7	80·3	73·5	68·0	64·2	58·1	62·7
20	77·6	81·5	75·9	71·1	66·1	60·6	65·7
22	79·6	82·6	78·1	74·0	68·0	63·1	68·6
24	81·5	83·6	80·3	76·9	69·7	66·9	70·4
26	83·3	85·4	82·1	79·3	71·4	68·9	72·2
28	85·0	86·0	83·8	81·4	74·7	70·8	74·0
30	86·0	86·6	85·4	83·2	75·9	71·1	75·2
100	100·0	100·0	100·0	100·0	100·0	100·0	100·0

1 Swanbourne 1761; 2 Winslow 1766; 3 Whitchurch 1771; 4 North Marston 1778; 5 Steeple Claydon 1795; 6 Padbury 1795; 7 Adstock 1797.
Source: Calculated from enclosure awards, *Bucks., C.R.O.*

Table 31. DATA ON LANDOWNERSHIP DISTRIBUTION AGGREGATED FOR 1760s, 1770s, AND THE WAR PERIOD

Percentage of owners	Percentage of land owned corresponding to percentage of owners for:		
	7 parishes enclosed in 1760s	11 parishes enclosed in 1770s	12 parishes enclosed during Napoleonic wars
2	27·2	20·7	14·3
4	40·7	37·0	26·5
6	47·5	47·9	37·0
8	54·1	54·1	43·6
10	58·2	59·0	49·6
12	62·2	63·7	55·3
14	66·5	67·5	59·7
16	69·1	70·1	63·4
18	71·6	73·0	67·0
20	74·8	75·3	69·5
24	78·6	79·5	73·9
28	81·7	82·0	77·8
100	100·0	100·0	100·0

Source: Calculated from enclosure awards, *Bucks, C.R.O.*

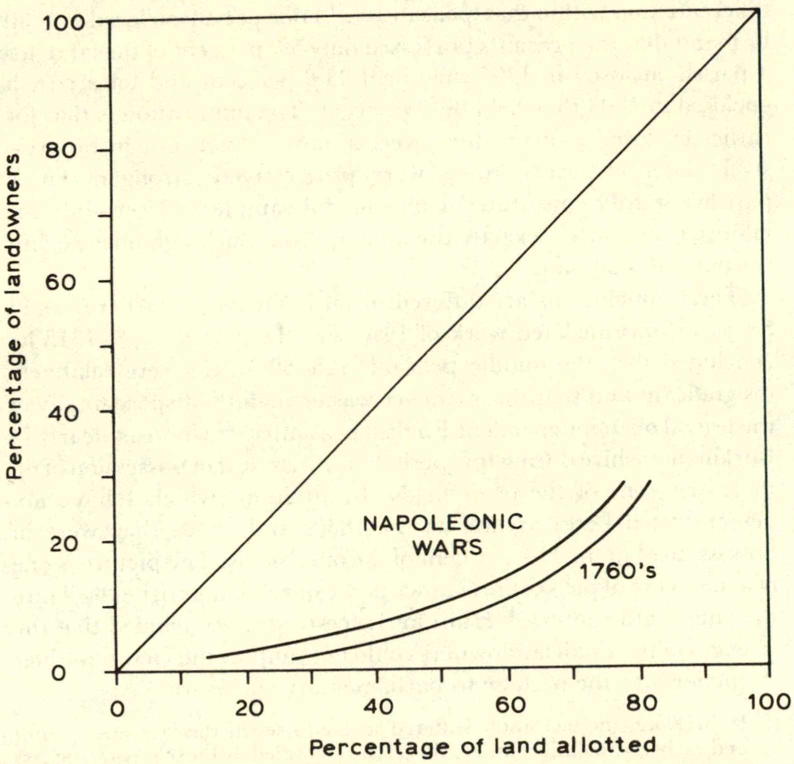

Fig. 20. Lorenz curves of landownership distribution for parishes enclosed in the 1760s and during the Napoleonic wars

Table 32. DISTRIBUTION OF LANDOWNERSHIP FOR 81 PARISHES ENCLOSED IN BUCKINGHAMSHIRE 1760–1819

Decade	Percentage over 500 acres	Percentage 200–500 acres	Percentage 50–200 acres	Percentage fewer than 50 acres
1760s	31·6	12·4	27·5	18·1
1770s	21·3	19·1	23·3	17·3
1780s	19·0	24·3	20·6	15·7
1790s	7·4	21·6	40·5	16·4
1800s	24·4	22·9	23·7	14·3
1810s	13·9	15·9	29·8	18·3

Source: Enclosure Awards, *Bucks., C.R.O*

Taking the Buckinghamshire enclosures as a whole one can see reflections of V. M. Lavrovsky's model, where for only three parishes enclosed between 1780 and 1803 he found elements of the 'peasantry' surviving into the nineteenth century and, what is more, a significant differentiation within that 'peasantry'.[21] For a parish enclosed in 1780 he found that the peasants possessed only 5·7 per cent of the land; for a parish enclosed in 1797 they held 23·8 per cent and for a parish enclosed in 1803 they held 39·7 per cent. The implication is that for earlier enclosed parishes they were almost extinct, but in progressively later enclosures they were progressively stronger. Three parishes hardly constitutes a meaningful sample and certainly his figures do not mirror exactly the findings from Buckinghamshire, but the pattern is similar.

These conclusions are different from Lavrovsky's earlier ones in his as yet untranslated work of 1940. For the period 1793–1815 he concluded that the middle peasants (25–50 acres) were relatively insignificant and that this evidence was enough to 'dispose finally of the legend of an independent English peasantry',[22] whereas clearly in Buckinghamshire during this period they were still in possession of up to 13 per cent of the open fields. In addition (which I have not demonstrated here) as late as the 1830s and 1840s they were in possession of up to 20·9 per cent of the open fields. The picture is one of a hard core of peasant resistance in the open field parishes well into the nineteenth century.[23] Hunt for Leicestershire concluded that the strength of the small landowners could not support the view that their extinction was the prelude to parliamentary enclosure:

> If therefore, the peasantry suffered severe losses in the late seventeenth and early eighteenth century, this class, identified as those possessing less than 100 acres, remained by the middle of the eighteenth century, collectively at least, as great in landowning strength as any other single class in many parishes.[24]

That any peasant-styled community could survive the late seventeenth and early eighteenth centuries during times of great scarcity for grazing lands and the resulting extensive enclosure, is surprising; that individual communities could survive when surrounded by enclosed or enclosing parishes is more surprising.[25] Perhaps the enclosing townships and resulting consolidation of holdings provided an experienced and growing supply of landless farmers; what better than to migrate to open field townships and strengthen the lower rungs of the agricultural ladder. This theory, however, still requires rigorous testing. The conclusion is, and surely Lavrovsky would agree, that the expropriation of the peasantry, supposedly complete by about 1780, was in Buckinghamshire, Leicestershire, and other counties incomplete as late as the mid-nineteenth century, and what is more crucial, it may have been instrumental in a relatively late chronology of enclosure.[26]

Owners, owner-occupiers and absentee ownership

By using the land tax records we are able to get away from the static situation imposed by using enclosure awards, and look at changing landownership patterns and also at the different sectors of ownership: owner-occupancy and absentee ownership. Table 33 summarises the landownership characteristics of 103 parishes in the years 1785 and 1825, using parishes from north Buckinghamshire, essentially the five northern hundreds in open fields at some stage prior to 1830. Problems encountered by other workers on the land tax have been considered.[27]

Table 33. SUMMARY OF OWNERS, OCCUPIERS AND OWNER-OCCUPANCY IN THE FIVE NORTHERN HUNDREDS OF BUCKINGHAMSHIRE BASED ON THE LAND TAX OF 1785 AND 1825

1785 Type of parish	Total no. of owners (average per parish)	Total no. of occupiers (average per parish)	Total no. of owner-occupiers (average per parish)	Owner-occupiers as percentage of owners	Owner-occupiers as percentage of occupiers
(1) 37 parishes of old enclosure	299 (8·1)	511 (13·8)	80 (2·2)	26·8	13·2
(2) 31 parishes enclosed pre-1780	957 (30·9)	1,036 (33·4)	337 (10·9)	35·2	32·5
(3) 20 parishes enclosed 1780–1800	721 (36·0)	642 (32·1)	261 (13·0)	36·2	40·7
(4) 15 parishes enclosed 1800–1820	524 (34·9)	443 (29·5)	189 (12·6)	36·1	42·6
1825 Type of parish	**Total no. of owners (average per parish)**	**Total no. of occupiers (average per parish)**	**Total no. of owner-occupiers (average per parish)**	**Owner-occupiers as percentage of owners**	**Owner-occupiers as percentage of occupiers**
(1) 37 parishes of old enclosure	208 (5·6)	447 (12·1)	89 (2·4)	42·8	19·9
(2) 31 parishes enclosed pre-1780	809 (26·1)	884 (28·5)	333 (10·7)	41·2	37·7
(3) 20 parishes enclosed 1780–1800	629 (31·5)	621 (31·0)	242 (12·1)	38·5	39·0
(4) 15 parishes enclosed 1800–1820	485 (32·3)	491 (32·7)	208 (13·8)	42·9	42·4

Source: Land tax returns for 1785 and 1825, *Bucks, C.R.O.*

In 1785, parishes of old enclosure or enclosed before 1780 had fewer landowners than those enclosed after 1780. This can be seen as a direct reason for delayed enclosure, that is the parishes of later enclosure had a larger differentiation and fragmentation of landownership, the late survival of the Buckinghamshire peasantry. The same conclusion can be inferred from the record of occupiers and owner-occupiers. In old enclosed parishes there were both fewer occupiers and fewer owner-occupiers. This finding differs significantly from Martin's conclusions in his study of Warwickshire where he found that in 1780 the owner-occupiers were strongest in parishes which were enclosed in the immediate thirty years.[28] On the other hand agreement can be found in the studies by Chambers and Davies. In fact Davies found that the majority of old enclosed parishes in his study had no owner-occupiers at all.[29] The parishes of old enclosure were therefore characterised by large holdings both as ownership and production units, and greater absentee ownership. The converse was true for parishes still open in 1785, that is there were generally more occupiers and owner-occupiers per parish, smaller ownership and farm units and less absentee ownership. All these factors may have caused delays in enclosure, in particular the degree of owner-occupancy; it was easier to petition Parliament when there were very few resident owners, or at least this is the conclusion used by Hunt to suggest that many of the leading promoters of parliamentary enclosure were absentee owners.[30]

Owner-occupiers as a percentage of all owners were strongest in the open field parishes; they were even stronger if taken as a percentage of all occupiers.[31] The percentage of land tax paid by owner-occupiers in 1785 can be summarised as follows.

Type of parish	Owner-occupiers as percentage of land tax owned and occupied	Owner-occupiers as percentage of all land tax paid	The difference
39 old enclosed	6·0	16·9	10·9
23 enclosed before 1780	16·4	27·5	11·1
16 enclosed 1780–1800	15·9	19·3	3·4
14 enclosed 1800–1820	21·2	34·7	13·5

The figures in the first column show the percentage of the land that the owner-occupiers both *owned and occupied*. This should be compared with the second column which shows the percentage of land that they actually owned. The third column therefore is the percentage of land that these owner-occupiers leased to others.

Old enclosed parishes were typified by greater absentee ownership. They were both numerically strong and owned a greater percentage of land in the parishes. In 1785 the owner-occupiers were strongest in those parishes that were to remain open until the nineteenth century and a relationship can be seen between this and the level of opposition to enclosure. The Stewkley land tax illustrates this quite well. In 1785 there were 98 owners and 69 occupiers, of whom 43 were owner-occupiers. The percentage of land that these owner-occupiers occupied was 31·5 per cent of the parish but the percentage of land that they actually owned was 49·1 per cent. In other words they leased out 17·6 per cent to tenants. There was opposition to enclosure in this parish from 1772 until the act was finally passed in 1811. The degree of owner-occupancy may have been instrumental in delaying this enclosure considering that a two-thirds to four-fifths majority by value was the necessary agreement required to petition Parliament successfully. At Bletchley in 1785 there were 37 owners and 13 owner-occupiers but they controlled 55 per cent of the parish. Enclosure here was delayed until 1810.

The Buckinghamshire figures for owner-occupancy do not compare very well with those for the neighbouring county of Oxfordshire as researched by Gray. For 1785 he found that only 9 per cent of the county was in the possession of independent farmers, although in common with the present study he did find that owner-occupiers were strongest in those parishes that remained open the longest.[32]

It is interesting to note that of all the parishes enclosed in Buckinghamshire, those in the period 1780–99 (16 in the sample above of which 12 were enclosed in the 1790s) had the lowest level of owner-occupancy. It was these parishes, enclosed during the early part of the French wars, which were dominated by absentee owners, and what is more, as the analysis from the awards showed, they were also dominated by owners of the lesser freeholder category. Possibly therefore it was a combination of lesser freeholders and absentee ownership, and the chance to capitalise during the inflation of the wars that inspired enclosure in these parishes.

By 1825 a number of changes in these general patterns had taken place. The number of owners per parish had decreased, but this applied to *all* types of parish. Similarly in Leicestershire, 'we can therefore hardly attribute this trend solely to parliamentary enclosure'.[33] The largest decreases were in parishes enclosed before 1800. Similarly the number of occupiers per parish had decreased, with the exception of those parishes enclosed in the first two decades of the nineteenth century, and the greatest decrease was for parishes enclosed before 1780. In other words there was a corresponding decrease in the number of landownership and farming units, a consolidation that could be seen in all types of parish but which was possibly strongest in parishes enclosed before 1780. The number of owner-occupiers did not vary very much from 1785 to 1825 although as a result of these other changes they became more important.[34]

The accompanying table summarises the position of the owner-occupiers in 1825. Compared with 1785 they had strengthened. Possibly this was as a result, not of continued prosperity for the ancient freeholder but more as a result of the extension of large-scale tenant farming and the tendency for landowners after about 1795, in the war period, to cultivate their own land.[35]

Type of parish	Owner-occupiers as percentage of land tax owned and occupied	Owner-occupiers as percentage of all land tax paid	The difference
39 old enclosed	7·1	18·3	11·2
23 enclosed before 1780	19·9	31·3	11·4
16 enclosed 1780–1800	19·5	32·1	12·6
14 enclosed 1800–1820	23·1	38·5	15·4

Such conclusions may be vitally important in answering the contentions of Marxist historians that the yeomanry had disappeared by the mid-eighteenth century. In many parishes they were still a very substantial element well into the nineteenth century and in fact had very often increased in strength. A similar conclusion was found by Chambers for Nottinghamshire.[36] The differentiation seen in the enclosure awards also demonstrates this survival, and even after 1785 the yeoman was able to maintain his position.[37]

The fact that the gap between owner-occupiers who owned and occupied their land and owner-occupiers who let their land widened by 1825 seems to demonstrate the emergence of capitalist farming, that is leasing landlords, but in fact even though the gap widened there was also an increase in the actual percentage that was owner-occupied, that is there appeared to have been an increase in the yeomanry. It appears on the face of all the evidence of this nature that the chronology of enclosure and variations in landownership distribution may have been related.

The year 1805 has also been studied and the findings are summarised in Table 34. For *parishes of old enclosure*, comparing 1805 with 1825 and 1785 it is clear that the main period of change for owners was after 1805, but for occupiers and owner-occupiers the main period of change was before 1805. In the late eighteenth century there was a consolidation of production units, possibly the continuation of a trend detectable before the land tax records are extant, followed by a consolidation of ownership units in the nineteenth century. For *parishes enclosed before 1780* there was a consolidation of both production and ownership units in the late eighteenth century, a trend which slowed down appreciably in the nineteenth century. Perhaps this period of change could be narrowed down to the fluid land market of the war period. In *parishes that were enclosed between 1780 and 1800*, there was a marked consolidation of ownership and production units before 1805. Perhaps this was an influence either of enclosure or the pending war. Of major importance was the increase in the number of owner-occupiers in the period before 1805 and their subsequent decline before 1825. Perhaps the economic effects of the war acted as an incentive to owner-occupancy and the elimination of the tenant farmer, albeit only for the duration of part or all of the war.[38] The post-war period on the other hand was a time of intermittent depression and this may have acted as a disincentive to owner-occupancy when the returns from the land were greater in terms of rent than in terms of the produce from the land. For *parishes enclosed between 1800 and 1820* there was a consolidation in ownership and production units in the late eighteenth century, and a decline in the numbers of owner-occupiers. Of the parishes that were enclosed in this period eight were enclosed after 1805 and seven before, as follows:

	7 parishes enclosed 1800–5 Numbers of			8 parishes enclosed 1806–19 Numbers of		
	Owners	Occupiers	Owner-occupiers	Owners	Occupiers	Owner-occupiers
1785	163	157	60	361	286	129
1805	136	143	44	336	278	116
1825	154	156	16	331	335	192

For the first group of parishes there was a large decrease in the numbers of owner-occupiers in the period *after* enclosure and a relatively large increase, or recovery, in the number of owners. The consolidation process before enclosure gave way to the fragmentation of holdings after enclosure, possibly as a result of the diminution of owner-occupiers. No single explanation seems satisfactory though possibly it was due to a combination of enclosure costs, the mortgaging of estates and the post-war depression. For the eight parishes

Table 34. SUMMARY OF OWNERS, OCCUPIERS AND OWNER-OCCUPANCY IN THE FIVE NORTHERN HUNDREDS OF BUCKINGHAMSHIRE BASED ON THE LAND TAX OF 1805

Type of parish	Total no. of owners (average per parish)	Total no. of occupiers (average per parish)	Total no. of owner-occupiers (average per parish)	Owner-occupiers as percentage of owners	Owner-occupiers as percentage of occupiers
37 parishes of old enclosure	297 (8·0)	446 (12·1)	90 (2·4)	30·3	20·9
31 parishes enclosed pre-1780	856 (27·6)	920 (29·7)	335 (10·8)	39·1	36·4
20 parishes enclosed 1780–1800	647 (32·4)	623 (31·2)	289 (14·5)	44·7	46·4
15 parishes enclosed 1800–1820	472 (31·5)	422 (28·1)	160 (10·7)	33·9	37·9
11 parishes enclosed after 1820	479 (43·6)	411 (37·4)	226 (20·5)	47·2	55·0

Source: Land tax returns for 1805, *Bucks, C.R.O.*

enclosed after 1805 there was a late eighteenth-century consolidation of ownership units but the number of farming units remained stable and the number of owner-occupiers declined slightly. In the period after 1805 there was little modification in ownership structure but a marked increase in the number of farming units and in the degree of owner-occupancy. This is an unexpected conclusion in the light of other research which tends to suggest that enclosure resulted in the consolidation of farming units, the so-called 'engrossment' that was supposed to follow enclosure. There is a suggestion that the huge increase in the number of owner-occupiers is an illusion; it may have been the result of enclosure or it may be related to the post-war depression. The retrospective evidence from the 1836 Select Committee on Agricultural Distress tends to support the latter as the most likely explanation; the farms were not so much owner-occupied as 'in hand'.[39]

Some conclusions

To draw general conclusions from the analysis in this chapter is very difficult. Different parishes enclosed at different times had different landownership characteristics at different periods. Whether this determines the chronology of enclosure or is determined by enclosure must remain speculative. Certainly the landownership and chronology of enclosure seemed both to influence and be influenced by each other to a greater or lesser degree, but the evidence that is available covers such an important economic period, the war and the subsequent post-war depression, that other influences must also be considered and given due weight.

The impression from Buckinghamshire is that strong owner-occupancy in the first main wave of enclosure activity held enclosure in abeyance, but in the absence of strong contemporary evidence it is a great deal short of conclusive. Certainly the *balance of power* if not the *absolute power* in the parishes filtered down the landownership spectrum the later the enclosure occurred. Apart from cases of known opposition and the details of landownership associated with that opposition, is there any other contemporary opinion to support this allegation? There is one important item but for reasons which will become apparent we may doubt its admissibility as evidence. The Select Committee of 1800, the evidence from which serviced the 1801 General Act, brought as witnesses many leading actors in the enclosure story, solicitors and commissioners, the most famous being

George Maxwell of Huntingdonshire who up to 1800 acted as a commissioner about 100 times. The committee reported that

> the great number of consents supposed to be necessary, according to the present practice of Parliament, whether three-fourths, according to the ideas of some, or four-fifths according to those of others (for there is no fixed rule) is a great bar to Inclosure. Your Committee are thence led to submit it to the wisdom of the House, whether it may not be expedient in future, to allow the proof of a less number of consents, provided they amount to a decided preponderance, to be sufficient for obtaining a Bill.[40]

The eight witnesses who were all asked the question about quantum of consent all replied that enclosures would be easier to obtain and the rate of enclosure increased if the quantum of consent was reduced to two-thirds. The risk of opposition to enclosure would be diminished, they felt. I suppose it stands as a platitude that the evidence of these men might not be admissible because they had such a strong vested interest, but they were saying that opposition to enclosure prevailed and stopped some enclosures from proceeding but that if the quantum of consent could be reduced by 10 or 15 percentage points things would proceed more smoothly. They did not specify where the opposition came from but the figures they mentioned would certainly be enough to swamp some of my Buckinghamshire recalcitrants. The report of the House came out in 1800 but the main wave of wartime enclosures in England came in the following fifteen years. The evidence therefore is retrospective of the first wave of enclosures and the early war enclosures.

8

Postscript

If the final chapter of a book is a conclusion in the sense of a résumé, as so often seems to be the case, or in the sense of drawing together reasonably hard and fast rules, then this will be no conclusion. Perhaps 'postscript' is a more appropriate heading because the one conclusion I will make is that we are a long way short of closing the file on the study of parliamentary enclosure, be we historical geographers or economic historians. Rather this book will close as an incomplete piece of work, and I will try to plot the immediate course of future research as I see it.

As the opening chapters indicated this book initially is a reference work; it is an improvement on the basic data we have perforce used in studying the spatial and temporal incidence of parliamentary enclosure. It could be treated therefore as a more reliable source than Slater and Gonner and others, but it must also be used cautiously because it is not yet complete. Nor indeed will it ever be complete as long as some few enclosures out of the 5,300 or so do not yield surviving documentation, nor as long as so many items of existing information are based on sometimes doubtful estimates such as are contained in many enclosure acts. But it is a consummation of more, and more reliable, items of information than heretofore has been achieved.

We must all wait for John Chapman to complete his 10 per cent sample of all the English and Welsh enclosures and hope that his sample will be representative. Needless to say, my personal hope is that Chapman's work will not seriously call into question the spatial and temporal history I have here portrayed. Nevertheless, the more recent work on parliamentary enclosure, say since the mid 1960s, has exposed our ignorance on the subject in a number of ways. Perhaps one of the most serious, and likely to be lasting, problems is the lack of contemporary observation and contemporary opinion of enclosures. This is particularly the case when the discussion turns to the reasons for enclosure, the determinants of enclosure. As we approach the fullest possible knowledge about the spatial and temporal details of enclosure our preoccupations will surely turn, as indeed they already have done so, towards the explicit social and economic questions which arise. One can envisage a revision of Beresford's catalogue of enclosure commissioners' minute books and working papers, of which many additional ones have been uncovered and deposited in record offices since he wrote in 1946.[1] If these documents can be used to write the biographies of enclosures, from the act of Parliament as the birth and the enclosure award as the death of the open fields and commons and wastes, then we also require information of an ante-natal character to discover the thoughts and reasoning of the promoters of enclosure, and also those who were in opposition. There is also a need to investigate the social and agricultural changes wrought by enclosure.

There is most immediately one area of future research which might bear fruit, and this surrounds the obvious periodisation of parliamentary enclosure. The idea is not new but perhaps it has been taken too much for granted. The mere identification of the two dominant periods of parliamentary enclosure, between about 1755 and 1780 and the Napoleonic war years is not enough in itself but should be a signal to us that those two periods must *always* be treated in total or near-total isolation from one another. I hope I have indicated this in a number of ways in this book, among them the increasing role of common and waste enclosure in the second period and the suggestion that the movement was nearly over in some counties whereas in others it had hardly begun by 1793. Even if my theory that there was a shortage of grazing land by about the mid-eighteenth century (and indeed sometime before) at a time when there was an increasing move towards pastoral or mixed farming in some areas is not wholeheartedly accepted, it certainly signals the dominant soil type of those early parliamentary enclosures. They occurred predominantly in the clay counties of the midlands. There is a major study awaiting a scholar in the investigation of the post-enclosure agricultural changes in those heavy-soiled regions. To what extent did they tumble to grass after enclosure and to what extent were they ploughed up again during the dearth years of the Napoleonic wars? As one who has followed the county approach as a PhD candidate, the plea must be that the next and successive monographs must disclaim the purely county approach. The wartime enclosures must also be studied without reference to the earlier period; they were different, they were increasingly concentrated on lighter soils and on marginal soils during a period of fierce inflation. Overriding this periodisation approach I would make a plea that future researchers bear in mind the landownership question, the extent to which enclosures might have been delayed because the quantum of consent was not obtained. We might therefore be able to identify some 'rogue' enclosures which came after 1793 but which in all but landownership characteristics more closely resembled most enclosures of the 1760s and 1770s.

Aspects of periodisation have been referred to by Crafts in terms of the concept of 'satiation stock'.[2] He postulates two models, a disequilibrium and an equilibrium model. For the former he postulates 'that it takes time for the use of a new producer good to reach an equilibrium level ("the satiation stock")'. In other words there is a learning process which determines the rate of diffusion of, say, parliamentary enclosure. The equilibrium model is a diffusion model which

> would propose an 'economic' explanation for the diffusion phenomenon postulating that adjustment to economic stimuli (say the availability of a new technique), is instantaneous but that there exists at any time a *distribution* of values of at least one economic variable pertinent to adoption decisions among potential users.

These theories might be relevant for parliamentary enclosure as follows. The ceiling of the satiation stock of enclosable land in the 1760s and 1770s was reduced as enclosure proceeded, as the declining profitability of arable farming was realised in the heavy-soiled areas of England. A certain amount of caution was exercised as some landowners observed the profitability of enclosure in neighbouring parishes or counties. Caution was also implicit in the different degrees of landownership distribution and density. Conversely, the wartime inflation of prices created a new ceiling, a new satiation stock of enclosable land in two directions. Existing arable land in light-soiled areas could be improved by farming in severalty; and the marginal lands, the commons and wastes which could be ploughed up, could be made to yield a profit even at low yields and high costs. The cost benefit analysis which these last ideas imply awaits rigorous research. It must be shown that the inflation in revenue from the land during the war years was greater than the inflation of costs. That will not be an easy task.

There is then considerable scope for future research in parliamentary enclosure. Provided the impetus of the last few years is maintained and economists, historians and geographers can exchange ideas there could be an exciting decade ahead of us.

Appendixes

Appendix 1. NUMBER OF PARLIAMENTARY ACTS – BY COUNTY[1]

County	A	B	C	D	E	F		Total
Beds.	82 (0)	4 (0)	4 (0)	2 (0)	5 (0)	2 (0)		99 (0)
Berks.	90 (5)	9 (2)	13 (0)	—	8 (0)	13 (0)		133 (7)
Bucks.	102 (1)	7 (0)	3 (0)	1 (0)	4 (0)	14 (0)		131 (1)
Camb.	104 (1)	12 (2)	8 (3)	—	9 (0)	3 (0)		136 (6)
Cheshire	1 (0)	36 (0)	—	1 (0)	—	17 (0)		55 (0)
Cornwall	— —	3 (1)	—	11 (3)	—	17 (1)		31 (5)
Cumb.	5 (0)	79 (0)	3 (0)	6 (0)	3 (0)	28 (0)		124 (0)
Derby.	71 (3)	61 (1)	2 (1)	—	—	7 (0)		141 (5)
Devon	— —	31 (2)	—	1 (0)	—	39 (0)		71 (2)
Dorset	48 (0)	19 (2)	—	16 (1)	3 (0)	19 (0)		105 (3)
Durham	5 (0)	34 (0)	1 (0)	—	—	1 (0)		41 (0)
Essex	12 (1)	28 (1)	6 (0)	—	12 (0)	18 (0)		76 (2)
Glos.	128 (32)	23 (6)	11 (8)	—	12 (0)	21 (0)		195 (46)
Hants.	58 (9)	38 (5)	5 (2)	2 (2)	2 (0)	59 (0)		164 (18)
I. of W.	— —	1 (0)	—	—	2 (0)	2 (0)		5 (0)
Hereford	24 (7)	24 (12)	3 (0)	1 (0)	4 (0)	16 (0)		72 (19)
Herts.	27 (0)	8 (2)	7 (0)	1 (0)	20 (0)	10 (0)		73 (2)
Hunts.	67 (2)	1 (0)	4 (1)	—	3 (0)	1 (0)		76 (3)
Kent	— —	17 (3)	—	—	—	17 (0)		34 (3)
Lancs.	— —	69 (2)	—	1 (0)	—	17 (0)		87 (2)
Leics.	150 (0)	4 (0)	1 (0)	—	—	—		155 (0)
Lincs.	264 (7)	49 (4)	—	31 (0)	6 (0)	12 (0)		362 (11)
Middx.	25 (1)	8 (0)	2 (0)	—	1 (0)	2 (0)		38 (1)
Mon.	1 (0)	3 (1)	—	—	3 (0)	6 (0)		13 (1)
Norfolk	187 (7)	99 (9)	1 (0)	—	4 (0)	31 (0)		322 (16)
Northampton	192 (3)	5 (0)	1 (0)	—	3 (0)	9 (0)		210 (3)
Northumberland	10 (0)	44 (2)	—	—	—	23 (0)		77 (2)
Notts.	115 (1)	17 (0)	8 (0)	2 (0)	3 (0)	7 (0)		152 (1)

Oxon.	127 (6)	7 (0)	14 (0)	1 (0)	21 (0)	16 (1)		186 (7)
Rutland	26 (3)	—	1 (0)	—	3 (0)	—		30 (3)
Salop.	7 (0)	42 (1)	—	—	—	19 (0)		68 (1)
Somerset	44 (3)	94 (6)	9 (3)	—	2 (0)	23 (0)		172 (12)
Staffs.	24 (1)	67 (0)	1 (0)	—	—	15 (0)		107 (1)
Suffolk	48 (0)	35 (0)	—	—	4 (0)	25 (0)		112 (0)
Surrey	22 (1)	30 (5)	2 (0)	—	5 (0)	18 (0)		77 (6)
Sussex	26 (0)	15 (0)	4 (0)	—	2 (0)	38 (0)		85 (0)
War.	132 (2)	23 (0)	3 (0)	—	8 (0)	11 (0)		177 (2)
West.	4 (0)	43 (9)	—	11 (0)	—	36 (0)		94 (9)
Wilts.	117 (4)	31 (0)	9 (0)	4 (0)	6 (0)	12 (0)		179 (4)
Worcs.	70 (3)	30 (1)	8 (0)	1 (0)	4 (0)	11 (0)		124 (4)
Yorks E.	149 (1)	20 (1)	10 (0)	1 (0)	3 (0)	3 (0)		186 (2)
Yorks N.	51 (2)	69 (4)	5 (0)	4 (0)	2 (0)	18 (0)		149 (6)
Yorks W.	163 (1)	149 (1)	9 (0)	—	2 (0)	39 (2)		362 (4)
England	2,778 (107)	1,388 (85)	158 (18)	98 (6)	169 (0)	695 (4)		5,286 (220)

But taking into account that some acts involved lands in more than one county; the revised England total eliminating this double counting is:

2,767 (107)	*1,381* (83)	*158* (18)	*98* (6)	*168* (0)	*695* (4)		*5,265* (218)

(A) Enclosure by parliamentary act containing some open field arable land.
(B) Enclosure by parliamentary act of common and waste only.
(C) Enclosure of open field arable under the General Act of 1836.
(D) Enclosure of common and waste under the General Act of 1840.
(E) Enclosure of open field arable under the General Act of 1845 et seq.
(F) Enclosure of common and waste under the General Act of 1845 et seq.
1. The figures in brackets indicate the number of enclosures for which, for whatever reason, an acreage value has not been obtained.

Appendix 2. NUMBER OF ACRES ENCLOSED BY PARLIAMENTARY ACT – BY COUNTY

County	A	B	C	D	E	F		Total
Beds.	128,612	2,638	3,757	1,697	8,192	892		145,788
Berks.	128,128	6,002	11,209	—	6,573	3,080		154,992
Bucks.	148,149	2,838	1,935	98	5,496	5,125		163,641
Camb.	233,886	42,300	6,325	—	8,138	1,668		292,317
Cheshire	126	26,998	—	21	—	2,034		29,179
Cornwall	—	3,942	—	1,178	—	5,419		10,539
Cumb.	6,837	220,144	184	661	5,067	36,971		269,864
Derby	101,192	45,309	400	—	—	2,486		149,387
Devon	—	30,115	—	241	—	11,287		41,643
Dorset	49,070	26,977	—	8,054	2,802	7,175		94,078
Durham	2,420	103,380	48	—	—	952		106,800
Essex	15,113	14,855	1,966	—	5,140	4,744		41,818
Glos.	180,541	12,126	11,843	—	5,138	3,687		213,335
Hants.	77,297	46,880	2,973	748	1,624	27,000		156,522
I. of W.	—	2,500	—	—	493	227		3,220
Hereford	22,978	5,782	743	206	442	2,821		32,972
Herts.	33,526	11,433	3,723	19	10,819	1,014		60,534
Hunts.	107,338	511	4,528	—	3,944	89		116,410
Kent	—	6,086	—	—	—	1,985		8,071
Lancs.	—	72,714	—	22	—	12,105		84,841
Leics.	217,907	20,246	242	—	—	—		238,395
Lincs.	494,405	148,555	—	14,790	5,592	3,757		667,099
Middx.	35,068	12,938	1,225	—	541	184		49,956
Mon.	780	12,300	—	—	531	2,759		16,370
Norfolk	313,059	92,793	212	—	7,323	6,976		420,363
Northampton	316,305	13,776	927	—	3,936	643		335,587
Northumberland	25,055	157,375	—	—	—	39,623		222,053
Notts.	164,322	17,342	3,860	1,667	1,864	3,630		192,685

Oxon.	200,906	10,460	12,954	1,798	25,261	2,567		253,946
Rutland	37,714	—	1,344	—	2,318	—		41,376
Salop	4,325	48,002	—	—	—	10,373		62,700
Somerset	37,243	118,515	900	—	63	14,513		171,234
Staffs.	23,911	57,410	91	—	—	12,632		94,044
Suffolk	69,257	20,298	—	—	2,824	2,230		94,609
Surrey	32,938	20,264	141	—	2,606	13,179		69,128
Sussex	20,084	9,387	1,109	—	261	10,128		40,969
War.	157,066	11,159	1,604	—	8,634	750		179,213
West.	320	76,229	—	1,118	—	28,487		106,154
Wilts.	219,625	15,652	10,012	1,461	4,062	4,306		255,118
Worcs.	62,680	16,003	2,697	623	1,233	1,882		85,118
Yorks E.	302,271	20,708	6,954	34	3,941	1,425		335,333
Yorks N.	84,710	126,542	1,235	1,549	1,037	39,677		254,750
Yorks W.	193,176	170,151	6,513	—	1,190	61,248		432,278
England	4,248,340	1,879,635	101,654	35,985	137,085	391,730		6,794,429

After the inclusion of interpolated acreages for the 218 enclosures for which acreage information is not available. The method of interpolation is given in the text.

(A) Enclosure by parliamentary act containing some open field arable land.
(B) Enclosure by parliamentary act of common and waste only.
(C) Enclosure of open field arable under the 1836 General Act.
(D) Enclosure of common and waste under the 1840 General Act.
(E) Enclosure of open field arable under the 1845 General Act et seq.
(F) Enclosure of common and waste under the 1845 General Act et seq.

Appendix 3. DENSITY OF PARLIAMENTARY ENCLOSURE AS MEASURED BY THE PERCENTAGE OF EACH COUNTY ENCLOSED

County	A	B	C	D	E	F		Total A+C+E	Total B+D+F	County Total
Beds.	43·5	0·9	1·3	0·6	2·8	0·3		47·6	1·8	49·3
Berks.	28·2	1·3	2·5	—	1·4	0·7		32·1	2·0	34·1
Bucks.	31·6	0·6	0·4	Neg.	1·2	1·1		33·2	1·7	34·9
Camb.	42·7	7·7	1·2	—	1·5	0·3		45·4	8·0	53·4
Cheshire	0·02	3·8	—	Neg.	—	0·3		0·02	4·1	4·12
Cornwall	—	0·5	—	0·1	—	0·6		—	1·2	1·2
Cumb.	0·7	22·6	0·02	0·1	0·5	3·8		1·2	26·5	27·7
Derby	15·7	7·1	0·1	—	—	0·4		15·8	7·4	23·2
Devon	—	1·8	—	0·01	—	0·7		—	2·5	2·5
Dorset	7·8	4·3	—	1·3	0·5	1·1		8·3	6·7	15·0
Durham	0·4	14·8	0·01	—	—	0·1		0·4	14·9	15·3
Essex	1·5	1·5	0·2	—	0·5	0·5		2·2	2·0	4·2
Glos.	22·3	1·5	1·5	—	0·6	0·5		24·4	2·0	26·3
Hants.	8·3	5·0	0·3	0·1	0·2	2·9		8·8	8·0	16·8
I. of W.	—	2·7	—	—	0·5	0·2		0·5	2·9	3·4
Hereford	4·3	1·1	0·14	0·04	0·1	0·5		4·5	1·6	6·1
Herts.	8·6	2·9	1·0	Neg.	2·8	0·3		12·3	3·2	15·5
Hunts.	46·6	0·2	2·0	—	1·7	0·04		50·2	0·3	50·5
Kent	—	0·6	—	—	—	0·2		—	0·8	0·8
Lancs.	—	6·0	—	Neg.	—	1·0		—	7·0	7·0
Leics.	42·6	4·0	0·1	—	—	—		42·7	4·0	46·6
Lincs.	28·7	8·6	—	0·9	0·3	0·2		29·0	9·7	38·7
Middx.	19·7	7·3	0·7	—	0·3	0·1		20·6	7·4	28·0
Mon.	0·2	3·6	—	—	0·2	0·8		0·4	4·4	4·7
Norfolk	23·2	6·9	0·02	—	0·5	0·5		23·7	7·4	31·1
Northampton	50·0	2·2	0·2	—	0·6	0·1		50·7	2·3	53·0
Northumberland	2·0	12·7	—	—	—	3·2		2·0	15·9	18·0

Notts.	31·1	3·3	0·7	0·3	0·4	0·7		32·1	4·3	36·4
Oxon.	43·0	2·2	2·8	0·4	5·4	0·6		51·2	3·2	54·3
Rutland	40·7	—	1·5	—	2·4	—		44·6	—	44·6
Salop.	0·5	5·6	—	—	—	1·2		0·5	6·8	7·4
Somerset	3·6	11·4	0·1	—	Neg.	1·4		3·6	12·7	16·4
Staffs.	3·3	7·9	0·01	—	—	1·7		3·3	9·6	12·9
Suffolk	7·3	2·2	—	—	0·3	0·2		7·6	2·4	10·0
Surrey	6·9	4·2	0·03	—	0·5	2·8		7·4	7·0	14·4
Sussex	2·2	1·0	0·1	—	0·03	1·1		2·3	2·1	4·4
War.	27·8	2·0	0·3	—	1·5	0·1		29·6	2·1	31·7
West.	0·1	15·0	—	0·2	—	5·6		0·06	20·8	20·9
Wilts.	25·3	1·8	1·2	0·2	0·5	0·5		26·9	2·5	29·4
Worcs.	13·5	3·5	0·6	0·1	0·3	0·4		14·4	4·0	18·4
Yorks E.	40·7	2·8	0·9	Neg.	0·5	0·2		42·2	3·0	45·2
Yorks N.	6·3	9·5	0·1	0·1	0·1	3·0		6·5	12·6	19·1
Yorks W.	10·9	9·6	0·4	—	0·1	3·4		11·3	13·0	24·3
England	13·1	5·8	0·3	0·1	0·4	1·2		13·8	7·1	20·9

(A) Enclosure by parliamentary act containing some open field arable land.
(B) Enclosure by parliamentary act of common and waste only.
(C) Enclosure of open field arable under the General Act of 1836.
(D) Enclosure of common and waste under the General Act of 1840.
(E) Enclosure of open field arable under the General Act of 1845.
(F) Enclosure of common and waste under the General Act of 1845.
(A+C+E) Total enclosure of open field arable.
(B+D+F) Total enclosure of common and waste.
TOTAL Total enclosure.
For the last three columns there are occasional rounding errors when a cross-column comparison is made.

Appendix 4. DENSITY OF ENCLOSURE – COMPARISON OF DIFFERENT BASE COUNTY ACREAGES AGAINST THE SAME ENCLOSURE ACREAGES

County	1		2		3		4		5	
Beds.	49·3		49·0		48·1		48·1		48·1	
Berks.	34·1		32·8		33·4		33·5		33·5	
Bucks.	34·9		35·3		34·1		34·4		34·1	
Camb.	53·4		54·5		52·7		53·2		52·8	
Cheshire	4·1		4·5		4·5		4·4		4·5	
Cornwall	1·2		1·2		1·2		1·2		1·2	
Cumb.	27·7		27·8		27·7		27·7		27·7	
Derby	23·2		22·5		23·2		22·7		22·9	
Devon	2·5		2·5		2·5		2·5		2·5	
Dorset	15·0		15·0		15·1		14·9		15·0	
Durham	15·3		15·7		16·5		16·5		16·5	
Essex	4·2		4·3		4·3		4·2		4·3	
Glos.	26·3		27·0		26·5		26·8		26·5	
Hants.	16·8		16·8		16·3		16·6		16·3	
I. of W.	3·4		3·4		3·4		3·4		3·4	
Hereford	6·1		6·1		6·1		6·1		6·1	
Herts.	15·5		15·1		15·0		14·9		15·0	
Hunts.	50·5		48·2		49·8		49·7		49·8	
Kent	0·8		0·8		0·8		0·8		0·8	
Lancs.	7·0		7·6		7·0		7·1		7·1	
Leics.	46·6		46·6		44·8		45·2		44·7	
Lincs.	38·7		40·2		39·3		39·5		39·5	
Middx.	28·0		27·8		22·4		27·6		22·4	
Mon.	4·7		5·1		4·7		4·8		4·7	
Norfolk	31·1		32·5		32·0		32·1		32·0	
Northampton	53·0		51·9		52·6		52·3		52·6	
Northumberland	18·0		19·1		17·2		17·2		17·2	
Notts.	36·4		36·7		35·7		35·7		35·7	
Oxon.	54·3		54·3		53·0		52·5		52·8	
Rutland	44·6		42·4		42·5		42·5		42·5	
Salop.	7·4		7·3		7·3		7·3		7·3	
Somerset	16·4		16·7		16·6		16·4		16·5	
Staffs.	12·9		12·8		12·7		12·6		12·6	
Suffolk	10·0		10·3		10·0		9·9		10·0	

Surrey	14·4	14·6	15·0	14·3	15·0
Sussex	4·4	4·5	4·4	4·4	4·4
War.	31·7	30·0	28·5	31·0	30·9
West.	20·9	21·8	21·1	21·1	21·1
Wilts.	29·4	29·3	29·6	29·0	29·5
Worcs.	18·4	18·5	19·0	17·7	17·7
Yorks E.	45·2	47·1	44·7	44·7	44·7
Yorks N.	19·1	20·0	18·7	18·7	18·7
Yorks W.	24·3	25·8	24·2	24·5	24·5
England	20·9	21·4	20·9		

(1) Using the 1873 base county as given in Stamp and Hoskins.
(2) Using the 1831 base county as found in the contemporary census.
(3) Using the 1956 base county as giving in Stamp and Hoskins.
(4) Using the 'Ancient County' as base as found in Bartholomew's Atlas.
(5) Using the 'Administrative County' as base as found in Bartholomew's Atlas.
Sources: Chapter 1, See notes 39–41.

Appendix 4a. RANK CORRELATION MATRICES BASED ON THE RANKINGS DERIVED FROM APPENDIX 4

KENDALL RANK CORRELATION COEFFICIENTS

Base County	1873	1831	1956	Bar 1	Bar 2
1873	1·000				
1831	0·981	1·000			
1956	0·971	0·969	1·000		
Bar 1	0·981	0·983	0·983	1·000	
Bar 2	0·975	0·978	0·993	0·990	1·000

SPEARMAN RANK CORRELATION COEFFICIENTS

Base County	1873	1831	1956	Bar 1	Bar 2
1873	1·000				
1831	0·999	1·000			
1956	0·996	0·996	1·000		
Bar 1	0·998	0·999	0·998	1·000	
Bar 2	0·997	0·998	0·999	0·999	1·000

Appendix 5. DENSITY OF PARLIAMENTARY ENCLOSURE WITH A PLUS AND MINUS 5 AND 10 PER CENT ERROR ADJUSTMENT

County	Minus 10%	Minus 5%	Actual density	Plus 5%	Plus 10%
Beds.	44·4	46·9	49·3	51·8	54·3
Berks.	30·7	32·4	34·1	35·8	37·5
Bucks.	31·4	33·2	34·9	36·7	38·4
Camb.	48·1	50·7	53·4	56·1	58·7
Cheshire	3·7	3·9	4·1	4·3	4·5
Cornwall	1·1	1·2	1·2	1·3	1·4
Cumb.	24·9	26·3	27·7	29·1	30·5
Derby	20·9	22·1	23·2	24·4	25·6
Devon	2·3	2·4	2·5	2·6	2·8
Dorset	13·5	14·2	15·0	25·7	16·5
Durham	13·7	14·5	15·3	16·0	16·8
Essex	3·8	4·0	4·2	4·4	4·6
Glos.	23·7	25·0	26·3	27·6	28·9
Hants.	15·1	15·9	16·8	17·6	18·4
I. of W.	3·1	3·3	3·4	3·6	3·8
Hereford	5·5	5·8	6·1	6·4	6·7
Herts.	13·9	14·7	15·5	16·3	17·0
Hunts.	45·5	48·0	50·5	53·0	55·6
Kent	0·7	0·8	0·8	0·8	0·9
Lancs.	6·3	6·7	7·0	7·4	7·7
Leics.	42·0	44·3	46·6	48·9	51·3
Lincs.	34·8	36·7	38·7	40·6	42·5
Middx.	25·2	26·6	28·0	29·4	30·8
Mon.	4·3	4·5	4·7	5·0	5·2
Norfolk	28·0	29·5	31·1	32·6	34·2
Northampton	47·7	50·3	53·0	55·6	58·3
Northumberland	16·2	17·1	18·0	18·9	19·8

Notts.	32·8		34·6		36·4		38·2		40·1
Oxon.	48·9		51·6		54·3		57·1		59·8
Rutland	40·2		42·4		44·6		46·9		49·1
Salop.	6·6		7·0		7·4		7·7		8·1
Somerset	14·8		15·6		16·4		17·2		18·0
Staffs.	11·6		12·3		12·9		13·5		14·2
Suffolk	9·0		9·5		10·0		10·5		11·0
Surrey	13·0		13·7		14·4		15·1		15·8
Sussex	4·0		4·2		4·4		4·7		4·9
War.	28·5		30·1		31·7		33·3		34·9
West.	18·8		19·9		20·9		21·9		23·0
Wilts.	26·4		27·9		29·4		30·8		32·3
Worcs.	16·5		17·4		18·4		19·3		20·2
Yorks E.	40·6		42·9		45·2		47·4		49·7
Yorks N.	17·2		18·1		19·1		20·1		21·0
Yorks W.	21·9		23·1		24·3		25·5		26·7
England	18·8		19·9		20·9		22·0		23·0

Appendix 6. DENSITY OF OPEN FIELD ARABLE ENCLOSURE DIVIDED INTO SPECIFIC TIME PERIODS (EXPRESSED AS A PERCENTAGE OF COUNTY AREA)

County	Pre-1793		1793–1815		1816–1829			Pre-1830		Post-1829
Beds.	7·9		31·9		1·6			41·5		6·1
Berks.	6·7		18·8		1·9			27·4		4·6
Bucks.	12·3		14·2		2·1			28·7		4·5
Camb.	1·1		27·9		1·8			30·8		14·6
Cheshire	—		0·2		—			0·2		—
Cornwall	—		—		—			—		—
Cumb.	0·2		0·5		0·05			0·7		0·5
Derby	5·9		9·0		8·0			15·7		0·1
Devon	—		—		—			—		—
Dorset	1·5		4·6		1·1			7·1		1·1
Durham	0·2		0·1		—			0·3		Neg.
Essex	—		1·2		0·2			1·4		0·9
Glos.	9·5		11·0		1·3			21·8		2·6
Hants.	4·0		3·3		0·7			8·0		0·7
I. of W.	—		—		—			—		0·5
Hereford	—		4·3		—			4·3		0·2
Herts.	1·0		6·8		0·4			8·2		4·1
Hunts.	14·1		29·0		1·3			44·4		5·8
Kent	—		—		—			—		—
Lancs.	—		—		—			—		—
Leics.	36·4		5·5		0·4			42·3		0·4
Lincs.	16·7		11·0		0·8			28·5		0·5
Middx.	1·3		17·0		1·3			19·7		1·0
Mon.	0·2		—		—			0·2		0·2
Norfolk	4·6		16·3		1·9			22·8		0·9
Northampton	32·7		12·3		2·8			47·8		2·9
Northumberland	0·8		1·1		—			1·9		0·1
Notts.	18·0		11·3		1·5			30·8		1·3

Oxon.	20·6		17·3		2·7			40·6		10·6
Rutland	18·9		18·8		2·1			39·8		4·8
Salop.	0·2		0·2		0·2			0·6		—
Somerset	0·0		3·1		0·4			3·4		0·3
Staffs.	1·3		1·5		0·1			2·9		0·4
Suffolk	0·4		5·5		1·1			6·9		0·8
Surrey	Neg.		6·5		0·3			6·8		0·6
Sussex	—		1·4		0·4			1·7		0·6
War.	20·6		5·9		1·1			27·6		2·0
West.	—		0·04		0·02			0·1		—
Wilts.	9·9		12·6		2·6			25·2		1·7
Worcs.	7·2		5·7		0·4			13·3		1·1
Yorks E.	26·0		12·4		1·7			40·1		2·1
Yorks N.	3·7		2·6		—			6·3		0·2
Yorks W.	4·2		5·3		1·2			10·8		0·5
England	5·7		6·1		0·7			12·6		1·3

Note: In some cases the aggregation of the first three columns to give the fourth column is plus or minus 0·1 per cent in error. This is due to rounding errors.

Appendix 7. DENSITY OF COMMON AND WASTE ENCLOSURE DIVIDED INTO SPECIFIC TIME PERIODS (EXPRESSED AS A PERCENTAGE OF COUNTY AREA)

County	Pre-1793	1793–1815	1816–1829	Pre-1830	Post-1820
Beds.	—	0·2	—	0·2	1·5
Berks.	0·6	0·7	—	1·3	0·7
Bucks.	—	0·4	0·1	0·5	1·2
Camb.	1·9	1·1	—	3·0	5·0
Cheshire	1·4	2·1	0·2	3·7	0·3
Cornwall	0·1	0·3	0·1	0·5	0·8
Cumb.	3·7	15·1	2·8	21·7	4·8
Derby	4·0	1·6	1·2	6·7	0·7
Devon	0·7	0·7	0·2	1·6	0·9
Dorset	1·7	2·0	0·6	4·3	2·4
Durham	7·4	5·9	0·1	13·5	1·5
Essex	0·1	0·5	0·2	0·8	1·2
Glos.	0·4	0·7	0·1	1·2	0·8
Hants.	0·9	3·2	0·8	4·9	3·1
I. of W.	—	2·7	—	2·7	0·2
Hereford	0·5	0·2	0·2	1·0	0·6
Herts.	1·3	1·7	—	2·9	0·3
Hunts.	—	0·2	—	0·2	0·04
Kent	0·1	0·4	0·1	0·5	0·3
Lancs.	1·3	3·8	0·8	5·9	1·2
Leics.	0·1	3·9	—	4·0	—
Lincs.	3·0	5·2	0·04	8·3	1·4
Middx.	5·9	1·3	—	7·3	0·1
Mon.	—	3·6	—	3·6	0·8
Norfolk	1·4	4·2	1·0	6·6	0·8
Northampton	0·1	1·0	1·1	2·2	0·1
Northumberland	9·7	2·4	0·3	12·3	3·6
Notts.	1·1	1·7	0·5	3·3	1·0

Oxon.	0·3		1·1		0·1			1·4		1·7
Rutland	—		—		—			—		—
Salop.	1·7		2·9		0·2			4·8		2·0
Somerset	5·8		4·5		0·4			10·7		2·1
Staffs.	2·7		4·6		0·4			7·7		1·9
Suffolk	0·1		1·8		0·3			2·2		0·2
Surrey	0·5		3·2		0·3			4·1		2·9
Sussex	0·4		0·5		0·2			1·0		1·1
War.	0·7		1·1		0·2			1·9		0·2
West.	3·5		6·8		1·8			12·1		8·8
Wilts.	0·5		1·1		0·2			1·8		0·7
Worcs.	1·8		1·1		0·4			3·3		0·7
Yorks E.	2·5		0·3		0·04			2·8		0·2
Yorks N.	4·2		4·8		0·5			9·4		3·2
Yorks W.	5·2		3·4		0·8			9·3		3·7
England	2·2		2·8		0·4			5·4		1·7

Note: In some cases the aggregation of the first three columns to give the fourth column is plus or minus 0·1 per cent in error. This is due to rounding errors.

Appendix 8. OPEN FIELD ARABLE ENCLOSURE DIVIDED INTO SPECIFIC TIME PERIODS EXPRESSED AS A PERCENTAGE OF *all* PARLIAMENTARY ENCLOSURE

County	Pre-1793	1793–1815	1816–1829	Pre-1830	Post-1829
Beds.	16·1	64·7	3·2	84·0	12·4
Berks.	19·6	55·3	5·7	80·6	13·6
Bucks.	35·3	40·7	6·1	82·1	13·0
Camb.	2·1	52·2	3·4	57·7	27·3
Cheshire	—	0·4	—	0·4	—
Cornwall	—	—	—	—	—
Cumb.	0·7	1·7	0·2	2·5	1·9
Derby	25·4	38·7	3·5	67·6	0·4
Devon	—	—	—	—	—
Dorset	9·8	30·6	7·2	47·6	7·5
Durham	1·6	0·7	—	2·3	0·05
Essex	—	28·1	4·6	32·7	20·5
Glos.	36·1	41·7	4·9	82·7	9·9
Hants.	24·1	19·7	4·1	47·9	4·4
I. of W.	—	—	—	—	15·3
Hereford	—	69·7	—	69·7	3·6
Herts.	6·3	44·1	2·5	52·9	26·5
Hunts.	27·9	57·4	2·6	87·9	11·6
Kent	—	—	—	—	—
Lancs.	—	—	—	—	—
Leics.	78·1	11·8	0·8	90·7	0·8
Lincs.	43·2	28·4	2·0	73·7	1·3
Middx.	4·7	60·7	4·8	70·2	3·5
Mon.	4·8	—	—	4·8	3·2
Norfolk	14·7	52·4	6·2	73·3	2·9
Northampton	61·7	23·2	5·3	90·3	5·4
Northumberland	4·7	6·0	—	10·7	0·6

Notts.	49·3		31·1		4·2			84·7		3·6
Oxon.	37·9		31·8		4·9			74·6		19·5
Rutland	42·4		42·0		4·8			89·2		10·8
Salop.	2·4		2·2		2·4			6·9		—
Somerset	—		18·6		2·2			20·8		1·7
Staffs.	10·1		11·3		0·7			22·1		3·4
Suffolk	3·5		54·5		10·5			68·4		7·8
Surrey	0·04		45·2		1·9			47·2		4·4
Sussex	—		31·1		8·1			39·1		13·3
War.	65·1		18·5		3·6			87·1		6·2
West.	—		0·2		0·1			0·3		—
Wilts.	33·8		43·0		8·9			85·7		5·9
Worcs.	39·4		31·0		2·0			72·3		5·9
Yorks E.	57·5		27·6		3·7			88·7		4·7
Yorks N.	19·5		13·7		—			33·1		1·0
Yorks W.	17·4		21·8		5·1			44·2		2·2
England	27·3		29·2		3·5			60·1		6·0

Note: In some cases the aggregation of the first three columns to give the fourth column is plus or minus 0·1 per cent in error. This is due to rounding errors.

Appendix 9. COMMON AND WASTE ENCLOSURE DIVIDED INTO SPECIFIC TIME PERIODS EXPRESSED AS A PERCENTAGE OF *all* PARLIAMENTARY ENCLOSURE

County	Pre-1793	1793–1815	1816–1829	Pre-1830	Post-1829
Beds.	—	0·5	—	0·5	3·1
Berks.	1·8	2·1	—	3·9	2·0
Bucks.	—	1·1	0·4	1·5	3·4
Camb.	3·6	2·1	—	5·7	9·3
Cheshire	34·8	52·3	4·1	91·2	8·4
Cornwall	9·4	21·8	6·2	37·4	62·6
Cumb.	13·5	54·5	10·3	78·2	17·3
Derby	17·2	6·8	5·0	28·9	3·1
Devon	26·1	26·8	9·7	62·6	37·4
Dorset	11·3	13·7	3·7	28·7	16·2
Durham	48·7	38·8	0·6	88·2	9·5
Essex	2·9	12·7	3·5	19·1	27·7
Glos.	1·7	2·5	0·2	4·4	3·0
Hants.	5·6	19·0	4·5	29·1	18·5
I. of W.	—	77·6	—	77·6	7·1
Hereford	8·9	4·0	3·5	16·4	10·3
Herts.	8·2	10·7	—	18·9	1·7
Hunts.	—	0·4	—	0·4	0·1
Kent	9·1	45·8	12·6	67·5	32·5
Lancs.	18·9	53·6	10·9	83·4	16·6
Leics.	0·1	8·4	—	8·5	—
Lincs.	7·8	13·4	0·1	21·4	3·7
Middx.	21·2	4·7	—	25·9	0·4
Mon.	—	75·1	—	75·1	16·9
Norfolk	4·6	13·5	3·2	21·3	2·4
Northampton	0·2	1·9	2·0	4·1	0·2
Northumberland	53·9	13·1	1·5	68·5	20·2

Notts.	2·9		4·5		1·5			9·0		2·8
Oxon.	0·6		2·0		0·1			2·6		3·2
Rutland	—		—		—			—		—
Salop.	23·7		39·2		2·7			65·7		27·4
Somerset	35·2		27·5		2·4			65·1		12·6
Staffs.	20·8		35·8		3·1			59·7		14·8
Suffolk	0·5		18·1		2·9			21·5		2·4
Surrey	3·7		22·4		2·3			28·3		20·1
Sussex	8·5		10·1		3·3			21·8		25·8
War.	2·2		3·3		0·4			5·9		0·7
West.	16·8		32·4		8·6			57·8		41·9
Wilts.	1·6		3·8		0·8			6·1		2·3
Worcs.	9·8		6·1		2·3			18·2		3·5
Yorks E.	5·5		0·6		0·1			6·2		0·4
Yorks N.	22·0		24·9		2·4			49·3		16·5
Yorks W.	21·2		13·8		3·3			38·3		15·2
England	10·4		13·3		2·1			25·9		8·1

Note: In some cases the aggregation of the first three columns to give the fourth column is plus or minus 0·1 per cent in error. This is due to rounding errors.

Appendix 10. APPENDIX TO ANSWER THE QUESTION, WHEN FOR EACH COUNTY WAS PARLIAMENTARY ENCLOSURE MOST IMPORTANT? TOTAL ENCLOSURE IN SPECIFIC TIME PERIODS EXPRESSED AS A PERCENTAGE OF PARLIAMENTARY ENCLOSURE

County	Pre-1793	1793–1815	1816–1829	Pre-1830	Post-1829
Beds.	16·1	65·2	3·2	84·5	15·5
Berks.	21·4	57·4	5·7	84·5	15·5
Bucks.	35·3	41·8	6·5	83·5	16·5
Camb.	5·7	54·3	3·4	63·4	36·6
Cheshire	34·8	52·8	4·1	91·6	8·4
Cornwall	9·4	21·8	6·2	37·4	62·6
Cumb.	14·2	56·1	10·4	80·7	19·3
Derby	42·6	45·5	8·4	96·5	3·5
Devon	26·1	26·8	9·7	62·6	37·4
Dorset	21·1	44·3	11·0	76·3	23·7
Durham	50·3	39·5	0·6	90·4	9·6
Essex	2·8	40·9	8·2	51·8	48·2
Glos.	37·8	44·2	5·2	87·2	12·8
Hants.	29·7	38·8	8·6	77·1	22·9
I. of W.	—	77·6	—	77·6	22·4
Hereford	8·9	73·7	3·5	86·1	13·9
Herts.	14·5	54·8	2·5	71·8	28·2
Hunts.	27·9	57·9	2·6	88·4	11·6
Kent	9·1	45·8	12·6	67·5	32·5
Lancs.	18·9	53·6	10·9	83·4	16·6
Leics.	78·2	20·2	0·8	99·2	0·8
Lincs.	51·0	41·9	2·1	95·0	5·0
Middx.	25·8	65·4	4·8	96·1	3·9
Mon.	4·8	75·1	—	79·9	20·1
Norfolk	19·3	65·9	9·4	94·6	5·4
Northampton	61·9	25·1	7·3	94·4	5·6
Northumberland	58·6	19·0	1·5	79·2	20·8

Notts.	52·3		35·7		5·7			93·7		6·3
Oxon.	38·5		33·8		5·0			77·3		22·7
Rutland	42·4		42·0		4·8			89·2		10·8
Salop.	26·1		41·4		5·1			72·6		27·4
Somerset	35·0		46·1		4·6			85·7		14·3
Staffs.	30·9		47·0		3·9			81·8		18·2
Suffolk	4·0		72·5		13·4			89·8		10·2
Surrey	3·7		67·6		4·2			75·5		24·5
Sussex	8·5		41·1		11·4			61·0		39·0
War.	67·3		21·8		4·0			93·0		7·0
West.	16·8		32·6		8·7			58·1		41·9
Wilts.	35·4		46·7		9·7			91·8		8·2
Worcs.	49·2		37·1		4·3			90·5		9·5
Yorks E.	62·9		28·2		3·7			94·9		5·1
Yorks N.	41·5		38·6		2·4			82·5		17·5
Yorks W.	38·7		35·6		8·4			82·6		17·4
England	37·7		42·6		5·6			85·9		14·1

Note: In some cases the aggregate of the first three columns to give the fourth column is plus or minus 0·1 per cent in error. This is due to rounding errors.

Appendix 11. OPEN FIELD ARABLE, HALF DECADE CHRONOLOGY OF ENCLOSURE, 1730–1849 NUMBER OF ACTS IN 24 HALF DECADES

County	1	2	3	4	5	6	7	8	9	10	11	12
Beds.	0	0	1	0	0	0	1	5	2	5	2	0
Berks.	0	0	2	1	0	1	1	0	5	7	1	2
Bucks.	0	1	2	0	0	0	4	9	12	8	2	2
Camb.	0	0	0	0	0	0	0	0	1	2	0	0
Cheshire	0	0	0	0	0	0	0	0	0	0	0	0
Cornwall	0	0	0	0	0	0	0	0	0	0	0	0
Cumb.	0	0	0	0	0	0	0	1	1	0	0	0
Derby	0	0	0	0	0	1	6	7	4	3	4	10
Devon	0	0	0	0	0	0	0	0	0	0	0	0
Dorset	1	1	0	0	0	0	2	1	0	1	0	2
Durham	0	0	0	0	0	0	0	1	0	0	2	0
Essex	0	0	0	0	0	0	0	0	0	0	0	0
Glos.	3	1	1	0	2	2	1	10	9	13	3	2
Hants.	0	0	3	1	0	3	0	0	1	1	4	6
I. of W.	0	0	0	0	0	0	0	0	0	0	0	0
Hereford	0	0	0	0	0	0	0	0	0	0	0	0
Herts.	0	0	0	0	0	0	0	3	0	1	0	0
Hunts.	0	0	0	0	0	0	2	3	10	2	2	1
Kent	0	0	0	0	0	0	0	0	0	0	0	0
Lancs.	0	0	0	0	0	0	0	0	0	0	0	0
Leics.	2	0	0	1	1	11	23	21	20	21	7	9
Lincs.	2	1	0	0	3	6	11	36	45	27	2	7
Middx.	0	0	0	0	0	0	0	0	1	0	1	1
Mon.	0	0	0	0	0	0	0	0	0	1	0	0
Norfolk	0	0	0	0	0	2	2	3	6	4	4	2
Northampton	1	0	1	2	5	7	16	18	21	40	8	2
Northumberland	0	0	1	0	0	1	1	0	0	1	1	0
Notts.	0	0	0	0	0	3	7	13	10	15	1	5

Oxon.	1	0	0	0	0	4	4	13	11	13	3	5
Rutland	0	0	0	0	0	4	2	1	5	0	0	0
Salop.	0	0	0	0	0	0	0	0	2	0	0	1
Somerset	0	0	0	0	0	0	0	0	0	0	0	0
Staffs.	0	0	0	0	0	0	0	1	5	0	1	1
Suffolk	0	1	0	0	0	0	0	0	1	1	0	0
Surrey	0	0	0	0	0	0	0	0	0	1	0	0
Sussex	0	0	0	0	0	0	0	0	0	0	0	0
War.	7	3	4	0	1	16	8	11	18	15	3	2
West.	0	0	0	0	0	0	0	0	0	0	0	0
Wilts.	1	0	1	2	0	0	0	2	2	14	7	6
Worcs.	0	0	0	0	0	0	3	2	13	12	2	2
Yorks E.	1	0	2	1	0	6	11	31	24	10	1	4
Yorks N.	0	0	0	1	0	6	0	6	4	5	2	3
Yorks W.	0	0	1	0	0	2	2	11	17	8	5	9
England	19	8	19	9	12	75	107	209	250	231	68	84

Appendix 11. (*cont.*)

County	13	14	15	16	17	18	19	20	21	22	23	24
Beds.	3	22	13	14	6	0	2	1	2	3	0	0
Berks.	2	3	20	8	23	4	1	4	1	0	2	1
Bucks	6	19	8	6	9	1	6	0	3	0	4	0
Camb.	1	9	17	18	21	2	2	4	3	14	8	2
Cheshire	0	0	0	1	0	0	0	0	0	0	0	0
Cornwall	0	0	0	0	0	0	0	0	0	0	0	0
Cumb.	0	0	0	0	2	0	0	1	0	0	0	0
Derby	5	5	5	7	3	6	3	0	1	0	0	0
Devon	0	0	0	0	0	0	0	0	0	0	0	0
Dorset	2	5	5	10	5	3	3	1	4	2	0	0
Durham	1	0	0	0	1	0	0	0	0	0	0	0
Essex	0	1	5	1	2	0	2	0	0	1	0	0
Glos.	10	13	8	13	15	4	1	1	5	5	1	0
Hants.	7	7	3	5	6	4	2	3	0	0	1	0
I. of W.	0	0	0	0	0	0	0	0	0	0	0	0
Hereford	1	4	2	4	13	0	0	0	0	0	0	0
Herts.	0	6	5	2	7	0	1	1	1	0	0	0
Hunts.	3	8	15	8	6	1	0	1	0	1	3	0
Kent	0	0	0	0	0	0	0	0	0	0	0	0
Lancs.	0	0	0	0	0	0	0	0	0	0	0	0
Leics.	15	6	5	2	2	0	1	1	0	0	1	0
Lincs.	23	22	32	16	14	10	1	3	0	0	1	0
Middx.	0	2	5	3	7	3	1	1	0	0	0	0
Mon.	0	0	0	0	0	0	0	0	0	0	0	0
Norfolk	5	14	30	40	44	11	5	7	0	3	5	0
Northampton	5	10	15	14	6	5	3	3	3	2	3	0
Northumberland	1	0	1	1	1	0	0	0	0	0	1	0
Notts.	10	17	16	8	2	3	2	1	0	1	0	1

Oxon.	11	6	15	6	13	5	5	2	2	2	5	0
Rutland	3	4	4	0	0	0	1	0	0	0	0	0
Salop.	1	0	0	1	0	2	0	0	0	0	0	0
Somerset	2	10	7	4	10	5	0	2	2	2	0	0
Staffs.	2	4	2	2	4	1	0	0	1	0	0	0
Suffolk	1	5	6	8	13	6	0	3	1	2	0	0
Surrey	0	1	6	6	3	2	1	1	0	0	0	0
Sussex	0	1	4	6	7	3	2	1	1	0	1	0
War.	8	7	8	6	4	4	1	2	2	0	0	0
West.	0	0	0	1	2	1	0	0	0	0	0	0
Wilts.	8	13	12	13	16	12	3	3	1	0	0	0
Worcs.	1	3	4	7	16	3	0	1	1	0	0	0
Yorks E.	12	3	19	4	8	3	4	0	3	0	2	0
Yorks N.	4	1	3	9	6	0	0	0	1	0	0	0
Yorks W.	15	17	21	16	18	11	1	5	1	2	0	0
England	168	248	321	270	315	115	54	53	39	40	38	4

Appendix 12. COMMON AND WASTE, HALF DECADE CHRONOLOGY OF ENCLOSURE, 1730–1849 NUMBER OF ACTS IN 24 HALF DECADES

County	1	2	3	4	5	6	7	8	9	10	11	12
Beds.	0	0	0	0	0	0	0	0	0	0	0	0
Berks.	0	1	1	0	0	0	0	0	0	2	0	0
Bucks.	0	0	0	0	0	0	0	0	0	0	0	0
Camb.	0	0	1	0	0	0	0	1	0	0	0	0
Cheshire	0	0	0	0	0	0	0	2	1	2	0	0
Cornwall	0	0	0	0	0	0	0	0	0	0	0	0
Cumb.	0	0	0	0	0	0	1	5	2	6	1	0
Derby	1	0	0	1	0	2	1	2	5	6	5	3
Devon	0	0	0	0	0	0	0	0	0	1	0	0
Dorset	0	0	0	0	0	0	1	1	0	1	0	0
Durham	0	0	0	0	0	3	5	4	4	0	0	1
Essex	0	0	0	0	0	0	0	1	0	1	0	0
Glos.	0	0	0	0	0	0	0	0	0	3	1	1
Hants.	1	2	4	1	1	3	0	0	1	2	4	6
I. of W.	0	0	0	0	0	0	0	0	0	0	0	0
Hereford	0	0	0	0	0	0	0	0	2	1	2	0
Herts.	0	0	0	0	0	0	0	0	0	2	0	0
Hunts.	0	0	0	0	0	0	0	0	0	0	0	0
Kent	0	0	1	0	0	0	1	0	0	0	0	0
Lancs.	1	0	0	0	1	1	4	4	2	4	0	4
Leics.	0	0	0	0	0	0	0	0	1	0	0	0
Lincs.	0	1	1	1	0	0	0	2	6	0	1	4
Middx.	0	0	0	0	0	0	0	1	0	1	0	0
Mon.	0	0	0	0	0	0	0	0	0	0	0	0
Norfolk	0	0	1	1	0	0	1	3	0	5	4	2
Northampton	0	0	0	0	0	0	0	0	0	0	0	0
Northumberland	0	0	0	0	5	0	0	3	1	8	1	1
Notts.	0	0	0	0	0	0	0	0	3	3	0	0

Oxon.	0	0	0	0	0	0	0	0	0	0	1	0
Rutland	0	0	0	0	0	0	0	0	0	0	0	0
Salop.	0	0	0	0	0	0	1	0	2	5	1	3
Somerset	0	0	0	0	1	0	0	1	3	7	5	6
Staffs.	1	1	0	0	0	1	0	1	6	5	3	2
Suffolk	0	0	0	0	0	0	0	0	0	0	0	1
Surrey	0	0	0	0	0	0	0	1	3	0	0	1
Sussex	0	0	0	0	0	0	0	2	0	1	0	1
War.	0	0	0	0	0	0	0	0	3	0	1	1
West.	0	0	0	0	0	0	0	2	5	3	0	0
Wilts.	1	1	0	0	0	0	0	0	1	1	0	1
Worcs.	0	0	0	0	1	0	1	0	5	1	3	0
Yorks. E.	0	1	1	1	1	0	1	1	2	2	0	1
Yorks N.	0	0	0	0	2	3	1	5	4	6	2	5
Yorks W.	0	0	0	0	2	6	5	12	8	12	6	10
England	5	7	7	4	14	16	23	54	69	90	37	48

Appendix 12. (*cont.*)

County	13	14	15	16	17	18	19	20	21	22	23	24
Beds.	0	1	0	2	0	0	0	0	0	0	1	0
Berks.	0	0	1	1	3	0	0	0	0	0	0	0
Bucks.	0	0	2	1	1	1	0	1	0	0	1	0
Camb.	3	0	1	1	1	0	0	0	2	1	1	0
Cheshire	6	2	1	7	8	1	2	3	0	1	0	0
Cornwall	0	0	0	1	0	2	0	0	0	0	0	0
Cumb.	0	4	5	12	23	6	7	3	1	0	3	0
Derby	4	3	7	2	3	3	2	5	1	3	2	0
Devon	0	0	3	6	8	4	1	3	1	2	2	0
Dorset	0	3	2	3	3	3	1	0	0	0	0	0
Durham	1	2	5	4	2	1	1	0	1	0	0	0
Essex	0	0	2	1	11	0	6	2	0	1	1	0
Glos.	0	0	2	1	4	1	0	4	0	0	1	0
Hants.	0	0	3	4	11	5	2	4	0	1	2	0
I. of W.	0	0	0	0	1	0	0	0	0	0	0	0
Hereford	0	1	1	5	4	4	0	0	2	0	0	0
Herts.	0	0	1	2	1	1	0	0	0	0	0	0
Hunts.	0	1	0	0	0	0	0	0	0	0	0	0
Kent	0	0	0	2	9	1	2	0	0	0	1	0
Lancs.	3	11	4	6	10	6	3	1	1	0	0	0
Leics.	0	0	1	2	0	0	0	0	0	0	0	0
Lincs.	5	4	6	3	6	1	0	1	3	0	0	1
Middx.	0	0	0	1	5	0	0	0	0	0	0	0
Mon.	0	0	0	1	2	0	0	0	0	0	0	0
Norfolk	2	6	20	11	22	7	5	3	1	1	0	2
Northampton	0	1	0	0	1	0	2	1	0	0	0	0
Northumberland	6	2	1	8	3	2	1	0	1	0	0	0
Notts.	2	3	0	3	1	1	0	0	0	1	0	0

Oxon.	0	0	0	1	1	3	0	0	0	0	0	0
Rutland	0	0	0	0	0	0	0	0	0	0	0	0
Salop.	0	3	5	8	4	4	2	0	0	3	0	1
Somerset	14	21	5	6	8	6	0	2	4	1	1	0
Staffs.	4	5	8	10	7	3	3	1	0	1	2	0
Suffolk	0	6	6	4	8	7	1	1	0	0	0	0
Surrey	1	0	6	5	5	1	5	1	0	0	1	0
Sussex	2	1	0	1	2	1	1	1	1	0	1	0
War.	0	2	3	1	4	5	0	1	1	0	1	0
West.	1	0	5	3	10	7	2	1	2	2	0	0
Wilts.	2	0	4	5	4	4	5	1	1	0	0	0
Worcs.	1	3	0	0	6	4	1	1	2	0	0	0
Yorks E.	2	0	1	3	1	0	0	1	0	0	0	0
Yorks N.	4	2	7	13	8	5	1	0	1	0	0	0
Yorks W.	4	9	11	10	21	17	5	6	1	1	3	0
England	67	96	129	160	232	117	61	48	27	19	24	4

Appendix 13. TOTAL ENCLOSURE, HALF DECADE CHRONOLOGY OF ENCLOSURE, 1730–1849 NUMBER OF ACTS IN 24 HALF DECADES

County	1	2	3	4	5	6	7	8	9	10	11	12
Beds.	0	0	1	0	0	0	1	5	2	5	2	0
Berks.	0	1	3	1	0	1	1	0	5	9	1	2
Bucks.	0	1	2	0	0	0	4	9	12	8	2	2
Camb.	0	0	1	0	0	0	0	1	1	2	0	0
Cheshire	0	0	0	0	0	0	0	2	1	2	0	0
Cornwall	0	0	0	0	0	0	0	0	0	0	0	0
Cumb.	0	0	0	0	0	0	1	6	3	6	1	0
Derby	1	0	0	1	0	3	7	9	9	9	9	13
Devon	0	0	0	0	0	0	0	0	0	1	0	0
Dorset	1	1	0	0	0	0	3	2	0	2	0	2
Durham	0	0	0	0	0	3	5	5	4	0	2	1
Essex	0	0	0	0	0	0	0	1	0	1	0	0
Glos.	3	1	1	0	2	2	1	10	9	16	4	3
Hants.	1	2	4	1	1	3	0	0	1	2	4	6
I. of W.	0	0	0	0	0	0	0	0	0	0	0	0
Hereford	0	0	0	0	0	0	0	0	2	1	2	0
Herts.	0	0	0	0	0	0	0	3	0	3	0	0
Hunts.	0	0	0	0	0	0	2	3	10	2	2	1
Kent	0	0	1	0	0	0	1	0	0	0	0	0
Lancs.	1	0	0	0	1	1	4	4	2	4	0	4
Leics.	2	0	0	1	1	11	23	21	21	21	7	9
Lincs.	2	2	1	1	3	6	11	38	51	27	3	11
Middx.	0	0	0	0	0	0	0	1	1	1	1	1
Mon.	0	0	0	0	0	0	0	0	0	1	0	0
Norfolk	0	0	1	1	0	2	3	6	6	9	8	4
Northampton	1	0	1	2	5	7	16	18	21	40	8	2
Northumberland	0	0	1	0	5	1	1	3	1	9	2	1
Notts.	0	0	0	0	0	3	7	13	13	18	1	5

Oxon.	1	0	0	0	0	4	4	13	11	13	4	5
Rutland	0	0	0	0	0	4	2	1	5	0	0	0
Salop.	0	0	0	0	0	0	1	0	4	5	1	4
Somerset	0	0	0	0	1	0	0	1	3	7	5	6
Staffs.	1	1	0	0	0	1	0	2	11	5	4	3
Suffolk	0	1	0	0	0	0	0	0	1	1	0	1
Surrey	0	0	0	0	0	0	0	1	3	1	0	1
Sussex	0	0	0	0	0	0	0	2	0	1	0	1
War.	7	3	4	0	1	16	8	11	21	15	4	3
West.	0	0	0	0	0	0	0	2	5	3	0	0
Wilts.	2	1	1	2	0	0	0	2	3	15	7	7
Worcs.	0	0	0	0	1	0	4	2	18	13	5	2
Yorks E.	1	1	3	2	1	6	12	32	26	12	1	5
Yorks N.	0	0	0	1	2	9	1	11	8	11	4	8
Yorks W.	0	0	1	0	2	8	7	23	25	20	11	19
England	24	15	26	13	26	91	130	263	319	321	105	132

Appendix 13. (*cont.*)

County	13	14	15	16	17	18	19	20	21	22	23	24
Beds.	3	23	13	16	6	0	2	1	2	3	1	0
Berks.	2	3	21	9	26	4	1	4	1	0	2	1
Bucks.	6	19	10	7	10	2	6	1	3	0	5	0
Camb.	4	9	18	19	22	2	2	4	5	15	9	2
Cheshire	6	2	1	8	8	1	2	3	0	1	0	0
Cornwall	0	0	0	1	0	2	0	0	0	0	0	0
Cumb.	0	4	5	12	25	6	7	4	1	0	3	0
Derby	9	8	12	9	6	9	5	5	2	3	2	0
Devon	0	0	3	6	8	4	1	3	1	2	2	0
Dorset	2	8	7	13	8	6	4	1	4	2	0	0
Durham	2	2	5	4	3	1	1	0	1	0	0	0
Essex	0	1	7	2	13	0	8	2	0	2	1	0
Glos.	10	13	10	14	19	5	1	5	5	5	2	0
Hants.	7	7	6	9	17	9	4	7	0	1	3	0
I. of W.	0	0	0	0	1	0	0	0	0	0	0	0
Hereford	1	5	3	9	17	4	0	0	2	0	0	0
Herts.	0	6	6	4	8	1	1	1	1	0	0	0
Hunts.	3	9	15	8	6	1	0	1	0	1	3	0
Kent	0	0	0	2	9	1	2	0	0	0	1	0
Lancs.	3	11	4	6	10	6	3	1	1	0	0	0
Leics.	15	6	6	4	2	0	1	1	0	0	1	0
Lincs.	28	26	38	19	20	11	1	4	3	0	1	1
Middx.	0	2	5	4	12	3	1	1	0	0	0	0
Mon.	0	0	0	1	2	0	0	0	0	0	0	0
Norfolk	7	20	50	51	66	18	10	10	1	4	5	2
Northampton	5	11	15	14	7	5	5	4	3	2	3	0
Northumberland	7	2	2	9	4	2	1	0	1	0	1	0
Notts.	12	20	16	11	3	4	2	1	0	2	0	1

Oxon.	11	6	15	7	14	8	5	2	2	2	5	0
Rutland	3	4	4	0	0	0	1	0	0	0	0	0
Salop.	1	3	5	9	4	6	2	0	0	3	0	1
Somerset	16	31	12	10	18	11	0	4	6	3	1	0
Staffs.	6	9	10	12	11	4	3	1	1	1	2	0
Suffolk	1	11	12	12	21	13	1	4	1	2	0	0
Surrey	1	1	12	11	8	3	6	2	0	0	1	0
Sussex	2	2	4	7	9	4	3	2	2	0	2	0
War.	8	9	11	7	8	9	1	3	3	0	1	0
West.	1	0	5	4	12	8	2	1	2	2	0	0
Wilts.	10	13	16	18	20	16	8	4	2	0	0	0
Worcs.	2	6	4	7	22	7	1	2	3	0	0	0
Yorks E.	14	3	20	7	9	3	4	1	3	0	2	0
Yorks N.	8	3	10	22	14	5	1	0	2	0	0	0
Yorks W.	19	26	32	26	39	28	6	11	2	3	3	0
England	235	344	450	430	547	232	115	101	66	59	62	8

Appendix 14. KEY TO HALF DECADES FOR APPENDIXES 11–13

1	1730–34
2	1735–39
3	1740–44
4	1745–49
5	1750–54
6	1755–59
7	1760–64
8	1765–69
9	1770–74
10	1775–79
11	1780–84
12	1785–89
13	1790–94
14	1795–99
15	1800–04
16	1805–09
17	1810–14
18	1815–19
19	1820–24
20	1825–29
21	1830–34
22	1835–39
23	1840–44
24	1845–49

Notes and References

Chapter 1: *Introduction*

1 From *Poems by William Cowper Esquire* (1814) vol 2, 'The Task', 40, 'Town and Country Contrasted'.
2 My interest in this poet and those lines of verse was first aroused by Professor H. C. Darby before I was ever interested in parliamentary enclosure. See Darby, 'On the relation of geography and history', *Transactions of the Institute of British Geographers*, (1953) **19**, 6.
3 Brown, E. H., 'Man shapes the Earth', *The Geographical Journal* (1970), **136**, 74–85, esp. 76–7.
4 Tate, W. E., *The English village community and the enclosure movements* (1967) 87–8.
5 For similar examples in Lincolnshire see Swales, T. H., 'The parliamentary enclosures of Lindsey', *Architectural and Archaeological Societies of Lincolnshire and Northamptonshire, Reports and Papers* (1937), **42**, 233–74 and new series (1938), 2, 85–120, esp. 115–19.
6 See also Tucker, D. N., 'Linear parishes and farm structures in the Vale of Pickering', *Geography* (1972), **57**, 111.
7 *Buckinghamshire County Record Office*, Bierton enclosure map, B.R.O. IR/Ia.
8 Hoskins, W. G., *The making of the English Landscape* (1965), 154–6.
9 See also Wilkinson, O., *The agricultural revolution in the East Riding of Yorkshire* (1956), 11–12.
10 As stated in *The Journal of the House of Commons* (22 April 1801), **56**, 26.
11 'Return of Commons (Inclosure Awards)', *Parliamentary Papers–House of Commons* (1904), **50**; 'Return of inclosure acts', *idem* (1914), **399**.
12 Gonner, E. C. K., *Common land and inclosure* (1912); Slater, G., *The English peasantry and the enclosure of common fields* (1907); Curtler, W. H. R., *The enclosure and redistribution of our land* (1920); Tate, W. E., *English village community*.
13 For example see Tate, W. E. (ed. Turner, M. E.), *A Domesday of English enclosure acts and awards* (1978), 21–2.
14 Williams, M., 'The enclosure and reclamation of waste land in England and Wales in the eighteenth and nineteenth centuries', *Transactions of the*

Institute of British Geographers (1970), **51**, 55–69; Williams, 'The enclosure of waste land in Somerset', in *Transactions* (1972), **57**, 99.

15 Or in Yelling's prefatory remarks, 'I have followed Slater rather than Gonner in omitting consideration of the enclosure of common wastes, other than those tracts that were an integral part of common-field husbandry.'

16 Darby, H. C., *Historical Geography of England before 1800* (1936), 400–1; Darby, *A new historical geography of England* (1973), maps, 323, 476, 479.

17 White, L. J., 'Enclosures and population movements in England, 1700–1830', *Explorations in Entrepreneurial History* (1968), **6**, 175–86; Williams, 'Enclosure and Reclamation of waste land'; Tucker, G. S. L., 'The old poor law revisited', *Explorations in Economic History* (1975), **12**, 233–52; Philpot, G., 'Enclosure and population growth in eighteenth century England', *Explorations in Economic History* (1975), **12**, 29–46; Deane, P. and Cole, W. A., *British economic growth, 1688–1959* (1969), 95, who use *British Parliamentary Papers* (1836), **8**, 501.

18 Martin, J. M., '*Warwickshire and the parliamentary enclosure movement*' (1965); Hunt, H. G., '*The parliamentary enclosure movement in Leicestershire*' (1956); Williams, 'Enclosure of waste land in Somerset' and his 'The enclosure and reclamation of the Mendip Hills', *Agricultural History Review* (1971), **19**, 65–81; Grigg, D. B., *The agricultural revolution in south Lincolnshire* (1966); Rodgers, W. S., '*The distribution of enclosure in the West Riding*' (1953).

19 For which see Tate, *Domesday*, 4–5; see also Brewer, J. G., *Enclosure and the open fields: a bibliography* (1972), 27–9.

20 By printed sources I am referring to the *Blue Books* and the *Journal of the House of Commons*, though it should be noted that by no means all acts or entries in the *Journal* give such information.

21 Tate's manuscripts are now to be found in the University of Reading Library, *Tate Mss.* 1093.

22 Tate, *Domesday*, 3–12.

23 Thompson, F. M. L., reviewing Perry, P. J., *British farming in the Great Depression, 1870–1914*, in *Agricultural History Review* (1977), **25**, 68.

24 In these respects a replica of the *Domesday of Enclosures*.

25 See Tate, 'English village community', 93.

26 Itemised in Tate, *Domesday*, 82, 99, 112, 121, 151, 171, 210, 240, 266–7 and 317–18.

27 Williams, 'Enclosure of Mendip Hills', 65.

28 As he seems to do in 'Enclosure in Somerset', 99–123.

29 The title of the conference was 'Enclosures reopened: recent developments in the enclosure debate'.

30 See also his 'Parliamentary enclosure in the uplands: the case of the North York Moors', *Agricultural History Review* (1976), **24**, 1–17.

31 Hodgson, R. I., 'The progress of enclosure in County Durham, 1550–1870' in Fox, H. S. A. and Butlin, R. A. (eds.), *Change in the countryside: essays on rural England, 1500–1900* (1979), 83–102.

32 But see the discussion later in this chapter and the results in Appendix 5 of a 5 and 10 per cent error test.

33 For example see Tate, *Domesday*, certain entries, 79, 94, 108–11, 138, 140, 147, 152, 154, 174, 188, 193, 204, 230, 244, 248–9, 262, 276, 283, 317–18.

34 *Domesday*, 65, 81, 83–4, 90, 113–14, 123, 131, 140, 152, 172, 219, 222, 227, 235, 241, 245, 250, 255, 263, 268–9, 284, 293, 301, 320. See also Lefèvre, G. J.

S. (Baron Eversley), *English Commons and Forests* (1894), especially chs. XVI and XX and Appendix II.

35 That is to say had not come to light by late September 1973 when the research for the Tate volume was completed.

36 i.e. (96, 916/68) × 71 acres.

37 Slater, *English Peasantry*, 140–7 and Appendix A, 267. There are fewer acts in Slater's total population because he failed to include the enclosure of common and waste.

38 Especially the act of 7 and 8 Victoria, c.61, 1844, by which detached parts of counties, which had already for parliamentary purposes been amalgamated with the county by which they were surrounded or with which the detached part had the longest common boundary, were annexed to the same county for all purposes.

39 For example see the *Census Enumeration Abstract*, vol. 1, 1831, the entry for Gloucestershire, 224–5, where we learn that 'the area of the county of Gloucestershire is 1,258 Square Statute Miles, and consequently 805,120 acres; while the area herein assigned to the several parishes amounts to no more than 790,470 acres; but no attempt to reconcile this apparent discrepancy has been deemed allowable'. I used these contemporary estimates of county acreage in my table of enclosure density in my 'Parliamentary enclosure and population change in England, 1750–1830', *Explorations in Economic History (1976)*, **13**, 464. The densities presented there do not differ very much from the revised estimates in Appendix 3.

40 Bartholomew, J. G., *The survey atlas of England and Wales* (1903), 13.

41 The 1873 Returns and the 1951 Census figures are itemised in Hoskins, W. G. and Stamp, L. D., *The common lands of England and Wales* (1963), 92–3 and 102–3 respectively.

42 This was a Kendall rank correlation test. With the Spearman test the coefficients in all cases were 0·99 (see Appendix 4a).

Chapter 2: *The spatial setting*

1 After Radipole there were very few other seventeenth-century enclosure acts. The full list is Radipole in Dorset 1604, Marden and other places in Herefordshire 1606, Malvern Chase in Gloucestershire, Herefordshire, and Worcestershire 1664, Horton in Gloucestershire 1668, West Derby and Wavertree in Lancashire 1677, Hambleton in Rutland 1692, and Salford in Oxfordshire 1696. The last two were for the enclosure of open field arable and the rest were for the enclosure of commons, forests, and wastes. They were all private acts except Radipole and Marden which were public acts. There is a good case for making the public act of 37 Henry VIII, c.2, 1545 the very first enclosure act. It is not usually included among local enclosure acts but it foreshadows the method of enclosure by commissioners which prevailed in the eighteenth century. It has some claims therefore to be regarded as the first local enclosure. It relates to the partition of Hounslow Heath in Middlesex and is described in detail in Scrutton, T. E., *Commons and Common Fields* (1887), 95. The last act of 1914 is identified as the enclosure of land, including open field arable in the Gloucestershire parish of Elmstone Hardwicke, under the 1845 General Act and its successors and pursuant to a Provisional Confirmation Order of 1914.

2 Though also where appropriate in accordance with the 1801 General Enclosure Act.

3 Base acreage for England as described in Chapter 1, taken as that recorded in the 1873 *Return of Waste Lands* and reprinted in Hoskins and Stamp, *The common lands*, 92–3. It should be noted here that historically, acres or measures that purport to be acres do not always conform to the official or statutory acre commonly used. In the present work this problem applies to Lancashire and to a lesser degree Cheshire, in both of which the enclosure acreages are recorded in the documents as Cheshire acres and customary acres as well as statutory acres.

4 *Ibid.*

5 For Devon see Hoskins, W. G., 'The reclamation of the waste in Devon, 1550–1800', *Economic History Review* (1943), **13**, 80–92, esp. 81 where we are told that open fields were very rare by 1550–1600.

6 See Orwin, C. S. and C. S., *The open fields* (1938); Chambers, J. D., *Laxton: the last English open-field village* (1964); Rundle, J. R., 'Laxton today', *Agriculture* (1955), **62**, 170–2.

7 See Swann, B., 'The historical background to the registration of common land', *The Amateur Historian* (1967), **7** (no. 6), 232–40.

8 Baker, A. R. H., 'Howard Levi Gray and English field systems: an evaluation', *Agricultural History* (1965), **39**, 86–91; Baker, 'Some terminological problems in studies of British field systems', *Agricultural History Review* (1969), **17**, 136–40; Butlin, R. A., 'Some terms used in agrarian history: a glossary', *Agricultural History Review* (1961), **9**, 98–104; Butlin, 'Recent developments in studies of the terminology of agrarian landscapes', *Agricultural History Review* (1969) **17**, 141–3. I am therefore open to the criticism expressed in this last reference of being labelled amongst those agrarian historians who 'appear to prefer not to know what they are talking about', 141; Adams, I. H., *Agrarian landscape terms: a glossary for historical geography* (1976).

9 Baker, A. R. H. and Butlin, R. A., (eds.), *Studies of field systems in the British Isles* (1973) 70 and 73.

10 Yorkshire West Riding is included with some reservations but justified because of the westward extension of the open fields in the Vale of York.

11 *Victoria County History for the County of Gloucestershire* (1907), **2**, 164.

12 Darby, *New historical geography*, ch. 5, Baker, A. R. H., 'Changes in the later middle ages', 213–14.

13 Williams, 'Enclosure in Somerset', 100.

14 Darby, *New historical geography*, ch. 6; Emery, F. V., 'England circa 1600', 255, 261–2 and 270.

15 *Victoria County History for the county of Hertfordshire* (1908), **2**, 129.

16 Young's emphasis: Young, A., *General View of the agriculture of the county of Hertford* (1804), 48.

17 *Victoria County History for the county of Middlesex* (1911), **2**, 97.

18 *Victoria County History for the county of Kent* (1932), **3**, 350.

19 Fox, H. S. A., 'The study of field systems', *Devon Historian* (1972), **4**, 7.

20 Baker and Butlin, *Studies of field systems*, ch. 2; Elliott, G., 'Field systems of north west England', 41–92; and ch. 3, Butlin, 'Field systems of Northumberland and Durham', 93–144.

21 See Roden, D., 'Enclosure in the Chiltern Hills', *Geografiska Annaler* (1969), **51**, 115–26.

22 The map was constructed from the awards and plans for those parishes in the Hundreds of Cottesloe and Aylesbury which share Chiltern and Vale topographies.
23 Coppock, J. T., 'Farms and fields in the Chilterns', *Erdkunde* (1960), **14**, 140; Coppock, *The Chilterns*, part 4 of Edwards, K. C. (ed), *British landscapes through maps* (1968), 14–15.
24 Baker and Butlin, *Studies of field systems*, ch. 8; Roden, D., 'Field systems of the Chiltern Hills and their environs', 366.
25 Havinden, M., 'Agricultural progress in open field Oxfordshire', *Agricultural History Review* (1961), **9**, 74.
26 See Grigg, D. B., *The agricultural revolution in south Lincolnshire* (1966), 14–16, for an illustration of the relationship between parish shape and topography.
27 *Buckinghamshire County Record Office*, Wendover enclosure award and map, B.R.O. IR/26.
28 Martin, J. M., 'The parliamentary enclosure movement and rural society in Warwickshire', *Agricultural History Review* (1967), **15**, 19.
29 Baker and Butlin, *Studies of field systems*, ch. 5; Roberts, B. K., 'Field systems of the west midlands', 191, 193, 204.
30 Yelling, J. A., 'Common land and enclosure in east Worcestershire, 1540–1870' *Transactions of the Institute of British Geographers* (1968), **45**, 157–68.
31 Roberts, 'Field systems of west midlands', in Baker and Butlin, *Field systems*, 209, also makes the suggestion that Staffordshire can be treated as a northern extension of the woodlands of Worcestershire and his map (p. 204) depicts it thus; see also Yates, E. M., 'Enclosure and the rise of grassland farming in Staffordshire', *North Staffordshire Journal of Field Studies* (1974), **14**, 46–60, and Thomas, H. R., 'The enclosure of open fields and commons in Staffordshire', *Collections for a History of Staffordshire* (1933), 55–99.
32 In general for the West Riding see Rodgers, W. S., 'The distribution of enclosure in the West Riding' (1953).
33 Williams, 'Enclosure in Somerset', 105.
34 Eyre, S. R., 'The upward limit of enclosure on the east moor of north Derbyshire', *Transactions of the Institute of British Geographers* (1957), **23**, 63.
35 It should be noted that the awards for the last three were not signed and sealed until 1819, 1820, and 1820 respectively, though apparently the awards for East and West and Wildmore Fens had still not been fully executed as late as 1844 owing to disagreements about the payment of costs. See Beckwith, I. S., 'The present state of enclosure studies in Lincolnshire', *Bulletin of Local History, East Midlands region* (1971), **6**, 21–40. Beckwith's note 29 on p. 38 is slightly ambiguous in view of the dates of the awards. Presumably what is meant is that even after the awards were signed and sealed there were post-award administrative problems not unlike those described in my 'The cost of parliamentary enclosure in Buckinghamshire', *Agricultural History Review* (1973), **21**, 35–46.
36 *Victoria County History for the county of Lincolnshire* (1906), **2**, 343, based on Wheeler, W. H., *A history of the fens of south Lincolnshire* (1868); see also Grigg, *Agricultural revolution*, 50, 52. In Holland 'the open fields had either never existed or had been enclosed at a very early date'. So whatever parliamentary enclosure there was, was mainly common and waste. In fact Grigg is in no

doubt that only common lands and not open fields remained in eighteenth-century Holland, which conflicts with the evidence here presented.

37 As Joan Thirsk does in her *English peasant farming: the agrarian history of Lincolnshire from Tudor to recent times* (1957); see also Beckwith, 'Enclosure studies in Lincolnshire', 30 and 33, Grigg, *Agricultural revolution*, and Johnson, S. A., 'Some aspects of enclosure and changing agricultural landscapes in Lindsey from the sixteenth to the nineteenth century', *Lincolnshire Architectural and Archaeological Society, Reports and Papers* (1962), **9**, 134–50.

38 See below, this chapter, 55–8.

39 Darby, *Historical geography*, ch. 7; Darby, H. C., 'The age of the improver', 341; Postgate, M. R., 'The field systems of Breckland', *Agriculture History Review* (1962), **10**, 80–101.

40 Postgate, 'Field systems of Breckland', 81 and in Baker and Butlin, *Field Systems*, ch. 7, 'Field systems of East Anglia', 282.

41 Postgate, 'Breckland', 83–4.

42 Thirsk, J. and Imray, J., *Suffolk farming in the nineteenth Century* (1958), 20.

43 Postgate, 'Field systems of East Anglia', 289.

44 Thirsk and Imray, *Suffolk farming*, 20.

45 Darby, 'Age of the improver', 340.

46 Postgate, 'Breckland', 85 and 'Field systems of East Anglia', 302.

47 Postgate, 'Breckland', 87.

48 Thirsk and Imray, *Suffolk farming*, 18, 20, and 22.

49 Hodgson, R. I., 'The progress of enclosure in county Durham, 1550–1870', 84–5 and 87–8, in Fox, H. S. A. and Butlin, R. A. (eds.), *Change in the countryside; essays on rural England, 1500–1900* (1979).

50 Elliott, 'Field systems of north west England', 75.

51 Slater, *English peasantry*, 73, 196, 197, 233; Rodgers, 'Enclosure in the West Riding', maps forming appendix and inserted into back cover; Hunt, H. G., 'The parliamentary enclosure movement in Leicestershire' (1956).

52 Quoted in Butlin, R. A., 'The enclosure of open fields and extinction of common rights in England, circa 1600–1750: a review', 73 and 69 respectively, in Fox and Butlin, *Change in the Countryside.*

53 Darby, *New historical geography*, 322.

54 Derby, *New historical geography*, 323 and ch. 6, Emery, 'England circa 1600'.

55 A ranking of counties in terms of density of open field arable enclosure is, Oxfordshire 50·3%, Northamptonshire 49·8%, Bedfordshire 47·2%, Huntingdonshire 48·5%, Cambridgeshire 45·9%, Yorkshire East Riding 44·2%, Leicestershire 42·6%, and Rutland 42·4%, in all of which over 40% of land area was open field arable enclosure.

56 Tate, *Domesday*, 72. To include old enclosures in the award was not unusual because allottees took advantage of enclosure to exchange land with each other for greater personal convenience, and it did not necessarily involve very many acres.

57 Darby, H. C. in *Victoria County History for the county of Cambridgeshire* (1948), **2**, 114, based on Vancouver, C., *General view of the agriculture of the county of Cambridge* (1794).

58 Whereas on the county basis the base acreage employed is the one for 1873.

59 Hoskins and Stamp, *The common lands*, 3.

60 Young, A., *Observations on the present state of the waste lands of Great Britain*, 37.
61 Williams, M., 'The enclosure and reclamation of waste land in England and Wales in the eighteenth and nineteenth centuries', *Transactions of the Institute of British Geographers* (1970), **51**, 55–69.

Chapter 3: *The temporal sequence*

1 Apart from Hunt's thesis cited in Chapter 1 see also his 'The chronology of parliamentary enclosure in Leicestershire', *Economic History Review* (1957), **10**, 265–72; see also Rodgers, 'The distribution of enclosure in the West Riding' (1953); Williams, 'Enclosure of Mendip Hills', 65–81; Slater, *English peasantry*; Gonner, *Common land and inclosure*.
2 Darby, *New historical geography*, 323, 476, 479, and see note 16, Chapter 1.
3 See my 'The cost of parliamentary enclosure in Buckinghamshire', *Agricultural History Review* (1973), **21**, 35–46.
4 Turner, 'Cost of parliamentary enclosure'.
5 Beresford, M. W., 'Commissioners of enclosure', *Economic History Review* (1946), **16**, 130–40, esp. 137; see also Swales, T. H., 'The parliamentary enclosures of Lindsey', *Architectural and Archaeological Societies of Lincolnshire and Northamptonshire, Reports and Papers* (1938), **2**, 96.
6 See Chapter 2, note 35 and associated text; Beckwith, I. S., 'The present state of enclosure studies in Lincolnshire', *Bulletin of local history, east midlands region*, **6**, 31, 39 and note 35; see also the many works by R. C. Russell on the county of Lincolnshire, some of which are itemised in Brewer, J. G., *Enclosure and the open fields: a bibliography* (1972), 9–11.
7 *British Parliamentary Papers* (1836), **8**, 501. The following is the first ten years in rank order of magnitude:

Year	No. of bills	Year	No. of bills
1812	133	1811	107
1802	122	1804	104
1810	122	1777	99
1814	120	1809	92
1813	119	1808	91

8 Deane, P. and Cole, W. A., *British economic growth, 1688–1959* (1969), 95.
9 Chambers, J. D. and Mingay, G. E., *The agricultural revolution, 1750–1880* (1966), 83; Pawson, E., *The early industrial revolution: Britain in the eighteenth century* (1979), 61.
10 Minchinton, W. E., 'Agricultural returns and the government during the Napoleonic wars', *Agricultural History Review* (1953), **1**, 29–43.
11 This seemed to be the case for Buckinghamshire, see my 'The 1801 crop returns for Buckinghamshire', *Records of Buckinghamshire* (1974), **19**, 471–82.
12 For the narrower period 1795–1814 there were 1,771 acts, or an annual average of 89.
13 Butlin, 'Enclosure of open fields' 70, in Fox and Butlin, *Change in the countryside*.
14 Hunt, 'Chronology of parliamentary enclosure', 266.

15 Hunt, 'Chronology', 266, 270, and 271 respectively.
16 Chambers, J. D., *Nottinghamshire in the eighteenth century* (1932), 150–4.
17 Hunt, 'Chronology', 270.
18 Darby, H. C., 'The age of the improver: 1600–1800', 325, being ch. 7 of Darby, *New historical geography*. He cites evidence from Marshall, W., *Rural economy of the midland counties* (1790), and Young, A., *Political arithmetic* (1774).
19 Hunt, 'Chronology', 270.
20 Martin, J. M., 'Warwickshire and the parliamentary enclosure movement' (1965), 45
21 Mills, D. R., 'Enclosure in Kesteven', *Agricultural History Review* (1959), **7**, 95.
22 Darby, *New historical geography*, 326, citing Donaldson, J., *General view of the agriculture of Northampton* (1974), 5.
23 Prince, H. C., 'England circa 1800', 403, being ch. 8 of Darby, *New historical geography*; on the conversion of arable to pasture in the period 1750–80, see also Gonner, *Common land*, 141.
24 I have transcribed and edited the entire collection of the 1801 crop returns for England from the originals in the *Public Record Office*, Home Office Papers, HO/67/1–26. See Turner, M. E., *The 1801 crop returns for England* (1978), 6–9, 25, 28, 35, 37, 199, 264, 268–9, 271, 273, 313, 353, 363–5, 399, 504, 508, 510, 512, 545, 547. This work awaits a publisher but three typescripts are available, one each at the Institute of Historical Research, the Public Record Office and on deposit with the Social Science Research Council. I would like to record my thanks to Prof. F. M. L. Thompson, director of the Institute, for a research fellowship in 1978 and to the Social Science Research Council for sponsoring the fellowship.
25 Turner, *1801 crop returns*, 264.
26 Turner, *1801 crop returns*, 268.
27 Turner, *1801 crop returns*, 364–5.
28 Turner, *1801 crop returns*, 512.
29 'Return of inclosure acts', *Parliamentary Papers, House of Commons* (1914), 399; Bowen, I., *The great enclosures of common lands in Wales* (1914), 47–56. There was a second peak of activity in Wales in the 1850s and 1860s when 89 acts were passed.
30 Young, A., *General view of the agriculture of Oxfordshire* (1813), 87.
31 Williams, 'Enclosure of waste land in England and Wales', **51**, 56.
32 Williams, 'Enclosure of waste land', 57, quoting from *Parliamentary Papers, Reports* (1795–6), **48**, papers 131, 33, and 19.
33 Billingsley, J., 'An essay on the best method of inclosing, dividing and cultivating waste-lands', *Letters to the Bath and West of England Agricultural Society* (1807), **11**, 2.
34 From Sinclair's memoirs reported in Halevy, E., *A history of the English people in the nineteenth century*, vol. 1, 'England in 1815' (1960), 230.
35 Minchinton, 'Agricultural returns'.
36 Galpin, W. F., *The grain supply of England during the Napoleonic Period* (1925), 28.
37 Galpin, *Grain Supply*, 194; see also Fussell, G. E. and Compton, M., 'Agricultural adjustments after the Napoleonic wars', *Economic History* (1939), **3**, 188.
38 Thirsk and Imray, *Suffolk farming*, 18 and 21–2.

39 Thomas, H. R., 'The enclosure of open fields and commons in Staffordshire', *Collections for a History of Staffordshire* (1938), 79.
40 Postgate, 'Field systems of East Anglia', 302, being ch. 7 of Baker and Butlin *Field systems in the British Isles.*
41 Turner, M. E., 'Some social and economic considerations of parliamentary enclosure in Buckinghamshire, 1738–1865' (1973), 65 and '1801 crop returns'.
42 Lambert, A., 'Oxfordshire circa 1800 A.D. A study in human geography', 70.
43 Chapman, J., 'Parliamentary enclosure in the uplands: the case of the North York Moors', *Agricultural History Review* (1976), **24**, 1–17, esp. 5.
44 Turner, *1801 crop returns*, 60.
45 Turner, *1801 crop returns*, 56.
46 Turner, *1801 crop returns*, 430 and 432. Holwell was subsequently transferred to Dorset.
47 Turner, *1801 crop returns*, 514.
48 Turner, *1801 crop returns*, 556 and 586.
49 Turner, *1801 crop returns*, 273.
50 Bailey, J. and Culley, G., *General view of the agriculture of Northumberland, Cumberland and Westmorland* 1805, 237.
51 See John, A. H., 'Farming in wartime: 1793–1815', 28–47 being ch. 2 of Mingay, G. E. and Jones, E. L. (eds.), *Land, Labour and Population during the Industrial Revolution: essays presented to J. D. Chambers* (1967).
52 Fussell and Compton, 'Agricultural adjustments', 201–2; Fussell, G. E. and K. R., *The English countryman, his life and work A.D. 500–1900* (1955), to name only two items from wider literature on the post-Napoleonic war depression.
53 Rounded down.
54 Rounded up.

Chapter 4: *The general determinants of enclosure*

1 For example the Turkdean, Gloucestershire enclosure act of 32 George III, c.21, 1792 says in the preamble, 'And whereas the Lands of the respective Proprietors, in the said Open Fields and Commonable Lands by this Act intended to be divided and inclosed, lie intermixed, and dispersed in small Parcels, and in their present Situation are incapable of any considerable improvement; but if the same were divided, and specific Parts or Shares thereof were allotted to and amongst the said Proprietors in Severalty, in lieu of, and in Proportion to their Lands, Tythes, Rights of Common, and all other Rights and Interests therein respectively, great advantage would arise to the Parties concerned.'
2 See Minchinton, 'Agricultural returns' 29–43; Turner, *1801 crop returns*, esp. introduction, i–xv.
3 *Public Record Office*, Home Office Papers, HO/42/37. Document of 5 Nov. 1795.
4 *Public Record Office*, HO/42/38/ Book of returns dated 14 Jan. 1796 but with reference to 1795 Inquiry.
5 Turner, *1801 crop returns*, 313 and 317–18.

6 Turner, *1801 crop returns*, 36, 118, 165, 197, and 527.
7 Turner, *1801 crop returns*, 546; Young, A., *The farmer's tour through the east of England* (1771), vol. 1, 20.
8 Davis, T., *General view of the agriculture of Wiltshire* (1811), 46.
9 Stone, T., *Suggestions for rendering the inclosure of common fields and waste lands a source of population and riches* (1787), 25.
10 Clare, J., from *The village minstrel and other poems* (1821); The Thornborough Lamentation or Gang Monday no more kept at Mill, *Buckinghamshire County Record Office*, B.R.O. AR/39/53, Dayrell Collection Mss. deposited by BAS, anonymous though possibly attributed to Henry Dayrell.
11 Mingay, G. E., *English landed society in the eighteenth century* (1963), 182–3; Thompson, F. M. L., *English landed society in the nineteenth century* (1963), 224; Beastall, T. W., *A north country estate: the Lumleys and Saundersons as landowners, 1600–1900* (1975), 92.
12 Beastall, *A north country estate*, 90–3 for some Lincolnshire examples.
13 *B.R.O.*, Grubb Mss., c.15, Risborough valuations; Young, *The farmer's tour*, 25.
14 Turner, M. E., 'Enclosure in Buckinghamshire', 360; for some Oxfordshire examples see Young, *Agriculture of Oxfordshire* 91–2 and 94.
15 Purdum, J. L., 'Profitability and timing of parliamentary land enclosures', *Explorations in Economic History* (1978), **15**, 314.
16 Young, *Agriculture of Oxfordshire*, 91, my emphasis.
17 Hunt, H. G., 'The chronology of parliamentary enclosure in Leicestershire', *Economic History Review* (1957), **10**, 271.
18 For example see Williams, 'Enclosure in Somerset', 100.
19 See the works by Chambers, Martin, Hunt and Lavrovsky itemised below in Chapter 7.
20 My emphasis.
21 Hunt, 'Chronology of parliamentary enclosure', 265 and 272 respectively.
22 McCloskey, D. N., 'The enclosure of open fields: preface to a study of its impact on the efficiency of English agriculture in the eighteenth century', *Journal of Economic History* (1972), **32**, 17.
23 McCloskey, D. N., 'The persistence of English common fields', in Parker, W. N. and Jones, E. L. (eds.), *European peasants and their markets: essays in agrarian history* (1975); McCloskey, 'English open fields as behaviour towards risk', *Research in Economic History* (1976), **1**, 124–70.
24 There is a growing literature on the effects of war on an economy; see in particular Winter, J. M. (ed.), *War and economic development: essays in memory of David Joslin* (1975), bibliography; Anderson, J. L., 'Aspects of the effect on the British economy of the wars against France, 1793–1815', *Australian Economic History Review* (1972), **12**, 1–20; Hueckel, G., 'War and the British economy, 1793–1815: a general equilibrium analysis', *Explorations in Economic History* (1973), **10**, 365–96.
25 Hueckel, 'War and the British economy', esp. 367–73, though in a subsequent study he fully recognises the effects of bad harvests: 'Relative prices and supply response in English agriculture during the Napoleonic wars', *Economic History Review* (1976), **29**, 401–14.
26 Board of Agriculture, *The agricultural state of the Kingdom, 1816* (reprinted with introduction by Mingay, G. E., 1970), VIII; Chambers and Mingay, *Agricultural revolution*, 113–15; other sources make 1796 a good or goodish

year, Lord Ernle says abundant, E. L. Jones says by no means good though not bad and Thomas Tooke says abundant: *English farming past and present*, (1922), 269; *Seasons and prices: the role of the weather in English agricultural history* (1964), 153–4; *A history of prices* (1857), **6**, 471.

27 Hueckel, 'War and the British economy', 369.

28 Chambers and Mingay, *Agricultural revolution*, 116, citing Olsen, M., *The economics of the wartime shortage* (1963), 65.

29 John, A. H., 'Farming in wartime: 1793–1815', 29, being ch. 2 of Jones and Mingay, *Land, labour and population.*

30 Tooke, *History of prices*, 476.

31 Minchinton, 'Agricultural returns', 38, citing the 'Second Report of the Lords' Committee on the dearth of provisions', *British Parliamentary Papers* (1801), **2**, 170.

32 Minchinton, 'Agricultural returns', 30.

33 Minchinton, 'Agricultural returns', and note 2 above; see also Galpin, *Grain supply of England.*

34 Priest, St John, *General view of the agriculture of the county of Buckingham* (1810), appendix 1, 367–72.

35 Retrospective evidence from 'Report from the select committee to whom several petitions which have been presented to the House in this session of Parliament, complaining of the depressed state of the agriculture of the United Kingdom were referred', *British Parliamentary Papers* (1821), **9**, 6.

Chapter 5: *The economic determinants of enclosure*

1 Chambers and Mingay, *Agricultural revolution*, 83.

2 Hunt, 'Chronology of parliamentary enclosure', 266–7.

3 Hunt, 'Chronology of parliamentary enclosure', 267.

4 Williams, 'Enclosure in Somerset', 101.

5 Yelling, J. A., *Common field and enclosure in England 1450–1850* (1977), 16 and 34 respectively.

6 McCloskey, 'Enclosure of open fields', 31.

7 Chambers and Mingay, *Agricultural revolution*, 84; Hunt, 'Chronology of parliamentary enclosure', 270.

8 Ashton, T. S., *An economic history of England: the eighteenth century* (1955), 40–1.

9 McCloskey, 'Enclosure of open fields'.

10 Crafts, N. F. R., 'Determinants of the rate of parliamentary enclosure' (1974), Warwick Economic Research Papers, **56** and *Explorations in Economic History* (1971), **14**, 227–49.

11 Beresford, M. W., 'Habitation versus improvement: the debate on enclosure by agreement', 56 in Fisher, F. J. (ed.), *Essays in the economic and social history of Tudor and Stuart England in honour of R. H. Tawney* (1961); see also Gonner, *Common land and inclosure*, 188.

12 See the notes attached to Table 18.

13 For a simple guide to regression theory see Floud, R. C. (ed.), *Essays in quantitative economic history* (1974), introduction, 19–30; for a more advanced guide see any standard statistics or econometrics text such as Johnston, J., *Econometric methods* (1972).

14 Wallis, K. F., *Introductory econometrics* (1972), 89.

15 Wonnacott, R. J. and T. H., *Econometrics* (1970), 136. With the number of observations I am using certainly, and in general, the nearer the DW statistic is to 2 the less likelihood there is of autocorrelation.

16 Wonnacott, *Econometrics*, explained in Chapter 5.

17 Wonnacott, *Econometrics*, 140.

18 See Crafts, 'Rate of parliamentary enclosure', 239, for an explanation of a similar problem that he encountered.

19 Wonnacott, *Econometrics*, 70, and Crafts, 246 where he eventually used a dummy variable but despite its coincidence with the war/non-war situation it was held to stand for something different.

20 McCloskey, 'Enclosure of open fields', 26–7.

21 Wilton, D. A., 'Structural shift with an interstructural transition function', *Canadian Journal of Economics* (1975), **8**, 424. My thanks to Adrian Darnell of the Department of Economics, University of Durham, for drawing my attention to this article.

22 Crafts, 'Rate of parliamentary enclosure', 16 and 239.

23 Wallis, *Introductory econometrics*, 89.

24 Mitchell, B. R., *Abstract of British historical statistics* (1962), 5–6 and 8.

25 Holderness, B. A., 'Capital formation in agriculture, 1750–1850', 159–83, esp. Table 1a, 163, in Higgins, J. P. P. and Pollard, S. (eds.), *Aspects of capital investment in Great Britain 1750–1850* (1971).

26 Turner, M. E., 'The cost of parliamentary enclosure in Buckinghamshire', *Agricultural History Review* (1973), **21**, 35–46.

27 The rate of increase in the Holderness index is faster than the corresponding rate for Buckinghamshire up to 1800 because it may underestimate the cost of the earlier enclosures: see Turner, 'Cost of parliamentary enclosure'.

28 McCloskey, 'Enclosure of open fields', 31.

29 Barnes, D., *A history of the English corn laws* (1930), 298, for the prices series.

30 Deane and Cole, *British economic growth*, 66; from my project on the 1801 crop returns as outlined in Chapter 3, note 24, from 371 parishes the mean wheat yield was 2¾ quarters (i.e. 22 bushels) per acre.

31 See again, McCloskey, 'Enclosure of open fields', 31.

32 Hammond, J. L. and B., *The village labourer* (1911), 25.

33 Crafts, 'Rate of parliamentary enclosure', 248.

Chapter 6: *Open field inflexibility and the shortage of pasture*

1 Beresford, M. W., 'Habitation versus improvement: the debate on enclosure by agreement', 40, in Fisher, *Essays in economic and social history.*

2 Beresford, 'Habitation', 41.

3 Beresford, 'Habitation', 54, my parenthesis. Beresford was commenting on John Shotbolt's plan for general permission to enclose as it was put to James I (in an undated document, *British Museum*, Royal Mss. 18A/XXV).

4 Beresford, 'Habitation', 64.

5 Havinden, M. A., 'Agricultural progress in open-field Oxfordshire', *Agricultural History Review* (1961), **9**, 73–83; Hoskins, W. G., 'The Leicestershire farmer in the seventeenth century', *Agricultural History* (1951), **25**, 9–20; Kerridge, E., *The agricultural revolution* (1967), esp. 91–113. Kerridge sees both

flexibility and inflexibility: 'An outstanding feature of common-field husbandry was its combination of inflexibility of field course with maximum freedom in cropping. The cultivator's liberty to choose what crops he liked in the cornfield of a two-field course or in the tilth and breach fields of the Midlands three-field course was nothing new and did not indicate that common-field husbandry was progressing or becoming more flexible or adaptable', 94–5; see also the review by J. M. Martin of Gonner, *Common land and inclosure*, in *Agricultural History Review* (1968), **16**, 72–4: 'Modern scholarship has very considerably diminished the significance of enclosure as an agent of change in agriculture and within the rural community. Common field farming was far less backward and inflexible than Gonner and his contemporaries believed.'

6 See Cossons, A., 'Early enclosures in Beeston', *Thoroton Society Transactions* (1958), **62**, 1–10, for an account of partial enclosures in Beeston in the seventeenth century. It seems to have been a three-field village, the Nether field was enclosed in the early Stuart period and the two remaining fields were subdivided to form three fields again.

7 In Staffordshire there was much enclosure that had taken place without the sanction of Parliament, evinced in the references to lands 'recently enclosed' in the successions of manorial rolls. See Thomas, H. R., 'The enclosure of open fields and commons in Staffordshire', *Collections for a History of Staffordshire* (1933), 79.

8 Beresford, M. W. and Hurst, J. G. (eds.), *Deserted medieval villages* (1971), particularly ch. 1, 3–75.

9 Swales, 'Parliamentary enclosures of Lindsey', 245.

10 Butlin, 'Enclosure of open fields'.

11 Gay, E. F., 'Inclosures in England in the sixteenth century', *Quarterly Journal of Economics* (1902–3), **17**, 576–97, in particular 581.

12 Gay, 'Inclosures', 581 and 585; see also Leonard, E. M., 'The inclosure of common-fields in the seventeenth century', *Transactions of the Royal Historical Society* (1905), **19**, 101–42, who argued against the popular belief of her day by saying that enclosure was common in the seventeenth century; see also Kerridge, E., 'The returns of the inquisitions of depopulation', *English Historical Review* (1955), **70**, 212–28 for a criticism of Leadham, I. S., Gay and others on their use of the 1517 and 1607 inquisitions as measures of enclosure. Leadham, I. S., *The domesday of inclosures*, 2 vols. (1897) and Gay, 'Inclosures'.

13 A failed bill of 1666 gives a retrospective insight into the first half of the seventeenth century: 'Within these forty, fifty and sixty years last past there have beene within this Kingdom multitudes of enclosures of commonable grounds wastes heaths fermgrounds and marshes', *House of Lords* Mss. (30 Oct. 1666).

14 See Chapter 2 above, 54; see also Tawney, R. H., *The agrarian problem in the sixteenth century* (1912), 218 which is a table from a sample of 47 demesne farms and shows that at a particular moment in time some were fully enclosed, some partially enclosed and others still in open fields.

15 See Beresford, 'Habitation versus improvement', 67–9; Thirsk, J., 'Agrarian History, 1540–1950', in *Victoria County History for the county of Leicestershire*, 2 (1954); Beresford, M. W., 'The Decree Rolls of Chancery as a source for Economic History, c.1547–c.1700', *Economic History Review* (1979),

32, 1–10; Kerridge, E., *Agrarian problems in the sixteenth century and after* (1969), esp. 103–18; and Clark, G. N., 'Enclosure by agreement at Marston, near Oxford', *English Historical Review* (1927), **42**, 87–94.

16 A transcript of the deed can be found in the Leckhamstead Parish Register, *Buckinghamshire County Record Office*, *B.R.O.*, PR/127/1/1, 133–4.

17 *B.R.O.*, PR/127/1/1, 230.

18 From the title deeds of the Napier and Utthwatt families. *B.R.O.*, AR/6/63–1/48/1. A map of 1641 confirms that only 20–25 per cent of Great Linford was still in common fields, *B.R.O.*, BAS 632/43. Three-quarters of the parish had been enclosed by the mid-seventeenth century.

19 *B.R.O.* AR/6/63–1, 1/48/3.

20 *B.R.O.*, Lee Mss. D/LE/1/307, agreement to enclose, 5 June 1669.

21 *B.R.O.*, Doddershall Mss. D/D Miscellaneous estate papers, no. 2, agreement to enclose, 20 Oct. 1669; *Hertfordshire County Record Office, H.R.O.*, Ashridge estate papers, AH 1163.

22 *H.R.O.*, AH 2358 and Act of 16 and 17 Victoria, c.20, 1853.

23 Campbell, M., *The English yeoman under Elizabeth and the early Stuarts* (1942), 90, quoting P.R.O., Star Chamber 8, 141/16. Loughton was enclosed by act of 8 George III, c.8, 1768.

24 Bateson, F. W., *A short history of Steeple Claydon* (no date), 9, citing *Claydon House*, Steeple Claydon Court Rolls.

25 Campbell, M., *The English Yeoman*, 91.

26 *B.R.O.*, BAS Miscellaneous 5.

27 Tawney, *The agrarian problem*, 151, states, 'at the very time when the peasantry agitated most bitterly they were often hedging and ditching their own little holdings and nibbling away fragments of the waste to be cultivated in severalty'.

28 *B.R.O.*, BAS Miscellaneous 5, agreement to enclosure, 30 Sept. 1687: A certain Richard Smallbrook enclosed one and a half acres of arable in Windmill field and one and a half acres of ley, all of which he had to fence within six months and for which he had to surrender his right of common for all manner of cattle in respect of the pieces enclosed, and also in respect of a further six acres in the open fields.

29 Kerridge, *Agrarian problems*, 99; Leonard, 'Inclosure of common fields', 110.

30 Campbell, *English yeoman*, 92.

31 *B.R.O.*, BAS Great Woolstone Deeds, 224/3, enclosure agreement of 7 Jan. 1674, cited in 'An agreement for the composition of tithe 5 January 1675'.

32 My emphasis, *B.R.O.*, Iver parish records, churchwardens' account book at a vestry held 30 Nov. 1776, PR/115/4/1.

33 Thirsk, J., 'The common fields', *Past and Present* (1964), **29**, 3–25; Yelling, J. A., 'Open field enclosure, and farm production in Worcestershire, 1540–1870' (1966), 237–9.

34 *Northamptonshire County Record Office, N.R.O.*, Articles of agreement of 1 Dec. 1702 referring to the Buckinghamshire village of Nash in the parish of Whaddon.

35 Hoskins, W. G., 'English agriculture in the seventeenth and eighteenth centuries', *Relazioni* (1955), **4**, 215.

36 Thirsk, J. (ed.), *The agrarian history of England and Wales* (1967), **4** (for 1500–1640), 202–3; *Tudor Enclosures* (1959). At Caythorpe in the Kesteven

Division of Lincolnshire as a means of procuring an enclosure agreement in the mid-seventeenth century, 'spies' were employed to stop unlawful trespass. The legal action that would result from trespass would be much more expensive for the encroaching small farmers and cottagers than the actual enclosure. Hosford, W. H., 'An eye witness account of a seventeenth century enclosure', *Economic History Review* (1951–2), **4**, 215–20; in the township of Leicester encroachments continued from the sixteenth century onwards, separate farms growing up within the open fields. Here there was a desperate shortage of pasture. Billson, C. J., 'Open fields of Leicester', *Transactions of the Leicester Archaeological Society* (1925–6), 14, 13.

37 Thirsk, J., 'Industries in the countryside', 83, in Fisher, *Economic and social history*.

38 Williams, 'Enclosure in Somerset', 101.

39 Hoskins and Stamp, *Common lands of England and Wales*, 44–60.

40 Holderness, B. A., 'Aspects of inter regional land use and agriculture in Lincolnshire, 1600–1850', *Lincolnshire History and Archaeology* (1974), **9**, 37.

41 Thirsk, J., 'Fenland farming in the sixteenth century', *University of Leicester, Department of English Local History, Occasional Papers* (1953), No. 3, 34–5, and Thirsk, *English peasant farming: the agrarian history of Lincolnshire from Tudor to recent times* (1957), 36–7.

42 Thirsk, *English peasant farming*, 81–2 and 97; Thirsk, 'Seventeenth century agriculture and social change', 152–3 of Thirsk, J. (ed.), *Land, church, and people: essays presented to Professor H. P. R. Finberg* (1970).

43 Leonard, 'Inclosure of common fields', 116 and 130–2.

44 Hoskins, W. G., *Provincial England*, ch. 8 (1963); Hunt, 'Chronology of enclosure in Leicestershire', 270.

45 Pettit, P. A. J., *The Royal forests of Northamptonshire; a study in their economy 1558–1714* (1968), 147; Lambert, A., 'Oxfordshire circa 1800 A.D. A study in human geography' (1953), 41–2.

46 Massingham, H. J., *Where man belongs* (1946), 121; Eland, G. (ed.), *Papers from an iron chest at Doddershall* (1937), 7 and 54.

47 *Birmingham City Library*, ref. 508622–25, list of demands, articles of agreement and answers made by freeholders of Aylesbury, Buckinghamshire, c.1600.

48 *B.R.O.*, Dormer estate Mss., D/93/Box 2, court roll of Ravensmere manor, Hughenden 1752; *B.R.O.*, Doddershall Mss., bundles 2 & 3.

49 Hyde, F. E. and Markham, S. F., *A history of Stony Stratford* (1948), 38; *P.R.O.*, Chancery Proceedings, Eliz. W.23, no. 55, 1580; Manorial Roll of 8 Oct. 1656, revised 18 April 1733 cited in Hyde and Markham, *Stony Stratford*, 42.

50 Thirsk, in *VCH for Leicestershire*, vol. 2, 1954, 202.

51 Chibnall, A. C., *Sherington: fiefs and fields of a Buckinghamshire village* (1965), esp. ch. 22, 'The battle against enclosure', 169–75.

52 Chibnall, *Sherington*, 173 and 199.

53 The glebe was still in open fields in 1674 and in 1700; Chibnall, *Sherington*, 173; *British Museum*, Cole Mss., Add. MS., 5839, f.393; Lipscomb, G., *The history and antiquities of the county of Buckinghamshire*, vol. 4 (1847), 379.

54 Tate, W. E., 'Inclosure movements in Northamptonshire', *Northamptonshire Past and Present* (1949), **1**, 26, mentions the open field bye-laws for the parish of Byfield in 1659; see also Barley, M. W., 'East Yorkshire manorial

bye-laws', *Yorkshire Archaeological Journal* (1943), **35**, 35–60, who uses the bye-laws from 1545 to 1856 and discusses stinting on pp. 38–9 and 53–6; see also Ault, W. O., 'Open-field husbandry and the village community, a study in agrarian bye-laws in medieval England', *Transactions of the American Philosophical Society*, **55** (1965). This is a study which leans heavily on Buckinghamshire manors for evidence; however, court rolls do not always give information about common field cultivation, those for the rectorial manor of Waddesdon in Buckinghamshire do not, see Ballard, A., 'Notes on the court rolls of the rectorial manor at Waddesden', *Records of Buckinghamshire* (1911), **10**, 98–100.

55 This control was never formally transferred from the court leet to the select vestry but it came about by an act of 13 George III, c.81, 1772–3, which entrusted the management of the common fields not to a true vestry but to a meeting of proprietors in which three-quarters majority in number and value would have the final determination on any issue of husbandry policy: Tate, W. E., *The parish chest* (1969), 256.

56 Ault, 'Open field husbandry', 12; Tawney, R. H. and Power, E., *Tudor economic documents* (1924), 59–60; the five sets of Steeple Claydon field orders begin in 1635 and finish in 1792: Bateson, *Steeple Claydon*, 10; for Leighton Buzzard the agreements for the management of the commons and open fields date from 1631 to 1834: *Bedfordshire County Record Office*, Boutwood Deposit, BO. 1324–40; for Cosgrove in Northamptonshire the field orders date from 1686: *N.R.O.*, Acc. nos. 1940/24 and 1943/4; for Berkshire several stinting agreements survive for the early eighteenth century, for Milton in 1712, North Moreton in 1719, Wadley in 1738 and Sparsholt in 1747: *Berkshire County Record Office*, D/EBt–E28, D/EB–E3, D/EB–E2 and D/ER–E5 respectively; the articles of agreement concluded at Cottenham in Cambridgeshire in 1597 continued to be the basis of the management of the common waste until the parish was enclosed by an act in 1842: Cunningham, W. (ed.), 'Common rights at Cottenham and Stretham in Cambridgeshire', *Camden Miscellany* (1910), **12**, 173–287; and at Leicester such regulations for the stinting of the pasture are earlier, from the fifteenth century and through the sixteenth century: Billson, 'Open fields of Leicester', 231.

57 *B.R.O.*, Nightingale deposit D/12/77, 'Agreement for stinting and regulation of commons in Cheddington, 22 April 1719'; *B.R.O.*, BAS 146/45, 'Articles of agreement regarding the use of common lands, 2 April 1772', in Ivinghoe Aston; *B.R.O.*, PR/235/3/3, Wingrave parish records, 'Articles orders and agreements made . . . 5 April 1777 . . . in the parish of Wingrave'; *B.R.O.*, BAS Miscellaneous 5, 414/44, 'A statement of Sherington commoners, 20 March 1722'; *Victoria County History for the county of Buckingham* (1927), **4**, 19.

58 Thirsk, *English peasant farming*, 116; Ault, W. A., 'Village bye-laws by common consent', *Speculum* (1954), **39**, 378–94.

59 *B.R.O.*, BAS Miscellaneous 5, 335/22, 'The case of North Crawley tenants, 20 August 1742'.

60 *B.R.O.*, letter of 4 Jan. 1772 from John Lord, a noted local enclosure commissioner.

61 *British Museum*, Add. MS., 37–9, 220, letter of 31 Dec. 1739 in papers relating to Whaddon.

62 Thirsk, *English peasant farming*, 100.

63 Martin, J. M., 'Warwickshire and the parliamentary enclosure movement' (1965), 14 and 30–3.
64 See the Northamptonshire example cited by Tate, 'Inclosure movements', 26, which concerned the intercommoning in 1650 between the villages of Little Houghton and Brafield; see also note 56 above for further examples.
65 *B.R.O.*, PR/67/1/2, 84–5, of Dunton parish register, rules numbers 14, 2, and 4 respectively, 'Orders agreed upon by us the parishioners of Dunton, 17 December 1652'.
66 On New College court rolls reprinted in Ault, 'Village bye-laws', 53–96; for a comparison see Barley, 'East Yorkshire manorial bye-laws', 35–60 and Barley, 'Parochial documents of the archdeaconry of the East Riding', *Yorkshire Archaeological Society, Record Series* (1939), **99**, XV.
67 Ault, 'Village bye-laws', 85, 94, and 96 respectively.
68 Anon., 'Grendon Underwood manor in 1678', *Records of Buckinghamshire* (1937), **13**, 285–6.
69 *B.R.O.*, AR/23A/66(L), Doddershall Mss., Miscellaneous item no. 13.
70 *B.R.O.*, D/104/1, Stowe estate miscellaneous.
71 Ward, W. H. and Black, K. S., *A history of the manor and parish of Iver* (1933), 221; *B.R.O.*, Iver parish records, Vestry book no. 5, 1779–97.
72 *Balliol College Muniments*, Snell Trust deeds, CI/70, 1641, 'Orders agreed upon by inhabitants of Ufton for the using of their fields to continue for one and twenty years from Michaelmas next ensuing'.
73 *B.R.O.*, PR/115/8/3, Iver parish records, 'Presentments of the manor of Iver', contained in Vestry book 5 and repeated unchanged from 1779 to 1797.
74 Chibnall, *Sherington*, 226 and appendix 283–5; *B.R.O.*, BAS 414/44.
75 Vinogradoff, P., 'An illustration of the continuity of an open-field system', *Quarterly Journal of Economics* (1907–8), **22**, 71.
76 Martin, 'Warwickshire and parliamentary enclosure', 16 and 30–1; Barrett, D. M., *Ecclesiastical terriers of Warwickshire parishes*, part 1 in vol. 22, 1955, part 2 in vol. 27, 1971).
77 *B.R.O.*, PR/235/3/3, Wingrave parish records.
78 *B.R.O.*, D/X, 534/95, 31 March 1781.
79 Hyde and Markham *Stony Stratford*, 79–80.
80 Hyde and Markham, *Stony Stratford*, 42, from the manorial court rolls of 8 Oct. 1656 and 18 April 1733.
81 Two of this list have not so far been cited, viz. *B.R.O.*, PR/162/28/1, Padbury parish collections, 'Regulations for the open-fields of Padbury agreed on at a manor court, 7 December 1779'; Eland, G. (ed.), *The Purefoy letters*, 1735–53, vol. 2, appendix A (1931), 434–9, 'Rules for management of open-fields, 12 March 1750', in the manor of Shalstone.
82 As an example of the collapse of co-operation, an act was passed in 1777 for the parish of Wendover to consolidate holdings in the open fields, though still maintaining the principles of open field husbandry, including the right to depasture stock at specific times of the year. It also agreed that clover and turnips could be sown as substitutes for the pasture of the balks (act of 17 George III, c.78, 1777). One owner disregarded these rules one year and folded his sheep on the turnips in May instead of at the agreed time, thereby ruining the crop: James, W. and Malcolm, J., *A general view of the agriculture of the county of Buckinghamshire* (1794), 29. But how successful had the open fields

been consolidated in Wendover? In 1794, the year that the Wendover enclosure act was passed, there was one owner at least whose lands were very widely scattered throughout the open fields, in fact 18 acres in 31 distinct parcels: Tate, W. E., *A handlist of Buckinghamshire enclosure acts and awards* (1946), 26.
83 The Shenley agreement of 1739 proposed to lay down for grass one tenth of the arable lands, to remain unploughed for 21 years, at the end of which period it could be ploughed again but had to be replaced by a tenth located elsewhere. In addition all 'lands' in the arable fields were to be two poles apart and these 'joynts' were to be laid down to grass: *British Museum*, Add. MS., 37069, 220 and following; at Sherington it was decided that each year greensward of 16½ feet in width would be set aside between the merestones and marks of each furlong to act as a pastured causeway, not to be ploughed for 21 years. There was to be one foot set aside of each half acre strip to be kept as greensward; where two adjacent half acres belonged to the same person there was to be two feet set aside, on the outside of each half acre; where there were three half acres together there were to be three feet set aside, on either side; where there were four half acres it was to be two feet on the outside and four feet between the two middlemost lands; in addition every sixth acre of arable was to be laid as greensward. *B.R.O.*, BAS. Miscellaneous 5, 414/44.
84 Martin, 'Warwickshire and parliamentary enclosure', 37.
85 See Thirsk, in *VCH* for Leicestershire, vol. 2, 224; in order to reduce the amount of fallow in the parish of Leighton Buzzard it was agreed as late as 1814 to divide the existing three fields into four and also to allow the introduction of turnips and potatoes as a substitute for the fallow. The parish was not enclosed until 1837–40: *Beds. R.O.*, Boutwood Deposit, BO/1334.
86 See Tawney, *Agrarian problem*, 312.
87 See Thirsk, *Tudor enclosures*, 5.
88 Evidence from several counties suggests that some early parliamentary enclosure was for the conversion of arable to pasture. To the instances already cited could be added. *Victoria County History* for the counties of Huntingdon, Nottingham, and Oxford, vols. 2 in each case (1932, 1910, and 1907), 94, 281 and 294, and 188; Arthur Young talks generally of the central counties, where enclosure involved the conversion of arable to pasture: see *VCH* for Huntingdon.
89 Butlin, 'Enclosure of open fields', 70.

Chapter 7: *Landownership and the chronology of enclosure*

1 Hammond, J. L. and B., *The village labourer* (1911), 25.
2 This was a customary rather than legal quantum of consent. See for example Homer, H., *An essay on the nature and method of ascertaining the specific shares of proprietors upon the inclosure of common fields* (1766), 36; The Hammonds, *Village labourer*, 25, talk in terms of a three-quarters to four-fifths quantum of consent as evinced in a Commons Select Committee of 1800.
3 Hunt, H. G., 'Landownership and enclosure, 1750–1830', *Economic History Review* (1958–9), **11**, 500; Turner 'Parliamentary enclosure in Buckinghamshire', 77–83 and 99–100.
4 Hunt, 'Landownership and enclosure', 497–505; Turner, 'Parliamentary enclosure in Buckinghamshire', 82; Martin, J. M., 'The parliamentary

enclosure movement and rural society in Warwickshire', *Agricultural History Review* (1967), **15**, 27.

5 See Tate, W. E., 'Parliamentary counter-petitions during the enclosures of the eighteenth and nineteenth centuries', *English Historical Review* (1944), **59**, 392–403; Tate, 'Opposition to parliamentary enclosure in eighteenth century England', *Agricultural History* (1945), **19**, 137–42; for some Buckinghamshire examples see Turner, 'Parliamentary enclosure in Buckinghamshire', 172–212.

6 For method of construction and problems encountered in construction see Turner, 'Parliamentary enclosure in Buckinghamshire', 77–9.

7 Martin, 'Parliamentary enclosure movement', 25, table 8.

8 Ashton, *Industrial revolution*, 19 (but my brackets).

9 Martin, 'Parliamentary enclosure movement', 26, table 9. This was in parishes where at least 75 per cent of the entire parish land was enclosed.

10 Hunt, 'Landownership and enclosure', 499; Martin, 'Parliamentary enclosure movement'.

11 My thanks to Mrs Jan Crowther for this information. She is working on the parliamentary enclosures of the East Riding and at the time of writing confirms this general picture of landownership distribution for the period before about 1780.

12 In fact in Buckinghamshire, the average size of the landowners of from 1–200 acres was at the lower end of the range. In the four decades up to 1800 the average sizes were respectively 138, 142, 124, and 139 acres.

13 Lavrovsky, V. M., 'Parliamentary enclosure in the county of Suffolk 1797–1814', *Economic History Review* (1937), **7**, 207–8.

14 See McCloskey, 'Enclosure of open fields', 15–35.

15 Turner, 'Parliamentary enclosure in Buckinghamshire', 172–212.

16 Lambert, S., *Bills and acts: legislative procedure in eighteenth century England* (1971), 133.

17 If those allotted over 200 acres are included the proportion only rises to 30 per cent.

18 Marx, K., *Capital* (1887), vol. 1, ch. 27; Habakkuk, H. J., 'English landownership 1680–1740', *Economic History Review* (1940), **10**, 2–17.

19 See Soltow, L., 'Long-run changes in British income inequality', *Economic History Review* (1968), **21**, 17–29.

20 See Dollar, C. M., and Jensen, R. J., *Historian's guide to statistics* (1971), 121–6.

21 Big peasants were defined as having over 50 acres, with an average sized holding of 108½ acres, having eliminated those defined by description as 'esquire' or 'gentleman'. See Lavrovsky, V. M., 'The expropriation of the English peasantry in the eighteenth century', *Economic History Review* (1956–7) **9**, 271–82.

22 Lavrovsky, V. M., *Parliamentary enclosure of the common fields in England at the end of the eighteenth century and beginning of the nineteenth* (1940), reviewed in Hill, C., *Economic History Review* (1942), **12**, 94.

23 Turner, 'Parliamentary enclosure in Buckinghamshire', 87 and 172–212.

24 Hunt, 'Landownership and enclosure', 501, citing Johnson, A. H., *The disappearance of the small landowner* (1909), 132.

25 See Chibnall, *Sherington*, 200.

26 By this it is not to suggest that the two centuries before 1750 were not ones

during which there was a savage reduction in the size of the peasantry, though this popular belief awaits further investigation. The contention is that there was a very late survival of this peasantry into the nineteenth century in many places. See in this connection Lavrovsky's revised ideas on the nineteenth century peasant in 'The great estate in England from the sixteenth century to the eighteenth century', in *First International Conference of Economic History* (1960), 353–65; see also the controversial essay by John Rae, 'Why have the yeomanry perished' *Contemporary Review* (1883), **44**, 546–65, an essay which in the light of the Buckinghamshire evidence might well be reconsidered.

27 These problems and imperfections have been highlighted by Grigg, D. B., 'The land tax returns', *Agricultural History Review* (1963), **11**, 82–94; Mingay, G. E., 'The land tax assessments and the small landowner', *Economic History Review* (1964), **17**, 381–8; Martin, J. M., 'Landownership and the land tax returns', *Agricultural History Review* (1966), **14**, 96–103. The main studies which have used the land tax since its existence was first highlighted by Johnson, have been Gray, H. L., 'Yeoman farming in Oxfordshire from the sixteenth century to the nineteenth', *Quarterly Journal of Economics* (1910), **24**, 293–326; Davies, E., 'The small landowner 1780–1832, in the light of the land tax assessments', *Economic History Review* (1927), **1**, 87–113; Chambers, J. D., 'Enclosure and the small landowner', *Economic History Review* (1940), **10**, 118–27; Payne, E. O., *Property in land in south Bedfordshire, 1750–1832* (1946); Hunt, 'Landownership and enclosure'; Martin, 'Parliamentary enclosure movement'; Turner, 'Parliamentary enclosure and landownership change in Buckinghamshire', *Economic History Review* (1975), **27**, 565–81; Walton, J., 'The residential mobility of farmers and its relationship to the parliamentary enclosure movement in Oxfordshire', in Phillips, A. D. M. and Turton, B. J., *Environment, man and economic change* (1975), 238–52.

28 Martin, 'Parliamentary enclosure movement', 32.

29 Chambers, 'Enclosure and the small landowner', 123; Davies, 'The small landowner', 103 and 105.

30 Hunt, 'Landownership and enclosure', 502.

31 For comparison the following were Martin's findings for Warwickshire, 'Parliamentary enclosure movement', 32.

in 56 old enclosed parishes	Owner-occupiers were 23% of all owners	
in 30 parishes enclosed 1730–79	do.	58%
in 13 parishes enclosed 1780–99	do.	47%
in 9 parishes enclosed 1800–22	do.	30%

32 Gray, 'Yeoman farming in Oxfordshire', 303–4; and Davies found that only about 10 per cent of the land tax was paid for by the independent farmer, 'The small landowner', 112.

33 Hunt, 'Landownership and enclosure', 503.

34 This differs markedly from the findings for Warwickshire.

Bucks. owner-occupiers (and as proportion of all owners)

	1785	1825
37 parishes old enclosed	80 (26·8%)	89 (42·8%)
31 parishes enclosed before 1780	337 (35·2%)	333 (41·2%)
20 parishes enclosed 1780–1800	261 (36·2%)	242 (38·5%)
15 parishes enclosed 1800–1820	189 (36·1%)	208 (42·9%)

Warwicks. owner-occupiers		
56 parishes old enclosed	106 (23%)	147 (34%)
30 parishes enclosed before 1780	502 (58%)	250 (44%)
13 parishes enclosed 1780–1800	209 (47%)	132 (34%)
11 parishes enclosed 1800–1820	66 (30%)	77 (47%)

Martin, 'Parliamentary enclosure movement', 32–3.

35 Davies has also remarked that the size of the individual owner-occupied estate was increasing: 'The small landowner', 94–105 and 110–11, conclusions which disagree with Marshall, D., *English people in the eighteenth century* (1956), 235.

36 Chambers, 'Enclosure and the small landowner', 127.

37 In this light perhaps it is worth reviewing John Rae's controversial and much criticised essay of 1883, 'Why have the yeomanry perished?', where he maintained a belief that if anything the yeoman had strengthened his position during the eighteenth century and that the source of his decline was the post-war depression after 1815 which followed nearly three decades of intensive investment by this class; Davies noted that in 1780 in the six counties that he studied, though owner-occupiers had ceased to be an outstanding feature the tendency in the next two decades at least was for their position to strengthen: 'The small landowner', 110; Grigg has shown that the small farms survived the period of enclosure and have survived into the twentieth century. His argument is that the cost of enclosure should have compelled the small owner-occupier to sell his farm and therefore enable the more prosperous farmer to expand his holdings. In this sense therefore enclosure would be incidental with large holdings. This was clearly not always the case: Grigg, 'Small and large farms in England and Wales', *Geography* (1963), **48**, 268–79; see also Mingay, 'The size of farms in the eighteenth century', *Economic History Review* (1962), **14**, 469–88 where he argues that there was a tendency for the number of small farms to decrease in the eighteenth century, but the process was neither rapid nor drastic but secular in character. Neither was the decline a result of enclosure but rather it had been at work well before the eighteenth century; see also Collins, K., 'Marx on the English agricultural revolution: theory and evidence', *History and Theory: Studies in the Philosophy of History*, (1967), **6**, 351–81: 'The evidence presented by recent research does, in fact, show that Marx's key factual statements concerning English agriculture in the eighteenth century are incorrect', 352, and see in particular 360–7 for a discussion of the disappearance of the yeoman.

38 'The war guaranteed that the 1790s were a golden age of agriculture for the new large-scale farmers and the smaller men alike . . . There was a marked increase in capital investment in farms', Briggs, A., *The age of improvement* (1959), 163; and in Leicestershire owner-occupiers increased in numbers during the war, 'reflecting the willingness of sitting tenants to purchase their farms during the period of agricultural prosperity'. Though the post-war period saw a reversal in this situation, as in Buckinghamshire. Hunt, 'Landownership and enclosure', 503–4; see also Davies, 'The small landowner', 98.

39 Meaning that the landowners may have found difficulty in finding tenants who were willing and able to take possession of the vacant farms. The land might therefore be returned for official purposes as 'in hand'. See 'Reports from the Select Committee appointed to inquire into the state of Agriculture; with the minutes of evidence and appendix', *British Parliamentary Papers* **8**,

(1836), 1st report questions 401, 1141, 1365, 1662, 1665, 1762–4, 3681 and 3rd report question 14137.

40 'Report from the Select Committee appointed to take into consideration the means of promoting the cultivation and improvement of the waste, uninclosed and unproductive lands in the Kingdom': *House of Commons Select Committee Reports*, first series, vol. 9 (1795–1801), 199.

Chapter 8: *Postscript*

1 Beresford, M. W., 'Bibliographical aids to research, no. XI: minutes of enclosure commissioners', *Bulletin of the Institute of Historical Research* (1946–8), **21**, 59–69. Professor Beresford detailed eight minute books for Buckinghamshire but there are now nearer thirty in the Buckinghamshire County Record Office, which covers about 20–25 per cent of all parliamentary enclosures in the county.

2 Crafts, N. F. R., 'Determinants of the rate of parliamentary enclosure', *Explorations in Economic History* (1977), **14**, 242–3.

Bibliography

Adams, I. H., *Agrarian landscape terms: a glossary for historical geography*, I.B.G. special publication no. 9 (London 1976).

Anderson, J. L., 'Aspects of the effect on the British economy of the wars against France, 1793–1815', *Australian Economic History Review*, **12**, 1–20 (1972).

[Anon], 'Grendon Underwood manor in 1678', *Records of Buckinghamshire*, **13**, 285–6 (1937).

Ashton, T. S., *The industrial revolution 1760–1830* (London 1948).

— *An economic history of England: the eighteenth century* (London 1955).

Ault, W. A., 'Village bye-laws by common consent', *Speculum*, **39**, 378–94 (1954).

— 'Open field husbandry and the village community, a study in agrarian bye-laws in medieval England', *Transactions of the American Philosophical Society*, **55** (1965).

Bailey, J. and Culley, G., *General view of the agriculture of Northumberland, Cumberland and Westmorland* (London 1805).

Baker, A. R. H., 'Howard Levi Gray and English field systems: an evaluation', *Agricultural History*, **39**, 86–91 (1965).

— 'Some terminological problems in studies of British field systems', *Agricultural History Review*, **17**, 136–40 (1969).

— 'Changes in the later middle ages' in Darby, H. C. (ed.), *A new historical geography of England*, 186–247 (Cambridge 1973).

— and Butlin, R. A. (eds.), *Studies of field systems in the British Isles* (Cambridge 1973).

Ballard, A., 'Notes on the court rolls of the rectorial manor at Waddesden', *Records of Buckinghamshire*, **10**, 98–100 (1911).

Barley, M. W., 'Parochial documents of the archdeaconry of the East Riding', *Yorkshire Archaeological Society, Record Series*, 99 (1939).

— 'East Yorkshire manorial bye-laws', *Yorkshire Archaeological Journal*, **35**, 35–60 (1943).

Barnes, D., *A history of the English corn laws* (London 1930).

Barrett, D. M., *Ecclesiastical terriers of Warwickshire parishes*, Dugdale Society

Publications, 22 and 27 (in two parts 1955 and 1971).

Bartholomew, J. G. (Director), *The survey atlas of England and Wales* (Edinburgh 1903).

Bateson, F. W., *A short history of Steeple Claydon* (Oxford no date).

Beastall, T. W., *A north country estate: the Lumleys and Saundersons as landowners 1600–1900* (London and Chichester 1975).

Beckwith, I. S., 'The present state of enclosure studies in Lincolnshire', *Bulletin of local history, east midlands region*, **6**, 21–40 (1971).

Beresford, M. W., 'Commissioners of enclosure', *Economic History Review*, **16**, 130–40 (1946).

— 'Bibliographical aids to research no. XI: minutes of enclosure commissioners', *Bulletin of the Institute of Historical Research*, **21**, 59–69 (1946–8).

— 'Habitation versus improvement: the debate on enclosure by agreement' in Fisher, F. J. (ed.), *Essays in the economic and social history of Tudor and Stuart England*, 40–69 (London 1961).

— 'The Decree Rolls of Chancery as a source for economic history, c.1547–c.1700', *Economic History Review*, **32**, 1–10 (1979).

— and Hurst, J. G. (eds.), *Deserted medieval villages* (London 1971).

Billingsley, J., 'An essay on the best method of inclosing, dividing and cultivating waste-lands', *Letters to the Bath and West of England Agricultural Society*, **11**, 2 (1807).

Billson, C. J., 'Open fields of Leicester', *Transactions of the Leicester Archaeological Society*, **14**, 3–29 (1925–6).

Board of Agriculture, *The agricultural state of the Kingdom, 1816* (London 1816).

Bowen, I., *The great enclosures of common lands in Wales* (London 1914).

Brewer, J. G., *Enclosure and the open fields: a bibliography* (Reading 1972).

Briggs, A., *The age of improvement* (London 1959).

Brown, E. H., 'Man shapes the Earth', *The Geographical Journal*, **136**, 74–85 (1970).

Butlin, R. A., 'Some terms used in agrarian history: a glossary', *Agricultural History Review*, **9**, 98–104 (1961).

— 'Recent developments in studies of the terminology of agrarian landscapes', *Agricultural History Review*, **17**, 141–3 (1969).

— 'Field systems of Northumberland and Durham' in Baker, A. R. H. and Butlin, R. A. (eds.), *Studies of field systems in the British Isles*, 93–144 (Cambridge 1973).

— 'The enclosure of open fields and extinction of common rights in England, circa 1600–1750: a review' in Fox, H. S. A. and Butlin, R. A. (eds.), *Change in the countryside; essays on rural England, 1500–1900*, 65–82, I.B.G. special publication no. 10 (London 1979).

Campbell, M., *The English yeoman under Elizabeth and the early Stuarts* (Yale 1942).

Chambers, J. D., *Nottinghamshire in the eighteenth century* (London 1932).

— 'Enclosure and the small landowner', *Economic History Review*, **10**, 118–27 (1940).

— *Laxton: the last English open-field village* (London 1964).

— and Mingay, G. E., *The agricultural revolution, 1750–1880* (London 1966).

Chapman, J., 'Parliamentary enclosure in the uplands: the case of the North York Moors', *Agricultural History Review*, **24**, 1–17 (1976).

Chibnall, A. C., *Sherington: fiefs and fields of a Buckinghamshire village* (Cambridge 1965).

Clare, J., *The village minstrel and other poems* (London 1821).

Clark, G. N., 'Enclosure by agreement at Marston, near Oxford', *English Historical Review*, **42**, 87–94 (1927).

Collins, K., 'Marx on the English agricultural revolution: theory and evidence', *History and Theory: Studies in the Philosophy of History*, **6**, 351–81 (1967).

Coppock, J. T., 'Farms and fields in the Chilterns', *Erdkunde*, **14**, 134–46 (1960).

— *The Chilterns* (Sheffield 1968).

Cossons, A., 'Early enclosures in Beeston', *Thoroton Society Transactions*, **62**, 1–10 (1958).

Crafts, N. F. R., 'Determinants of the rate of parliamentary enclosure', *Explorations in Economic History*, **14**, 227–49 (1977).

Cunningham, W. (ed.), 'Common rights at Cottenham and Stretham in Cambridgeshire', *Camden Miscellany*, **12**, 173–287 (1910).

Curtler, W. H. R., *The enclosure and redistribution of our land* (Oxford 1920).

Darby, H. C. (ed.), *Historical geography of England before 1800* (Cambridge 1936).

— 'On the relation of geography and history', *Transactions of the Institute of British Geographers*, **19**, 1–11 (1953).

— (ed.), *A new historical geography of England* (Cambridge 1973).

Davies, E., 'The small landowner 1780–1832, in the light of the land tax assessments', *Economic History Review*, **1**, 87–113 (1927).

Davis, T., *General view of the agriculture of Wiltshire* (London 1911).

Deane, P. and Cole, W. A., *British economic growth, 1688–1959* (Cambridge 1969).

Dollar, G. M. and Jensen, R. J., *Historian's guide to statistics* (New York 1971).

Donaldson, J., *General view of the agriculture of Northampton* (London 1794).

Eland, G. (ed.), *The Purefoy letters, 1735–53* (London 1931).

— (ed.), *Papers from an iron chest at Doddershall* (Aylesbury 1937).

Elliott, G., 'Field systems of north west England' in Baker, A. R. H. and Butlin, R. A. (eds.), *Studies of field systems in the British Isles*, 41–92 (Cambridge 1973).

Emery, F. V., 'England circa 1600' in Darby, H. C. (ed.), *A new historical geography of England*, 248–301 (Cambridge 1973).

(Lord) Ernle, *English farming past and present* (London 1922 ed.).

Eyre, S. R., 'The upward limit of enclosure on the east moor of north Derbyshire', *Transactions of the Institute of British Geographers*, **23**, 61–74 (1957).

Fisher, F. J. (ed.), *Essays in the economic and social history of Tudor and Stuart England* (London 1961).

Floud, R. C. (ed.), *Essays in quantitative economic history* (Oxford 1974).

Fox, H. S. A., 'The study of field systems', *Devon Historian*, **4**, 3–11 (1972).

— and Butlin, R. A. (eds.), *Change in the countryside: essays on rural England, 1500–1900*, I.B.G. special publication no. 10 (London 1979).

Fussell, G. E. and Compton, M., 'Agricultural adjustments after the Napoleonic wars', *Economic History*, **3**, 184–203 (1939).

Fussell, G. E. and Fussell K. R., *The English countryman his life and work A.D. 500–1900* (London 1955).

Galpin, W. F., *The grain supply of England during the Napoleonic period* (New York 1925).

Gay, E. F., 'Inclosures in England in the sixteenth century', *Quarterly Journal of Economics*, **17**, 576–97 (1902–3).

Gonner, E. C. K., *Common land and inclosure* (London 1912).

Gray, H. L., 'Yeoman farming in Oxfordshire from the sixteenth century to the nineteenth', *Quarterly Journal of Economics*, **24**, 293–326 (1910).

Grigg, D. B., 'The land tax returns', *Agricultural History Review*, **11**, 82–94 (1963).

— 'Small and large farms in England and Wales', *Geography*, **48**, 268–79 (1963).

— *The agricultural revolution in south Lincolnshire* (Cambridge 1966).

Habakkuk, H. J., 'English landownership 1680–1740', *Economic History Review*, **10**, 2–17 (1940).

Halevy, E., *A history of the English people in the nineteenth century* (London edn. 1960).

Hammond, J. L. and Hammond, B., *The village labourer* (London 1911).

Havinden, M., 'Agricultural progress in open field Oxfordshire', *Agricultural History Review*, **9**, 73–83 (1961).

Higgins, J. P. P. and Pollard, S. (eds.), *Aspects of capital investment in Great Britain 1750–1850* (London 1971).

Hill, C., reviewing Lavrovsky, V. M., *Parliamentary enclosure of the common fields in England at the end of the eighteenth century and beginning of the nineteenth* (Moscow–Leningrad 1940), *Economic History Review*, **12**, 92–5 (1942).

Hodgson, R. I., 'The progress of enclosure in county Durham, 1550–1870' in Fox, H. S. A. and Butlin, R. A. (eds.), *Change in the countryside: essays on rural England, 1500–1900*, 83–102, I.B.G. special publication no. 10 (London 1979).

Holderness, B. A., 'Capital formation in agriculture, 1750–1850' in Higgins, J. P. P. and Pollard, S. (eds.), *Aspects of capital investment in Great Britain 1750–1850*, 159–83, (London 1971).

— 'Aspects of inter regional land use and agriculture in Lincolnshire, 1600–1850', *Lincolnshire History and Archaeology*, **9**, 35–41 (1974).

Homer, H., *An essay on the nature and method of ascertaining the specific shares of proprietors upon the inclosure of common fields* (Oxford 1766).

Homer, S., *A history of interest rates* (New Brunswick, New Jersey 1963).

Hosford, W. H., 'An eye witness account of a seventeenth century enclosure', *Economic History Review*, **4**, 215–20 (1951–2).

Hoskins, W. G., 'The reclamation of the waste in Devon, 1550–1800', *Economic History Review*, **13**, 80–92 (1943).

— 'The Leicestershire farmer in the seventeenth century', *Agricultural History*, **25**, 9–20 (1951).

— 'English agriculture in the seventeenth and eighteenth centuries', *Relazioni*, **4**, 205–26 (1955).

— *Provincial England* (London 1963).

— *The making of the English landscape* (London 1965).

— and Stamp, L. D., *The common lands of England and Wales* (London 1963).

Hueckel, G., 'War and the British economy, 1793–1815: a general equilibrium analysis', *Explorations in Economic History*, **10**, 365–96 (1973).

— 'Relative prices and supply response in English agriculture during the Napoleonic wars', *Economic History Review*, **29**, 401–14 (1976).

Hunt, H. G., 'The parliamentary enclosure movement in Leicestershire, 1730–1842' (University of London unpublished PhD thesis 1956).

— 'The chronology of parliamentary enclosure in Leicestershire', *Economic History Review*, **10**, 265–72 (1957).

— 'Landownership and enclosure, 1750–1830', *Economic History Review*, **11**, 497–505 (1958–9).

Hyde, F. E. and Markham, S. F., *A history of Stony Stratford* (Wolverton 1948).

James, W. and Malcolm, J., *A general view of the agriculture of the county of Buckinghamshire* (London 1794).

John, A. H., 'Farming in wartime: 1793–1815' in Jones, E. L. and Mingay, G. E. (eds.), *Land, labour and population during the industrial revolution*, 28–47 (London 1967).

Johnson, A. H., *The disappearance of the small landowner* (Oxford 1909).

Johnson, J., *Econometric methods* (London 1972).

Johnson, S. A., 'Some aspects of enclosure and changing agricultural landscapes in Lindsey from the sixteenth to the nineteenth century', *Lincolnshire Architectural and Archaeological Society, Reports and Papers*, **9**, 134–50 (1962).

Jones, E. L., *Seasons and prices* (London 1964).

— and Mingay, G. E. (eds.), *Land, labour and population during the industrial revolution* (London 1967).

Kerridge, E., 'The returns of the inquisitions of depopulation', *English Historical Review*, **70**, 212–28 (1955).

— *The agricultural revolution* (London 1967).

— *Agrarian problems in the sixteenth century and after* (London 1969).

Lambert, A., 'Oxfordshire circa 1800 A.D. a study in human geography' (University of London unpublished PhD thesis 1953).

Lambert, S., *Bills and acts* (Cambridge 1971).

Lavrovsky, V. M., 'Parliamentary enclosure in the county of Suffolk 1797–1814', *Economic History Review*, **7**, 186–208 (1937).

— *Parliamentary enclosure of the common fields in England at the end of the eighteenth century and beginning of the nineteenth* (Moscow–Leningrad 1940).

— 'The expropriation of the English peasantry in the eighteenth century', *Economic History Review*, **9**, 271–82 (1956–7).

— 'The great estate in England from the sixteenth century to the eighteenth century', *First International Conference of Economic History*, 353–65 (Stockholm 1960).

Leadham, I. S., *The domesday of inclosures* (London 1897).

Lefèvre, G. J. S., *English commons and forests* (London 1894).

Leonard, E. M., 'The inclosure of common-fields in the seventeenth century', *Transactions of the Royal Historical Society*, **19**, 101–42 (1905).

Lipscomb, G., *The history and antiquities of the county of Buckinghamshire* (London 1874).

McCloskey, D. N., 'The enclosure of open fields: preface to a study of its impact on the efficiency of English agriculture in the eighteenth century', *Journal of Economic History*, **32**, 15–35 (1972).

— 'The persistence of English common fields' in Parker, W. N. and Jones, E.

L. (eds.), *European peasants and their markets: essays in agrarian history*, 73–119 (Princeton 1975).

— 'English open fields as behaviour towards risk', *Research in Economic History*, **1**, 124–70 (1976).

Marshall, D., *English people in the eighteenth century* (London 1956).

Marshall, W., *Rural economy of the midland counties* (London 1790).

Martin, J. M., 'Warwickshire and the parliamentary enclosure movement' (University of Birmingham unpublished PhD thesis 1965).

— 'Landownership and the land tax returns', *Agricultural History Review*, **14**, 96–103 (1966).

— Reviewing Gonner, E. C. K., *Common land and inclosure* (London 1966 edition), *Agricultural History Review*, **16**, 72–4 (1968).

— 'The parliamentary enclosure movement and rural society in Warwickshire', *Agricultural History Review*, **15**, 19–39 (1967).

Marx, K., *Capital* (English edition, London 1887).

Massingham, H. J., *Where man belongs* (London 1946).

Mills, D. R., 'Enclosure in Kesteven', *Agricultural History Review*, **7**, 82–97 (1959).

Minchinton, W. E., 'Agricultural returns and the government during the Napoleonic wars', *Agricultural History Review*, **1**, 29–43 (1953).

Mingay, G. E., 'The size of farms in the eighteenth century', *Economic History Review*, **14**, 469–88 (1962).

— *English landed society in the eighteenth century* (London 1963).

— 'The land tax assessments and the small landowner', *Economic History Review*, **17**, 381–88 (1964).

Mitchell, B. R., *Abstract of British historical statistics* (Cambridge 1962).

Olsen, M., *The economics of the wartime shortage* (Durham, North Carolina 1963).

Orwin, C. S. and Orwin, C. S., *The open fields* (Oxford 1938).

Parker, W. N. and Jones, E. L. (eds.), *European peasants and their markets: essays in agrarian history* (Princeton 1975).

Pawson, E., *The early industrial revolution: Britain in the eighteenth century* (London 1979).

Payne, E. O., *Property in land in south Bedfordshire, 1750–1832* Bedfordshire Historical Record Society Publications no. 23 (1946).

Pettit, P. A. J., *The royal forests of Northamptonshire: a study in their economy 1558–1714* (Northamptonshire Record Society no. 23 for 1963 but published 1968).

Phillips, A. D. M. and Turton, B. J., *Environment, man and economic change* (London 1975).

Philpot, G., 'Enclosure and population growth in eighteenth century England', *Explorations in Economic History*, **12**, 29–46 (1975).

Poems by William Cowper (London 1814).

Postgate, M. R., 'The field systems of Breckland', *Agricultural History Review*, **10**, 80–101 (1962).

— 'Field systems of East Anglia' in Baker, A. R. H. and Butlin, R. A. (eds.), *Studies of field systems in the British Isles*, 281–324 (Cambridge 1973).

Priest, St John, *General view of the agriculture of the county of Buckingham* (London 1810).

Prince, H. C., 'England circa 1800' in Darby, H. C. (ed.), *A new historical geography of England*, 389–464 (Cambridge 1973).

Purdum, J. L., 'Profitability and timing of parliamentary land enclosures', *Explorations in Economic History*, **15**, 313–26 (1978).

Rae, J., 'Why have the yeomanry perished?' *Contemporary Review*, **44**, 546–65 (1883).

Roberts, B. K., 'Field systems of the west midlands' in Baker, A. R. H. and Butlin, R. A. (eds.), *Studies of field systems in the British Isles*, 188–231 (Cambridge 1973).

Roden, D., 'Enclosure in the Chiltern Hills', *Geografiska Annaler*, **51**, 115–26 (1969).

— 'Field systems of the Chiltern Hills and their environs' in Baker, A. R. H. and Butlin, R. A. (eds.), *Studies of field systems in the British Isles*, 325–76 (Cambridge 1973).

Rodgers, W. S., 'The distribution of enclosure in the West Riding' (University of Leeds unpublished M. Comm thesis 1953).

Rundle, J. R., 'Laxton today', *Agriculture*, **62**, 170–2 (1955).

Scrutton, T. E., *Commons and common fields* (Cambridge 1887).

Slater, G., *The English peasantry and the enclosure of common fields* (London 1907).

Soltow, L., 'Long-run changes in British income inequality', *Economic History Review*, **21**, 17–29 (1968).

Stone, T., *Suggestions for rendering the inclosure of common fields and waste lands a source of population and riches* (London 1787).

Swales, T. H., 'The parliamentary enclosures of Lindsey', *Architectural and Archaeological Societies of Lincolnshire and Northamptonshire, Reports and Papers*, **42**, 233–74 (1937) and new series, **2**, 85–120 (1938).

Swann, B., 'The historical background to the registration of common land', *The Amateur Historian*, **7**, 232–40 (1967).

Tate, W. E., 'Parliamentary counter-petitions during the enclosures of the eighteenth and nineteenth centuries', *English Historical Review*, **59**, 392–403 (1944).

— 'Opposition to parliamentary enclosure in eighteenth century England', *Agricultural History*, **19**, 137–42 (1945).

— *A handlist of Buckinghamshire enclosure acts and awards* (Aylesbury, 1946).

— 'Inclosure movements in Northamptonshire', *Northamptonshire Past and Present*, **1**, 19–33 (1949).

— *The English village community and the enclosure movements* (London 1967).

— *The parish chest* (Cambridge 1969 edition).

— (edited by Turner, M. E.), *A domesday of English enclosure acts and awards* (Reading 1978).

Tawney, R. H., *The agrarian problem in the sixteenth century* (London 1912).

— and Power, E., *Tudor economic documents* (London 1924).

Thirsk, J., 'Fenland farming in the sixteenth century', *University of Leicester, Department of English Local History, Occasional Papers No. 3* (Leicester 1953).

— *English peasant farming: the agrarian history of Lincolnshire from Tudor to recent times* (London 1957).

— *Tudor enclosures* (Historical Association general series no. 41 (London 1959).

— 'Industries in the countryside' in Fisher, F. J. (ed.), *Essays in the economic and social history of Tudor and Stuart England*, 70–88 (London 1961).

— 'The common fields', *Past and Present*, **29**, 3–25 (1964).

— (ed.), *The agrarian history of England and Wales*, **4** (London 1967).

— 'Seventeenth century agriculture and social change' in Thirsk, J. (ed.), *Land, church, and people*, 148–77 (Reading 1970).

— and Imray, J., *Suffolk farming in the nineteenth century* (Suffolk Record Society 1958).

Thomas, H. R., 'The enclosure of open fields and commons in Staffordshire', *Collections for a History of Staffordshire*, volume for 1931, 55–99 (but not published till 1933).

Thompson, F. M. L., *English landed society in the eighteenth century* (London 1963).

— Reviewing Perry, P. J., *British farming in the Great Depression, 1870–1914* (Newton Abbot 1974), in *Agricultural History Review*, **25**, 67–8 (1977).

Tooke, T., *A history of prices*, 6 (London 1857).

Tucker, D. N., 'Linear parishes and farm structures in the Vale of Pickering', *Geography*, **57**, 105–19 (1972).

Tucker, G. S. L., 'The old poor law revisited', *Explorations in Economic History*, **12**, 233–52 (1975).

Turner, M. E., 'The cost of parliamentary enclosure in Buckinghamshire', *Agricultural History Review*, **21**, 35–46 (1973).

— 'Some social and economic considerations of parliamentary enclosure in Buckinghamshire, 1738–1865' (University of Sheffield unpublished PhD thesis 1973).

— 'The 1801 crop returns for Buckinghamshire', *Records of Buckinghamshire*, **19**, 471–82 (1974).

— 'Parliamentary enclosure and landownership change in Buckinghamshire', *Economic History Review*, **27**, 565–81 (1975).

— 'Parliamentary enclosure and population change in England, 1750–1830', *Explorations in Economic History*, **13**, 463–8 (1976).

— (ed.), *Tate, W. E., A domesday of English Enclosure acts and awards* (Reading 1978).

— (ed.), *The 1801 crop returns for England* (Typescript copies available at the Public Record Office, the Social Science Research Council and the Institute of Historical Research 1978).

Vancouver, C., *General view of the agriculture of the county of Cambridge* (London 1794).

Victoria County History for the county of Lincolnshire, 2 (London 1906).

— Gloucestershire, 2 (London 1907).

— Oxfordshire, 2 (London 1907).

— Hertfordshire, 2 (London 1908).

— Nottinghamshire, 2 (London 1910).

— Middlesex, 2 (London 1911).

— Buckinghamshire, 4 (London 1927).

— Huntingdonshire, 2 (London 1932).

— Kent, 3 (London 1932).

— Cambridgeshire, 2 (London 1948).

— Leicestershire, 2 (London 1954).

Vinogradoff, P., 'An illustration of the continuity of an open-field system', *Quarterly Journal of Economics*, **22**, 62–82 (1907–8).

Wallis, K. F., *Introductory econometrics* (London 1972).

Walton, J., 'The residential mobility of farmers and its relationship to the parliamentary enclosure movement in Oxfordshire' in Phillips, A. D. M.

and Turton, B. J., *Environment, man and economic change*, 238–52 (London 1975).

Ward, W. H. and Black, K. S., *A history of the manor and parish of Iver* (London 1933).

Wheeler, W. H., *A history of the fens of south Lincolnshire* (London 1868).

White, L. J., 'Enclosures and population movements in England, 1700–1830', *Explorations in Entrepreneurial History*, **6**, 175–86 (1968).

Wilkinson, O., *The agricultural revolution in the East Riding of Yorkshire* (East Yorkshire Local History Society 1956).

Williams, M., 'The enclosure and reclamation of waste land in England and Wales in the eighteenth and nineteenth centuries', *Transactions of the Institute of British Geographers*, **51**, 55–69 (1970).

— 'The enclosure and reclamation of the Mendip Hills', *Agricultural History Review*, **19**, 65–81 (1971).

— 'The enclosure of waste land in Somerset', *Transactions of the Institute of British Geographers*, **57**, 99–123 (1972).

Wilton, D. A., 'Structural shift with an interstructural transition function', *Canadian Journal of Economics*, **8**, 423–32 (1975).

Winter, J. M. (ed.), *War and economic development* (Cambridge 1975).

Wonnacott, R. J. and Wonnacott, T. H., *Econometrics* (New York 1970).

Yates, E. M., 'Enclosure and the rise of grassland farming in Staffordshire', *North Staffordshire Journal of Field Studies*, **14**, 46–60 (1974).

Yelling, J. M., 'Open field, enclosure and farm production in Worcestershire, 1540–1870' (University of Birmingham unpublished PhD thesis 1966).

— 'Common land and enclosure in east Worcestershire, 1540–1870', *Transactions of the Institute of British Geographers*, **45**, 157–68 (1968).

— *Common field and enclosure in England 1450–1850* (London 1977).

Young, A., *The farmer's tour through the east of England*, 1 (London 1771).

— *Observations on the present state of the waste lands of Great Britain* (London 1773).

— *Political arithmetic* (London 1774).

— *General view of the agriculture of the county of Hertford* (London 1804).

— *General view of the agriculture of Oxfordshire* (London 1813).

Index

Reference to authors is made only where they are mentioned by name in the text, or in tables or cited as references in tables. Place and county names are also indexed where referred to in the text or in the tables and maps. Reference to county names in the appendixes is not given here because the counties are mentioned in all of the appendixes. The use of the words 'England', 'act of Parliament', 'parliamentary enclosure', 'open field arable' and 'common' and 'waste' is so ubiquitous in this book as to defy satisfactory indexing.

C

D

Y